WINNING
THE STRESS
CHALLENGE

WINNING THE STRESS CHALLENGE

Highly Successful Stress-Management and Wellness Programs

NICK HALL, PhD

MEDIA

Published 2019 by Gildan Media LLC
aka G&D Media
www.GandDmedia.com

FIRST EDITION 2019

Front Cover design by David Rheinhardt of Pyrographx

Interior design by Meghan Day Healey of Story Horse, LLC

Library of Congress Cataloging-in-Publication Data is available upon request

ISBN: 978-1-7225-0022-1

10   9   8   7   6   5   4   3   2   1

Contents

Acknowledgments

've drawn from so many sources of information and personal experiences in putting this book together that I am at a loss to know where to begin in thanking all those who have contributed to this effort. The one exception is my loving wife, Hazel, whose contributions clearly outshine all others. Her patience and understanding while I was researching this topic kept me grounded and sane. This included keeping the home fires stoked while I was off on some adventure, testing the ideas discussed in this book. Also my two daughters, Rachele and Stephanie, each of whom has performed alligator wrestling shows with their dad at the Black Hills Reptile Gardens in South Dakota.

They've also shared cross-country motorcycle and bicycle adventures with me, which is how I learned that the rules of dealing with stress change when loved ones are involved. I'm also indebted to the wisdom and example set by my mother, Eileen, who, for 93 years, behaved like a woman in her twenties, thereby, serving as an inspiration for all who encountered her. Finally, my stepfather, Max, whose hard work and dedication to his adopted family were unparalleled.

A large number of people have assisted with the preparation of the material used in writing this book. I'm especially indebted to Barbara Furtek, who expertly set about the task of correcting the numerous grammatical blunders and misspellings, which were scattered about draft copies of this effort. I'd also like to acknowledge her astute ability to spot statements with meanings other than the ones intended, along with the literary solutions. In addition, Betty LeDoux-Morris, a Certified Meeting Professional, has been instrumental in forging the corporate connections that have kept this book grounded in pragmatism.

Others have helped shape some of the described concepts. The conclusions of Dr. Irv Dardik, expressed in his Wavenergy Theory, have made me realize that stress is good for you and that it is only when stress is unabated by recovery that health will be impaired. Dr. Phil Hayden's research and insights into the ways elite FBI agents cope with stress under extreme circumstances have taught me that academic models have little relevance when you find yourself in a rapidly failing environment. I am particularly grateful for having had the opportunity to work with Dr. Jim Loehr, whose insights pertaining to stress and performance in athletes have demonstrated that there are viable strategies which can be employed to prevent stress from impacting performance. Some of the strategies involving exercise and acting are based upon those insights. I'm particularly grateful for the recommendations of Dr. Gerald Iwerks, a professional mediator, whose discussions on the subject of conflict have proved invaluable in formulating the strategies for coping with adversity. Dr. Blake Anderson served as a consultant and contributor to the audio program Prescription for Burnout, parts of which have been incorporated into this book. Also, Paula Stahil, who edited an earlier edition of this book, titled Orchestrating the Mind and Body. Finally, I am indebted to the professional insights of Geneele Crump, a highly skilled Licensed Clinical Social Worker, who has made valuable suggestions pertaining to the recommended behavioral-interventions and has assisted with the editing and organization of the chapters.

In addition to acknowledging those who gave direct input while I was writing this book, I wish to acknowledge those who indirectly provided assistance. Steve Isaac, founder of the organization WaterTribe, has provided me with the opportunity to test under extreme conditions while participating in WaterTribe sponsored Challenges the recommendations I describe in these pages. Also, I wish to acknowledge my many friends at Nightingale-Conant, publishers of my audio programs, from which some of the material in this book has been drawn. Finally, I wish to acknowledge the National Institutes of Health, which, over a span of nearly four decades, has provided generous funding for my own mind-body research, as well as the research of others, which has been incorporated into the following chapters.

Introduction

Former prisoners of war and the survivors of concentration camps who showed adeptness in coping with stress shared certain characteristics in
common according to research carried out at Stanford
University:

- They did not surrender or give up their spirit.
- They maintained a sense of control no matter
  how bad it got. Despite everything going on
  around them, they could still control their own
  thoughts.
- They attributed some important meaning to
  their suffering and pain.
- They focused on good or positive things
  throughout each day. For example, "I got some
  food today," or "I didn't get beaten today."
- They maintained a strong sense of purpose and
  resolve to make it through the ordeal.

This research clearly shows that it is how you respond to the challenges you face that determines their impact upon your health. Your perception, your cognitive appraisal, and your interpretation are what matter most. These are the fundamental skills you need to have in order to win the stress challenge. And where do they come from? Simply put, they are acquired. Taking responsibility for how you react to the things that happen to you is the first step. Choosing not to see yourself as a victim and maintaining control is step two. Step three is to intentionally and habitually start thinking and acting in ways that keep you positive, engaged, empowered, and resilient. This is the winning formula, and this book will show you how to make it work for you.

You will begin by identifying the amount and types of stress that currently exist in your life. Next, you will learn the basic skills you'll need to identify the warning signs so you can take preventative action and reduce the probability that stressors even will arise. Then you will be guided through a series of scientifically grounded strategies to help you better manage life's challenges. Skeptical? Then you can delve into the references at the end of this book, which will provide whatever documentation you are seeking.

No two people respond in the same way to a stressor, and no two people will benefit in the same way from a stress management program.

Protocols have to be highly customized to meet your specific needs. This program is designed to provide you with the tools to identify the root causes of your stress-related problems as well as a menu of healthy responses so that you can customize your own personal program.

Many of the sections contain questions to help you distinguish between the stressor, your perception of events, your emotional response, and some of the secondary issues such as inherent conflicts between your response and your value system. Take time to carefully consider each question, and write or verbalize the answer to yourself or a trusted friend. This process will enable you to organize your thoughts. You will also gain insights by viewing the problem from a fresh perspective.

Instead of simply responding to the emotional fallout, you will now have an opportunity to view the problem through the spoken or written word. If nothing else, just this process is healing because you are gaining a measure of control. You are no longer helpless. You soon will come to realize that you alone can empower or derail your healing system.

Identifying the key components of your stress response through introspection, however, is not enough unless you take steps to create a healthier response. This book offers a variety of options. You will be provided with guidelines to engage in healthier dietary habits, to improve the quality of your sleep, and to use exercise to train for stress recovery. The health benefits of friendship, steps you can take to cope better with burnout, and ways to energize yourself also will be discussed.

What Are Your Stressors?

One of the greatest arenas for stress for many people is their work. Complete this brief questionnaire to determine if you might be suffering from job-related stress.

1. Do you believe that you have very little control over circumstances at work?
2. Could you do a better job with more time in which to do it?
3. Do you have difficulty making decisions at work?
4. Are you performing below your full potential?
5. Has new technology (computers, for example) exceeded your capacity to do your job efficiently? Are you concerned hat your job may be threatened because of a merger or because there are more talented people with whom you work?

6. Do you sometimes suspect that a supervisor or co-workers are conspiring or are biased against you?

7. Do you sometimes have a difficult time motivating yourself to go to work?

8. Do you lose your temper over trivial events at work?

9. Have you become more accident-prone?

10. Are you turning to drugs to deal with the problems at work? For example, do you find that you need extra coffee to get going in the morning? Or do you have to have a drink as soon as you get home from work?

11. Do you have headaches or other physical symptoms when you are at work?

If you answered yes to three or more of these questions, you are at risk for experiencing job burnout. If you answered yes to five or more of these questions, then the amount of job stress that you are experiencing probably is sufficient to impact on your future career and, even more seriously, on your physical and mental health.

Let's get specific. It is highly improbable that the entire job is stressful. Instead, it is more likely to be a specific aspect of the job. Use the following scoring system to narrow the problem down and then write the number in the space next to the category in the listing of specific sources of stress:

No problem/not applicable	0
Slight	1
Somewhat	2
Moderate	4
Exceeding	6
Overwhelming	10

Expectations at work

Requirements	_____
Workload	_____
Schedule	_____
Compensation	_____
Total Score	_____

Infrastructure

Physical environment	
Organizational climate	_____
Politics	_____
Total Score	_____

Relationships

Superiors	_____
Subordinates	_____
Peers	_____
Clients	_____
Total score	_____

The object of this exercise is to localize the major sources of your stress. Nothing else matters except for your perception of the events as being stressful. Irrespective of the appropriateness of your emotional and actual response, realize that your perception of events is all that counts. Note that the scoring system is not linear. Neither is the impact of stress upon your health.

Self-Evaluation

1. "Overall, I believe that my score is higher than others in my position, average, or lower."
   Why do you believe this?

2. "I experience the most stress with _____."
   Why do you think this is such a problem?

3. "I have the least stress with _____."
   Why?

In general, stressors arise from one of the following four categories:

- Inevitable transitions: Leaving home, marriage, having a child, etc.
- Unexpected events: Losing a job, divorce, accidents, etc.
- Unrelenting conflict: Incompatibility with spouse or coworkers, abuse, etc.
- Personal: Low self-esteem, unmet needs, chronic illness, etc.

As you contemplate the stressors in your life, ask, "Why is this a problem for me?" If the problem is overwhelming, start by dissecting it into its component parts. You will discover that while some solutions may lie beyond your control, others may have easy fixes.

What Is Stress?

During the 1970's and 1980's, there was a growing body of evidence supporting the existence of a powerful mind-body connection. An international gathering, hosted by the Belgian Royal Family, was convened in Brussels for the purpose of discussing the health ramifications of the emerging field called Psychoneuroimmunology. There was no disagreement that stress was a major factor, since there already was substantial literature documenting the links between emotional upheaval and illness. However, there was irreconcilable disagreement over how the word should be defined.

Should it be defined in chemical or psychological terms? Is it experienced in the same way by all people? How should it be measured? Is it the emotion or the response to the emotion that's the problem? Or perhaps the emotion is part of the response. "Are you afraid because you are running away, or are you running away because you are afraid?" is a question contemplated by the likes of Walter Canon and Claude Bernard, and which was now being paraphrased to accommodate a definition not of emotion, but rather the events associated with the expression of emotion. The discussion came to a sudden halt at the direction of the chairperson. He declared that it was a waste of time to continue, since it was apparent that consensus would not be reached in the allotted time. It was acknowledged that each person participating knew from personal experience and observation what stress was, and that each of us should embrace that understanding during the course of the subsequent discussions. We all agreed, pleased to have a quick way out of this intellectual quagmire. What does stress mean to you? In 2008, it meant impaired health to many Americans. The economic signs clearly indicated that not only the United States, but the world was in the midst of an unprecedented financial crisis. And according to the American Psychological Association, 60 percent of Americans reported irritability or anger; 53 percent were fatigued; 52 percent had difficulty sleeping; and 48 percent engaged in unhealthy eating. These percentages were up substantially when compared with the 2007 findings. Of course, one size does not fit all. Chances are, if you feel distressed, yet you don't experience any of these widely reported symptoms, it's probably because you manifest stress in other ways. Here are some of the options:

Physical Symptoms Of Stress

Tension headaches

Frowning

Trembling of lips or hands

Heartburn

Stomach cramps

Muscle tension

Neck aches

Back pain

Aggressive body language

Jaw pain

Increased sensitivity to
    light and sound

Lightheadedness, faintness,
    or dizziness

Ringing in the ears

Enlarged pupils

Blushing

Dry mouth

Problems swallowing

Frequent colds or bouts
    with flu

Nausea

Difficulty breathing

Restlessness

Trouble concentrating

    Heart and chest pain

Increased perspiration

Night sweats

Cold, sweaty hands

Cold hands and feet

Flatulence or belching

Frequent urination

Constipation

Nervous diarrhea

Decreased sexual desire

Difficulty reaching orgasm

Appetite change

Fatigue

Hives

Insomnia or hypersomnia

Rashes

Weight change

Chills or goose bumps

Digestive upset

Pounding heart

Rapid heart beat

Shortness of breath

Autoimmune symptoms

Mental Symptoms Of Stress

Anxiety   Loneliness
Guilt   Dulled senses
Increased anger   Poor concentration
Frustration   Low productivity
Moodiness   Negative attitude
Depression   Defensiveness
Nightmares   Suspiciousness
Trouble learning   Whirling mind
Forgetfulness   No new ideas
Disorganization   Boredom
Confusion   Feeling overwhelmed
Indecision   Discontentment
Fear of closeness to people   Spacing out
Suicidal thoughts

Behavioral Symptoms Of Stress

Inattention to grooming   Overspending
Increased tardiness   Edginess
Serious appearance   Overreaction
Unusual behavior   Prone to minor accidents
Nervous habits   Perfectionism
Making excuses   Reduced productivity
Lying   Fast or mumbled speech
Rushing around or pacing   Unusual risk-taking
Increased alcohol use   Gritting of teeth
Increased tobacco use   Social withdrawal
Gambling   Self-pity

Strained communication	Easily discouraged
Frustration	Stuttering
Mood swings	Procrastination
Bad temper	Nervous laughing
Crying spells	Nail-biting

Undoubtedly, the word stress is one of the most misused words in the bio-medical sciences. It's used as a noun, a verb, as well as an adjective. Claude Bernard, a renowned physiologist, defined stress as "an adaptive response to an external stimulus." In other words, he defined the word stress as the changes which occur within the organism in response to some external signal. Walter Cannon, an equally renowned physiologist, defined stress as the stimulus. There is nothing wrong with either of these definitions. However, it is important to exercise caution in defining how the word is being used in a particular context. Physicists use the word stressor to describe the external event. For example, a stressor would be the force acting on an airplane wing or the uspension of a bridge. The word strain is used to describe the rearrangement of molecules within that structure. I will use stressor when referring to the triggering event and then, when appropriate, describe the specific chemical changes which are responsible for impairing your health.

General Adaptation Response: Even though there are many definitions, most people agree with the basic concepts that were put forward by Hans Selye when he described the general adaptation response. He described the stress response as being comprised of three phases. First, was the alarm or emergency phase, during which a person recognizes a potential threat to their well-being. Second, was the adaptation or resistance phase, during which chemical changes occur in order to allow you to return to a state of homeostasis or normalcy. This was followed y the exhaustion or illness phase, which Selye defined as the using up of the chemicals responsible for maintaining homeostasis. We now know the opposite is true. Problems arise from excessive production of stress-induced chemicals within the body—not their exhaustion.

Operational Definition Of Stress: A very practical definition of stress was put forward by Richard Lazarus when he stated, "It seems wise to use stress as a generic term for the whole area of problems that includes the stimuli producing stress reactions, the reactions themselves, and the various intervening processes. It defines a large, complex, amorphous, interdisciplinary area of interest and study." It is not a good definition because it is too broad. However, it does address all the important variables which you have to take into account when using the word stress. For example, everybody manifests a stress response. It may differ somewhat from one individual to another. Some people, when confronted with a major stressor, may experience a very rapid increase in heart rate, perhaps even to the point of experiencing tachycardia. For other individuals, their stomach might turn into knots with a major impact on their gastrointestinal system. Yet others may experience tension headaches or muscle tension. All these symptoms have a tendency to occur, but different individuals will have a predominance of one type of symptom or another. Furthermore, the type of response you have is the one you likely will manifest, regardless of the stressor. If your supervisor at work has just given you a letter informing you that your services are no longer needed just a couple of years before retirement, you are likely to experience a stress response. And whatever the type of response, it's the same one you will experience if you get cut off while driving down the interstate.

Types of Stress

Acute Versus Chronic Stress: Acute stressors are those which occur for a short period of time and, eventually, go away. That is precisely the type of stress with which the body has learned to deal. It is when the stressor persists over a long period of time that it is referred to as chronic; which is when health-related problems can arise.

Anabolism Versus Catabolism: If you took a course in Biochemistry when you were in high school or college, you might have spent an enormous amount of time studying enzymatic reactions, memorizing sequences of pathways, as well as examining chemical structures. Forget all of that. There are just two chemical reactions in the context of stress that are important. They are those dealing with anabolism, which is a fancy chemical term used to describe building processes, versus catabolism, which describes the breaking down of products. During the stress response, there is a shift from anabolic to catabolic processes, and the reason is quite logical. Why build for the future if there isn't going to be a future? For the same reason that you would not build a summer cottage on the seaside when a hurricane were bearing down on the lot, your body is not going to waste valuable time and resources on reproduction and other construction projects when the future is uncertain. In the short term, halting unessential building projects will not be harmful. For a period of days, even weeks, the changes are actually very beneficial. Problems occur when you switch from anabolic to catabolic processes over an extended period of months, or even years. That is when stress-related illness can result.

You also can view the stress response as a series of chemical reactions which are designed to provide energy: a process for extracting glucose and other energy substrates from storage. Glucose is not the only substrate. Other substrates might be needed as well, but glucose is one of the primary substrates, especially for the muscles and the central nervous system. However, converting glucose from stored energy sources and then putting what you didn't require back into storage is very wasteful. About 30 percent of the usable energy is lost, which is why many people under chronic stress suffer from fatigue. This is so common that I have devoted an entire section to stress-related sleep and fatigue problems. But don't worry. There are several things you can do to energize yourself, no matter what is happening.

Somatic Versus Psychogenic Stress: There are many ways of categorizing the stress response. There are somatic stressors, which result in physical injury to the body. Chemical changes occur within the body, the tissue is repaired, and, eventually, unless damage is very severe, things will return to some sort of a homeostatic balance. It is the psychogenic stressors which cause problems. The anticipation of something that is perceived to be injurious to the body—even though it is not—can result in physiological changes. This is a bit misleading because a somatic stressor clearly will impact upon your psychological well—being, as well. Likewise, a psychogenic stressor will affect a number of nervous system pathways that are capable of impacting the body. Here is a listing of some of the potential ways you might respond when faced with uncertainty or threat.

Molecular Stress: Escaping your conscious awareness is the fact that a relentless stressor is at work, even as you breathe. It's estimated that between three to five percent of the oxygen you take in with each breath is converted into oxidative metabolites, which are more commonly referred to as free radicals.

Free radicals are unstable molecules, due to the fact that they are missing an electron. Like all things in nature, they seek stability by grabbing an electron from the most convenient source. This can be beneficial to your health when the electron is taken from a bacteria or virus. That's part of the mechanism whereby you rid yourself of an infection, and it is the reason why you need a certain number of free radicals in order to remain healthy. Problems arise when you have too many, through smoking, living in a polluted environment, or eating more than your fair share of fatty foods. Now, the extra free radicals take the electrons from healthy cells. If that happens inside the blood vessel wall, it may give rise to arteriosclerosis. Or in the brain, it may contribute to Alzheimer's disease. Even some forms of cancer have been linked with excess free radicals. In addition, oxidative injury has been implicated in degenerative diseases, epilepsy, trauma, and stroke. It is a threshold phenomenon that occurs after antioxidant mechanisms are overwhelmed. Oxidative stress occurs when there's an imbalance between the rates of free radical production and their elimination.

Fortunately, there are a number of mechanisms within the body that serve to counter the damage done by free radicals. Antioxidant defenses include the enzymes superoxide dismutase, glutathione peroxidase, and catalase, as well as the low molecular weight reductants alpha-tocopherol (vitamin E), glutathione, and ascorbate (reduced vitamin C). This is why eating foods that are rich in these ingredients is such a healthy pursuit. There are many antioxidants available through the foods we eat. These include, amongst others, vitamins A, C, and E, which basically donate an electron, thereby sparing your healthy cells.

In a perfect world, you probably would get enough of these vitamins by eating a well-balanced diet. That doesn't always happen under stress. Chemicals in the

brain prompt you to eat unhealthy proportions of carbohydrates, seek out fatty foods that make you feel good,
and then store the excess fat in the abdominal region,
where it has been correlated with cancer and heart disease. In addition, some people do not have the financial
resources or time to eat in a healthy manner. That's why
so many people turn to supplements that are rich in antioxidants, especially when they have reason to believe
they have more than their fair share of these potentially
harmful molecules.

How Stress Affects Your Body

Stress affects the body and mind through two primary mechanisms—the neuroendocrine pathways. Each will be discussed briefly to provide you with a better understanding of what is happening behind the biological scenes.

Autonomic Nervous System: During the course of a stress response, there are two primary circuits that become activated. One is the autonomic nervous system, and the other is referred to as the neuroendocrine circuit. The autonomic nervous system can be divided into two branches: the sympathetic and the parasympathetic. When you find yourself in a stressful situation, you might observe that your pupils begin to dilate. Salivation is stopped. You experience an increase in respiration and heartbeat. There is an inhibition of digestion and perhaps a relaxation of the bladder. Your body experiences an outpouring of catecholamines, epinephrine, and norepinephrine. These are all changes that are regulated by the sympathetic branch of the autonomic nervous system. The parasympathetic branch, however, is doing pretty much the opposite. For example, parasympathetic activation causes constriction of the pupils. It stimulates salivation, slows respiration and heart rate, and stimulates digestion.

Although it is not entirely correct, a general rule of thumb is those changes that occur as a result of sympathetic activation, are those that are most often associated with the stress response. The parasympathetic reactions are those that normally are associated with the relaxation response.

Neuroendocrine Circuits: The other major conduit by which the brain is able to regulate various organs is the neuroendocrine circuits. When the stressful event is first perceived, it acts on neurons in the central nervous system, and from there the signals are transported to endocrine tissues, hence neuro-endocrine. In the context of stress, the major circuit is the hypothalamic-pituitary-adrenal axis. The initial signal is corticotropin releasing factor, which is produced by neurons in the hypothalamus. This chemical makes its way through the blood stream to the pituitary gland, where it stimulates the release of two hormones. One is called adrenocorticotropin hormone, and the other is beta-endorphin. Adrenocorticotropin hormone travels through the body and makes its way to the adrenal gland, where it stimulates the release of cortisol. Cortisol is the major hormone produced in the wake of stress, and, because it is responsible for mobilizing glucose, is referred to as a glucocorticoid.

It is the release of endorphin that is primarily responsible for the reduction in pain sensitivity during stress. Many people, when they are in a car accident or have been wounded on a battlefield, do not realize the severity of their injuries until sometime later. The reason for this is because beta-endorphin, which means endogenous morphine, is released. It is a very potent painkiller, which makes sense. You don't want to be preoccupied with pain if you need to have your wits about you to extricate yourself from an emergency. You need to be able either to fight the threat or to escape from it, or as Walter Cannon described it, engage the fight or flight response.

Other changes may occur as well, depending upon the type of stress. Some people may have a release of growth hormone and prolactin. There also are interactions between the stress circuits and the reproductive axes. For example, corticotropin releasing factor and beta-endorphin both are capable of suppressing reproductive hormones, which is one of the reasons why amenorrhea is a common symptom in women under chronic stress and why impotence is not an uncommon symptom in men. This all makes sense. If you are living with chronic stress, one of the last things you need to be bothered with is raising offspring.

Growing Through Crisis And Change: Crisis and change, capable of giving rise to stress, are a part of life. Indeed, they are a necessary part of life, providing the motivation to grow. There really is no way to grow without dealing with life's difficulties and changes. You have the basic choice of learning and growing through the difficult times or more rigidly adhering to your familiar ways of doing things. The key is learning to accept that life is difficult, but trusting that you have the resources to make it through the tough times. Times of crisis and change can be viewed as threats or as challenges. It really depends on how you choose to view them.

Your resilience or ability to adapt to change often centers on your self-esteem. If you see yourself as powerless or unworthy, change can be very threatening, and you may fear not being able to deal with the changes. That is when an inner sense of worth is important. When you have come to trust your inner worth, the changes and tough times in life are less unsettling because you know you can rely on your inner resources. If you don't have a solid sense of who you are, you may adopt a rigid approach to life that freezes you in time, making it less likely that you will cope effectively when challenged by life's difficulties. As you feel more confident in yourself, you simultaneously feel safer and better equipped to deal with the challenges in life, whether it be death, the loss of a job, a move, or a divorce.

Most difficulties in life involve losses, and, as such, your response to them often depends on how you have dealt with past losses. If losses in the past have overwhelmed your ability to cope or simply come too soon or too fast, loss may terrify you. Often a new loss will confront you with your past experiences with loss and lead to feelings of powerlessness or helplessness. It is the experience of loss that all of us must deal with at many points in life. Most changes involve something lost and something gained. If you lose sight of what is gained and focus only on the loss, the prospect of change invariably will evoke fear.

Many events can throw you off course in life. If your feet are firmly planted on the ground—that is, you value yourself as a person, feel in your heart that basically you are a good person, and have a sense of stability—it is less likely that you will get swept away by life's challenges.

This isn't to say you won't be distressed at times—fear is a normal reaction to change. In the right proportion, it is fear that prepares us to cope better. To deal with crisis and change in life, it is important to look inward to work on ways of taking care of yourself with the support of people who are close to you, accepting the cycle of loss. In this way, you can keep pace with change. By looking for the "opportunities within the crisis," you can begin to grow through them.

Emotions

Scientists, philosophers, and artists have never been able to reach agreement on the true definition of emotions. What has been agreed upon, at least within the scientific community, is that there are generally six recognized families of emotion:

- Anger
- Disgust
- Fear
- Joy
- Love
- Sadness

Some would argue that this list needs to be expanded to include shame and guilt. However, I would regard these as subcategories of fear: fear of social rejection or of punishment. Likewise, rage and adoration are degrees of anger and love respectively, although some people might consider them as separate emotions.

Tune Into Your Feelings: It is very important that you understand why you are responding in the manner that you are. Too often, you respond only to the emotion. Or, you might focus upon only your behavioral response or the social consequences. Before you can modify your response, you first must identify it to gain an understanding of why it is occurring. Ultimately, realize that the purpose of stress-induced emotions and behavior is to provide balance. The experience of emotions helps you either to reduce the sadness, to eliminate the trigger of disgust, or to counter the threat.

Consider a symphony orchestra in performance before an attentive audience. I will use the orchestra to represent the mind and the audience to represent the body. The musicians are the brain cells, while the notes they play are the chemicals which now will affect the body. When the orchestra performs synchronically and in harmony, its effect upon the audience (the body) will be the desired interpretation of the music. The strains of a gentle etude induce relaxation, while The 1812 Overture will elicit arousal, and the intentional, intermittent Discordance of The Rite of Spring might elevate such arousal to a level of discomfort for some.

Yet, the audience also plays a role in the workings of the performance. Under optimal circumstances, it responds in balance with the effort of the orchestra. But the actions of individuals strongly can impact the rest of the audience as well as the performers themselves. There is a woman seated nearby who repeatedly snaps her purse open and shut as she consumes candy wrapped in extremely crinkly paper. This distraction significantly interferes with the ability of those around her to concentrate fully on the music. A man in the audience suffers from a hacking cough and sneezes loudly. Those nearby must contend with the distraction of the noise as well as that of being exposed to the man's illness. Instead of remaining in synch with the music, their attention is diverted. Furthermore, members of both the audience and the orchestra may be distracted by emotions associated with recent events in their personal lives, such as the second violinist who's concerned her contract won't be renewed and has no idea that the head cold she currently suffers from took hold because she's run down from worry.

Every element of the performance's outcome, for both orchestra and audience, is interwoven. While extremely simplified, it is analogous with the subtle interaction which constantly occurs between your mind and body. By understanding the impact of external and internal events, and, to a great degree, learning to control the stressors influencing them, you can better orchestrate your own health and well-being.

- Emotions are more than 'all in your head' as biological pathways link the brain and the body.
- Emotions can arise as a result of real or perceived events.
- Genetics and early life experiences play a role in shaping your emotions.
- The body can be trained to experience particular emotional and physical responses to events.

Emotions play a very important role in modulating the balance between good health and disease. When you can freely access emotions, you can experience the richness and passion of life, be it pleasure or pain. Some people are under the impression that they can somehow block out only the painful emotions, while preserving the more pleasurable ones. Normally, when you block emotions, you block them all, both pleasurable and painful. Feelings of numbness and depression can be signs that you tend to block your emotions.

A highly effective way of coping with stress is to deal directly with emotions. First, pay attention to how you may distract yourself from your feelings. Do you do any of the following?

- Keep busy?
- Watch too much TV?
- Reach for something o eat or drink?
- Sleep too much?
- Intellectualize?
- Focus on other people?
- Engage in excessive shopping?

Whichever your preferred method, interrupt the process by stopping and spending five or ten minutes of quiet time to focus on what you are feeling. If you are not used to dealing with emotions, you may find it helpful to focus on your body and determine which of the following emotions you are experiencing: anger, sadness, or fear. In some instances, you will be feeling a combination of these. Try not to judge or filter the emotions—simply let them come up to the surface. Then stay with the emotion for longer periods of time. Just let it happen, don't try to make it happen, and do not confuse thinking about emotions with feeling emotions. These are entirely different processes. Feeling is a freeing, spontaneous experience which, unlike conscious thought, cannot be forced.

Getting To Know Me: Your responses to stress are shaped by your thoughts and feelings. As you develop a greater awareness, you will begin to realize that your thoughts and feelings about stressful events are not automatic, but, at some level, involve a choice. The key is to be aware of this and make a choice to engage in a different thought process.

Build your confidence by thinking of a time in your life when you made a decision to do something. A time when you were committed to a particular course of action and believed, without a doubt, that you could accomplish your goal. A time when you were determined. Imagine how you felt at that time. If you cannot think of a decision you made, imagine something that you strongly believe in with no reservations. Then, imagine feeling as committed to changing your unhealthy patterns of behavior. Now create this same feeling of conviction with respect to changing your response to stressful events.

After you have taken some time to identify the patterns of dealing with stress that you wish to change, and have reinforced your commitment to actually making these changes, you can now begin to focus specifically on making changes.

Stress can be broken down into three parts: the trigger, the interpretation, and the resulting emotion. The trigger is the external event that you are dealing with; the interpretation is how you size it up; and the emotion is what follows. Of course, all of these components affect each other. You can change your stress response by directly focusing on one of these three components. The easiest place to focus is on the triggers. Then fill in the rest of the following table.

Personal Stressors		
Trigger	**Interpretation**	**Emotion**
Supervisor	*Unrealistic demands*	*Anger*

- *What conclusions can you draw about the situations that are particularly difficult for you?*
- *Are they ones that you could avoid?*
- *Are you distressed because particular people in your life are critical of you or question your judgment?*
- *Are there people in your life you can never please?*
- *Do you find your job leaves you feeling unhappy and unfulfilled?*

If these are some of the triggers, it might be possible to make some direct changes to eliminate or reduce them. You are the only one who can decide whether they are so unhealthy and damaging to your health that you should make some major changes in your life, or whether they are necessary evils that you cannot avoid and which you must learn to deal with. Alternatively, it may be your interpretation of events that is in need of change.

Just My Style

Do you fit into one of the following categories?

APPREHENSIVE

- What if something happens to me?
- What if I can't finish it?
- What if I lose control?

These are the typical thoughts of the apprehensive person. Their favorite statement is "what if " as they constantly anticipate the worst case scenario and create exaggerated images of failure. This type of person will be in a constant state of stress while engaging in this process.

FAILURE

- Why am I so clumsy?
- Why can't I get it right?
- Why didn't I do it that way?

Listen for the word 'why,' and chances are you have identified a person who considers himself to be a failure. He compares himself with others, and he constantly focuses upon weaknesses instead of strengths. This individual is unlikely ever to achieve high self-esteem or success.

CASUALTY

- I can't do that, so why bother trying?
- I'm too uncoordinated to attempt that.
- It won't make any difference.

Unfortunately, the real obstacle preventing a 'casualty' from achieving his objective is a pessimistic attitude. He always will find an obstacle and, invariably, will blame circumstances outside himself. In other words, there's nothing he can do. The result? Flight, often leading to a constant feeling of helplessness and depression.

INTOLERANT

- You must do it this way.
- This has to be done again
- I should always be perfect

Such a person often sets unrealistic goals and then considers himself to be a failure if he does not accomplish his objective. He is a perfectionist and intolerant of failure. You'll often hear the word 'must' in such a person's dialogues.

Changing Unhealthy Thoughts

Do you see yourself in one or more of the previous categories? If yes, ask yourself the following questions:

- "Will I accomplish anything worthwhile by continuing this process?"
- "Do I want to continue feeling the way I do?"
- "Are these thoughts justified?"

Now, write down each negative thought and answer the following questions.

- "What are the chances the scenario I am preoccupied with will really unfold?"
- "Is what I am thinking always true, or just sometimes?
- "If I do this, what is the worst that could happen?"
- "If the worst case scenario does occur, will it really be that bad? What would my options be?"
- "Am I considering all the information available to me?"
- "Am I considering all the information with equal importance, or am I twisting facts to fit my preconceived notions?"
- "What is the evidence my thoughts are justified?"

Next, replace each negative thought with a positive one. For example, "I'll never be able to do this" can become, "If I take time to learn this particular skill, I will be able to do this."

Or, "I'll be useless tomorrow if i don't fall asleep soon" can become, "Even lying in bed awake is a form of rest. I've functioned before with minimal sleep; I can do it again." As you replace the negative thoughts with positive ones, remember the following simple rules:

- Avoid using words with negative connotations.
- Stay in the present.
- Use the personal pronoun whenever you can.

Remember that your response to any event will be triggered by the image you create in your mind. That image will be shaped by your biases, your expectations, and your past experiences. They may be hard to rearrange. There's an old Chinese proverb:

"What your eyes see and your ears hear is what is already in your mind."

In addition to changing your thoughts, you also can work to change your emotions.

- If you feel sad, frightened, or defeated, the first step is to acknowledge it rather than make it go away. Then you can begin to change the feeling.
- If you are frightened or overwhelmed, focus on a time in your life when you felt safe or in control. Focus on how it feels to be safe or in control.
- Imagine you can make this feeling of being in control ten percent stronger, then twenty percent stronger, then fifty percent stronger. Repeat this

process throughout the day. Soon you will find that you can change your emotional response to events.

In those circumstances that are clearly out of your control, there are other approaches you can use. First, it is sometimes very helpful simply to accept the fact that the situation is out of your hands. Let it go. People tend to labor over how to control a situation out of their control, which just makes them more upset. When you begin to feel anxious or distressed, that is when it is probably time to simply set it aside for a while and come back to it later.

Another approach is to focus on the piece you can control. In some cases, the only thing you really can control is your attitude. Some people surrender their sense of personal control by believing other people always must approve of their actions, or that they never can make mistakes, or that they never can be vulnerable. These mindsets or beliefs insure that you will have little control over major aspects of your life. By changing these expectations or beliefs and by developing inner strength, you will find that you are faced with fewer out of control situations in life.

What types of beliefs do you maintain that keep you feeling unhappy and powerless? Be aware of how these beliefs operate in your life, and confront them when they occur.

Achieving Goals

Many people make the mistake of defining their goal in unrealistic ways, or else they confuse a reward for having achieved a goal with the actual goal. I once spoke at a large convention attended by several thousand entrepreneurs, who were being worked into a frenzy by their successful colleagues. Each began by describing the Mercedes or yacht now parked at their multi-million dollar mansion. Then, the eager attendees were instructed to cut out pictures of Rolex watches, their dream car, or other expensive possessions and place them in highly visible locations around the house. The idea was to be constantly reminded of their goal and of what life would be like when it was achieved. But the car or mansion morphed into the goal, when it should have been viewed as the reward. If a goal is truly worthwhile, the rewards will come automatically. By taking their sight off their goal, they were more likely missing their opportunities.

Goals should be things such as building a flourishing business, exceeding your sales quota, or paying off your debt. A goal must be defined in ways that easily can be measured, and in a manner that can be charted along the way. Think about it. That car is all or nothing. You don't acquire small pieces as you make progress. A correctly defined goal will enable you to identify progress each and every day. And one more thing. Make sure that you have defined a goal in a manner that you have control over.

What Are Your Values And Beliefs? Having goals that are inconsistent with your values will be a constant source of conflict. What are your primary values?

Refer to the following list; subtract from it or add to it if what you value is not listed. Create a personal list beginning with the values that are Most important to you, and then determine if they are compatible with your goals.

VALUES	
Wealth	*Material Possessions*
Love	*Friendship*
Power	*Career*
Altruism	*Family*
Labor	*Higher Power*

In addition to identifying your goals and values, you also need to identify your belief system. How would you complete these statements?

- Life is _____.
- People are _____.
- Stress is _____.
- Relationships are _____.
- The world would be a Better place to live if ____.
- I am _____.

And now ask yourself:

- Are these your beliefs or those of someone else?
- Are your beliefs based upon consistent experience?
- Can you think of times in your life when your belief system was challenged by reality?
- Have beliefs ever kept you from achieving a goal?
- Are certain themes reflected in your beliefs?
- Are you willing to change one or more of your beliefs if they are obstacles to your goals?

Now that you have pondered these questions, make a list of those beliefs that are most dear to you, making sure that they are rational and yours. Then, re-examine your goals, making certain that there are no conflicts between your beliefs and your long-term objectives.

Plan of Action

Write down your goals. Remember to use positive state-ments, be realistic, and establish a timetable.

- My goal is to _____.
- The following are potential obstacles that might interfere with my achieving my goal. _____.
- I am willing to take the following steps to minimize the effects of these obstacles. _____.
- By _____, I will be halfway to having completed my goal.
- By _____, I will have achieved it.

Be prepared to modify these dates. The unexpected will occur, and you Need to make allowances. You might consider giving yourself more time than you think you really need. This way, you won't be disappointed by fail-ing to meet a deadline; and if you reach the milestone sooner than projected, relish your triumph.

Helpful Hints!

- **Ritualize** your behavior by setting aside a time of day when you take steps to achieve your goal. Make sure you do something each day so that through conditioning, the clock will become a gentle reminder.
- **Remain** focused on the objective. If it seems overwhelming at times, then divide the task

into manageable steps. Remember, a journey is completed one small step at a time.

- **Restate** your goal, taking into account shifting priorities and unexpected changes in your life.
- **Redefine** the objective as a Challenge.
- **Resolve** to stay the course, and, if you deviate, remind yourself about the benefits of accomplishing your objective.
- **Reward** yourself as you make quantifiable progress toward your goal.

Organize Your Life: Most people underestimate the time that is required to complete a task. A study of under-graduate students conducted by Roger Buehler of Simon Frazer University has revealed that estimates are off by almost three weeks for long term projects. The problem is what is referred to as an optimistic bias. People tend to focus primarily upon their future plans and pay very little attention to relevant experience. Furthermore, people tend to ignore the obstacles that prevented them from completing a similar task on time in the past and blindly assign unrealistic deadlines. Here's what you can do.

- How you handle the optimistic bias depends upon what the consequences of underestimation might be. If missing a deadline is going to place you in a lot of hot water, then you might want to get some input from someone who knows not only about your past performance but about your future plans as well. Chances are your boss meets those criteria. It's interesting that studies have shown that while people often will underestimate their own completion dates, they generally will overestimate the finish times of others. So, if you want to get the most accurate time of completion, take into account your estimate and your boss' estimate, which probably will be overly conservative, and then split the difference.

- When a supervisor is not available, then you have to mull over your own track record and identify the rate limiting steps that will prevent you from completing the task. For example, if you have to rely upon input from a co-worker who is often unavailable, then that has to be factored in.

- If there will be no consequences for missing the target date, then there's no point in being optimistic about the completion time. The bottom line is that if missing a deadline is going to spell trouble, then consider your past experiences. If there will not be consequences, then just plow on with the project.

A major cause of burnout in the work place as well as in your personal endeavors is failure to achieve goals. Many books have been written on the subject about how to manage your time, and there are numerous seminars that are offered to help you get motivated. In general, the advice is basically the same. You need to have a general idea of what it is that needs to be accomplished in defined units of time, and then you need to set priorities. It also is a good idea to apply some of the same goal—achieving behaviors that you use in the work setting in your personal life, as well.

Everyone ought to have objectives that they want to achieve in order to provide some purpose to their lives. And whatever dream that happens to be, it should be realistic, and it should be something that you want, and not something that you are doing to please other people. Did you know that just thinking about a goal or writing that goal down will facilitate your accomplishing it? Once you've identified what it is you want to achieve, it becomes easier to identify information and circumstances that you can use to help you achieve that goal. From this point on, though, you need to be careful.

Keep in mind that I did not write this book. I wrote sentences, which came together as paragraphs, which then became chapters. If I had set about to write a book, I doubt I would have even started. Finding the time to take on such a project would have been daunting. But finding time to research a topic, and then knocking out a few paragraphs was never a problem. Do the same thing. Divide your ultimate goal into its component parts. As each part is completed, you will feel successful, which will make you act successful, and, before you know it, you're there.

Winning the Mental Challenge

Don't Worry; Be Happy: There are some people who can't seem to help worrying. About 30 percent of us are non-worriers, 15 percent are chronic worriers, and the rest fall somewhere in between. If you happen to be a chronic worrier, and you have tried everything you can to change, at least work to gain some control over your worrying behavior. After all, it's not how much you worry, but whether your worrying is interfering with your ability to function. Is it distracting you, keeping you from engaging in work or performing well in school? Is it causing you to lose sleep? One way to gain control over your worrying is to simply set aside a period of time when you are going to worry.

Select a time when worrying is least likely to be disruptive. It should be a period that is going to last about 30 minutes. Less or more time actually may intensify your worrying. Be careful where you do it. Don't sit in your favorite chair. Don't lie in bed worrying. Otherwise, you will turn the bedroom or your favorite location into reminders that later will evoke the same worrying behavior.

The objective of setting aside periods of time to worry is to break the worry cycle and to keep it from interfering with other activities. It's based on the principle of habituation. Think for a moment about your favorite meal. If you were to eat that food for breakfast, lunch, and dinner, chances are you wouldn't be able to stand even being in the same kitchen where it was being prepared after a few days. In very much the same way, setting aside periods of time during the day when you are going to worry, will enable you to habituate yourself. By designating time in the day when that's all you are going to do, it decreases the probability that the worrying will interfere with what you really need to be getting on with in your life. In short, take control over your worrying.

Stop Thinking About It: There's a significant difference between choosing to let something go and avoiding it. Choosing puts you in control, while evading the subject lets the problem have control over you.

When you're faced with a conflict, ask yourself this simple question:
"Is there anything I can do right now about this problem that I have not already done?"

If there is, then do it. Take some type of appropriate action immediately. Then once you have taken action, set the matter aside. If there is nothing else you can do, then let it go. Ruminating or obsessing about events rarely leads to any real solutions. Some of us are afraid to let go because of the belief that we are somehow working on the problem by worrying about it. Remember the wisdom of Reinhold Niebuhr:

"God, grant me the serenity to accept the things I cannot change, courage to change the things I can, and wisdom to know the difference."

- Many of your worries are related to past events you can no longer control.
- Most of the rest are related to what may occur in the future, of which at least half won't happen.
- Focus your resources on today. That's what you are most likely to have control over.

Resolve Situations As They Arise: The ability to rapidly resolve conflicts reflects a healthy state of mind. Anxiety and feelings of sadness or depression are sometimes the product of unresolved conflicts. The emotional residue of each circumstance may be stored and may interfere with feelings of contentment and peace. It is easy to carry around these unresolved feelings and become fatigued and burdened by 46 them. The more effectively you resolve situations as they arise, the more effectively you can live in the present and be unencumbered by the past. Patterns of resolving or not resolving conflict are often a function of early experiences, particularly very traumatic experiences.

To resolve particularly difficult conflicts may require professional assistance.

Ask Yourself:

- Do I tend to resolve situations as they arise?
- Do I find myself regretting not having said important things to people during past episodes of my life?
- Do I tend to 'smooth over' conflict when it occurs in relationships?
- Do I avoid conflict at all costs?
- Is it difficult for me to express emotions?
- Do I tend to rehash the events in my life, or, perhaps, preview possible solutions over and over in my mind, but never progress to the point where I take concrete action?

Take a moment to focus on how you feel when you avoid dealing with important situations. Focus on an image in the past week when you know you would have been better off to have brought something up that was bothering you, or when you regretted leaving something undone that you would have preferred to do. Let this feeling serve as a cue to practice resolving conflicts in the present. Stop and think of what you can say or do to reach some resolution, if only on a temporary basis. It may simply involve saying to someone, "Hey, I would like to talk about what just happened; do you have some time tomorrow?" Do something; do anything. Otherwise, you will reinforce your feelings of helplessness.

Resolving situations as they arise will probably confront you with your fears of failure or shame. People often avoid dealing with conflict because they do not believe their actions will be effective, or they are worried that others will respond negatively towards them. Ironically, avoiding conflict often sabotages relationships and makes life even more difficult. Soon, you actually do become ineffective, and, as a result, people no longer respond to you in a positive way. It becomes a self-fulfilling prophecy. This does not mean that it is best for you to analyze or to talk about every minor difficulty; it does mean that you take every step to resolve uncomfortable feelings as they arise in your life by either resolving your own inner feelings or by taking some concrete action.

Remember:

- You always have choices. If nothing else, you can choose your attitude.
- You always will act in accordance with your beliefs.
- Your stress decreases as your sense of control and optimism increases.

Get It Off Your Chest: Writing about the experiences in your life can be quite an effective strategy for reaching resolution and expressing emotions. Writing is simple and can be done almost anywhere, anytime. There is something about putting your thoughts and feelings on paper that helps. Sometimes, it simply helps you to break the cycle of ruminating about the event. Other times, it helps you to express important emotions. Or, it may help you to organize your feelings. Regardless, you will be surprised at the effectiveness of this technique.

The first step is to set aside fifteen or twenty minutes each day to write. Choose a time when you can be alone with your thoughts and feelings, free from distractions. Find a place and a time to do this each day and do it consistently. Simply write whatever comes to mind. You might focus on the events of the day or on an ongoing problem; you might reflect on a difficult event during your childhood, or you might write about a very happy experience in your life. Do not censor what you write: just write. In essence, you will be practicing free association. You write whatever comes to mind. If you find this hard to do, imagine writing to a friend, one you know very well. Tell her everything about your day, everything about your life, everything about yourself. Write about your joy, your fear, your anger, or your pain.

Talk Things Out With Yourself: There are many times in life when you may feel pressured to make a decision. Few decisions in life come without some degree of doubt, and conflict is a part of life. Dialogues, in written or spoken form, are useful in resolving these conflicts. Basically, this technique involves letting yourself experience two opposite sides of a conflict or quandary, like taking both sides in a debate. Imagine two opposing personalities or voices. Each personality gets the opportunity to discuss fully their side of the argument or their reason for making a particular choice, and the other gets to respond. This technique gives words to emotions, allowing feelings to be expressed and alternatives to be explored. You probably will feel silly at first, but give this exercise a fair chance. It really does work.

The sharing of feelings has proven to be highly therapeutic, leading to long-term gains in well-being. Under controlled conditions, undergraduate college students were asked to recall verbally the most traumatic event in their lives. One group narrated only the factual occurrences of the event, with no mention of their feelings about it. A second group described both the event and their feelings. A control group was asked to simply state what they were wearing or some other circumstantial element that had no emotional connotation. Those people who recalled their feelings about the events experienced an initial episode of increased anxiety as well as a decline in their immune systems. But over the course of the semester, it was the members of this group whose immune systems became more robust, resulting in fewer visits to the student health center. There was something about the act of disclosure that was both emotionally therapeutic and had an impact upon the immune system's ability to rebound.

How Disclosure Of Emotions Works: Several explanations have been offered. Among the most plausible is that when speaking or writing about a problem, you are forced to slow down. Information which has been ricocheting around the emotional brain is delayed during its translation into language. Your thoughts become organized. The problem is then perceived through different sensory pathways—through your eyes in the case of written disclosure, through your ears in the case of verbal disclosure. Each form of processing also takes time, adding a third modality, and it requires physical movement, adding a fourth. As a result, your mind often finds it easier to recognize potential solutions to improve or to overcome the perceived difficulty.

Desensitization is another hypothesis. Through the repetitive act of expressing your feelings, the emotional edge eventually wears off. Like watching re-runs of the same television program over and over again, you become tired of rehashing the same feelings and are able to distance yourself from their impact. (But this can also have the potential result of re-traumatizing a person, depending on the setting and the reception s/he receives.)

- Language provides a means of emotional expression.
- Language allows you to express your emotions in a controllable format.
- Putting your emotions into words allows you to perceive them from a new perspective.
- Simply changing the words you use can alter your emotional response to past or present events.

Some people have a difficult time disclosing emotion. Divulging your feelings is, in a sense, counter to being in control. You have a tendency to feel vulnerable. Furthermore, the longer a feeling has been suppressed, the more likely it is to emerge with a vengeance. By virtue of differences in temperament or early learning experiences, some people have difficulty accessing their emotions. In some cases, this stems from a fear of not being in control, or from a resistance to feel pain. You may have experienced an extraordinarily painful experience early in life and were so overwhelmed by the feeling that you learned to shut down the emotions whenever they began to surface. Write down those feelings you experienced in association with a recent stressor.

Language is both expressive of emotion, and it is a means through which emotion is expressed. Through the use of words, your expressing your feelings is extremely beneficial to both your mental and physical well-being. Maladies in many forms can arise when emotions constantly are repressed. It may seem that by ignoring your feelings, you are maintaining control over them, but actually the opposite, eventually, becomes true. The buried emotions find other ways to make themselves known. It may be through recurrent nightmares for the adult who believes he or she is over the sexual abuse that occurred in childhood. Anger, when turned inwards, eventually may manifest itself as a heart attack. In one way or another, your emotions will demand to be acknowledged. Why not do it on your terms and make emotions work for, instead of against, you?

Social Support

Loneliness is a major risk factor for disease. Indeed, it is suspected that one of the reason's people who believe in voodoo die after they learn a curse has been placed upon them is because they are shunned when the news spreads. Human contact is not only pleasurable; it is one of the most effective buffers against stress available to you.

- Associating with other living things produces beneficial emotional and physical results.
- Family, friends, pets, and plants provide emotional benefits by connecting you to the world outside yourself.
- Caring for others provides you with a sense of control over events.
- The behaviors associated with caring for people, pets, or plants reinforce a responsibility for your own wellbeing.

Assessing Your Social Safety Net:

Answer the following questions as true or false:

1. If I needed an emergency loan of $100, there is someone from whom I could get it.
2. There is someone who takes pride in my accomplishments.
3. I often meet or talk with family or friends.
4. Most people I know think highly of me.

Add up the number of true answers you recorded to these first four questions. Now continue.

5. If I needed an early morning ride to the airport, there's no one I would feel comfortable asking to take me.

6. I feel there is no one with whom I can share my most private worries and fears.

7. Most of my friends are more successful in making changes in their lives than I am.

8. I would have a hard time finding someone to go with me on a day trip to the beach or to the country.

Add up the number of times you responded with 'false' to the last four questions. And now add the number of 'true' responses to the first four questions to the number of 'false' responses to the second four. If your score is three or less, then you probably have inadequate social support. If it's four or more, then you likely have a good social safety net.

Barriers To Friendship: Some people create personal barriers to meaningful relationships. Because of unhealthy beliefs, they go to great lengths to avoid contact with others, although not in all circumstances. You may be outgoing in the workplace, where your role in the hierarchy is well defined, but you may feel ill at ease at a party. If there ever are circumstances under which you have difficulty communicating with others, it may be due to one of the following beliefs:

I don't want to appear silly or intrusive.
I'm concerned about sexual overtones.
I feel unworthy to be speaking to that person.

Respond to each that applies, as well as to others with which you identify, by asking the same questions that you would use to probe other beliefs:

- Are these your beliefs or those of someone else?
- Are your beliefs based upon experience?
- Can you think of times in your life when your belief system was challenged by reality?
- Have your beliefs ever kept you from achieving a goal?
- Are certain themes reflected in your beliefs?
- Are you willing to change one or more of your beliefs if they are obstacles to your goals!

When you make contact with others, let them know what you need from them. Some people intuitively will know how to support you; others will not. Some people will try to give advice; some people will talk about their own problems; others will try to cheer you up. While these responses can be helpful, it is better to talk with someone who knows how to listen.

Usually, what you need most when distressed is someone who can listen without judging. They don't have to solve your problem; they simply are there to hear you out. This provides you with an opportunity to express your thoughts and emotions, something that is extremely important when you are feeling distressed. If you don't have a partner, a family member, or a friend who can do this, you might want to talk with a professional therapist. The key is talking with someone who will allow you to express your feelings.

Remember to reciprocate. No one is devoid of hardship. Become a resource for those upon whom you depend. The following guidelines will greatly enhance your listening skills:

- Focus upon the other person's words and body language.
- Show interest by raising your eyebrows in response to what is being said.
- Use facial gestures, such as a smile, to convey empathy.
- Seek clarification when appropriate.
- Summarize.

Dealing with Burnout

Burnout is due to the cumulative effect of stress. It most often occurs in the workplace or home setting. While each situation requires a customized approach for dealing with it, there are some general guidelines that work for most people:

- **Set Priorities:** Insufficient time to complete tasks is a major contributor to stress and burnout. You have to set priorities. You can't do everything, so you have to determine those things that absolutely must be done first. And write them down on a piece of paper—one of those little sticky notes works well. When you complete the task, either check it off or crumple up the piece of paper and throw it away. Each of those strategies gives you a feeling of accomplishment.

- **Learn To Set Limits:** It's important to learn to say 'no' when you might be asked to engage in some behavior that you know in advance is going to cause you some distress. A lot of people make the mistake of saying yes when they really want to say no. Learning how to say no is perhaps one of the most important steps in dealing with stress, whether it is occurring in your personal life or whether it's occurring in your professional environment. If you say yes too often, you also rob yourself of precious recovery time.

- **Seek Advice:** Don't be afraid to ask questions. Seek out advice from your co-workers or people who might have more experience dealing with a particular problem that you have. Remember, you are allowed to share your problems with people and to talk things out.

- **Delegate:** You need to delegate responsibility and not believe you have to be the one who has to carry the full weight of the problem on your shoulders. No one can handle everything.

- **Set Realistic Goals:** You have to be realistic about meeting objectives. There are certain things that just can't be done with the resources available to you or completed within a given deadline.

Put On A Happy Face: For several years, I was engaged in research attempting to find out if people can use acting skills as a means by which to change their personalities. The study came about as a result of an observation I made many years earlier of a person who had been diagnosed with Multiple Personality Disorder, now referred to as Dissociative Identity Disorder. This is a rare condition where several distinct personalities, each residing within the same body, are exhibited. An experiment was designed where a small amount of blood was drawn before and after each personality exhibited itself. Profound changes were observed in the number of cells in the immune system after certain types of personalities had been expressed.

This led to a study designed to determine if a mentally healthy person could 'act' like a particular personality and elicit changes in his or her physiology. Two actors were chosen to play contrasting roles (one very negative and depressing, the other uplifting) in a 30-minute scene. After a brief intermission, a second 30-minute play was performed, and the actors switched roles. The program was presented nightly for two weeks before live audiences. Before and after each of the performances, blood samples were drawn from both the actors and the audience members. My research team was amazed to note that several changes occurred in the immune system, which were consistent with observations reported in the medical literature, indicating that depression was correlated with impaired immunity. In short, by simply acting in a depressed way, certain measures of the immune system are decreased.

Many people, when they hear the word acting, think automatically of faking it. I use the word acting to describe a process whereby a person elicits a true emotion in order to achieve a particular physiological response—acting like a winner to become a winner. The signals transmitted to this person's brain are very similar to those that would be transmitted if that person were experiencing the same emotion in response to something occurring within his environment. The emotion this person elicits through acting is a true emotion.

It's easy to observe such emotional alternation within ourselves. First, put a deep frown on your face, and count to ten. Now, observe how you feel, both physically and mentally. Next, move your facial muscles into the form of a smile. Again, count to ten, and observe the changes experienced in both your mind and body. Try it.

The way you behave can contribute to the severity of symptoms that you might experience in illness. By employing acting skills, you may be able to modify your body in ways that will decrease the probability of becoming ill.

- Acting using particular emotion can fool the body into experiencing the physiological changes that occur when actually experiencing that emotion.
- Negative emotions suppress the immune system, which can lead to physical and mental illnesses.

Whenever I Feel Afraid, I Hold My Head Erect: problems arise when an emotion is expressed inappropriately. This can include unleashing an emotional response at the wrong target or when emotional expression interferes with your ability to perform.

When you assume a certain body posture, feedback signals are transmitted back into your body, eliciting a physiological state to match what is on the surface. So, basically, wearing a mask of confidence elicits a state of confidence. Use these body language tips to perform more effectively:

- Stand or sit with your back straight.
- Hold your shoulders back.
- Relax your arms and hands.
- Lift your chin.
- Focus your eyes on the person with whom you're dealing.
- Hold this pose—even a brief lapse can be sufficient to cause you to lose your confidence.

Your physical stance can impact your emotional response to stressful events. If the situation involves another person, your body language also can impact their emotional responses.

Bottom Line

- You always have choices. If nothing else, you can choose your attitude.
- You always will act in accordance with your beliefs.
- Your stress decreases as your sense of control and optimism increases.

If We Couldn't Laugh, We Would All Go Insane: There is nothing more effective to reduce blood pressure and relax muscles than having a good laugh. It may stimulate endorphin release within the brain, which would certainly explain the feeling of wellbeing that is associated with humor; but, at the very least, it's a brief diversion from the stressors in your life.

How is it that some people are able to relate the most dreadful experiences in such a way that they and everyone around them dissolve into spasms of laughter? When telling of their home being destroyed by a fire, they focus on the scent of barbecued beef wafting up from the freezer after it exploded. Or they can aptly recall the children's bath toys floating off in a flotilla after the flood. It certainly isn't that they are immune to devastation and loss or the incredible problems they face in putting their lives back together. Instead, they understand, even subconsciously, that how they choose to perceive the problem, whether through weirdness or woe, has an impact upon how well they cope. As Carol Burnett said, "Comedy is tragedy plus time."

Norman Cousins, the late editor of *The Saturday Review*, wrote *Anatomy of an Illness* and described how he used humor to overcome an incapacitating degenerative disease. His physicians had diagnosed him with an untreatable condition and told him that he faced years of increasing pain until his death. Cousins flatly refused to accept this prognosis. Instead, being a typically difficult-to-manage patient, he angered his doctors by checking out of the hospital and into a nearby hotel. There, he did two things. He undertook a regular program of exercise and good nutrition, and he spent a lot of time watching comic movies. He soon found that after a good dose of humor, he was able to sleep and rest without pain. Cousins then became adamant about being surrounded by hilarity in the form of old movies and records. Within months, the symptoms were in remission. It was the use of humor which he most greatly credited with his recovery.

Why is laughter such good medicine? Some research indicates that there is an increased level of a particular antibody secreted in the saliva following episodes of laughter. It's also been correlated with elevated levels of beta-endorphin in the bloodstream. Both the antibody and the beta-endorphin are released during periods of exercise, which hearty laughter actually is since it moves the entire chest and abdominal area.

There's also the fact that the focus of the humor creates a diversion, thereby masking opposing, more painful emotions, such as sadness or anger. When you laugh, it creates a condition of emotional interference by overriding the brain's ability to produce an opposing emotion, such as sadness.

Since we seldom laugh without stimulation from others, there is an element of socialization involved, as well, even if the person who's making us laugh is Allan King's voice on the radio or Groucho Marx's face on the movie screen. It doesn't matter that neither is alive because their wit and slapstick antics still are.

Realize that from birth your body has learned to associate smiling with warmth and security. From the moment you smiled at your mother, and she smiled back, the configuration of the facial muscles has taught your brain that you are experiencing a state of positive feelings. In the same way that the sound of the bell caused

Pavlov's dogs to salivate, it may be that smiling triggers the emotion of pleasure.

Gallows humor is something we all experience at one time or another, and it often frightens us. No matter how inappropriate you may believe it is to laugh in the midst of tragedy, nor how rationally insensitive it may seem, release through the occasional sick joke is actually a coping skill, enabling you to balance the horror of the situation while keeping your emotions under control.

Try this to experience how effective it is. Force yourself to laugh. It needn't be laughter caused by actual mirth. Just smile and begin to emit the sound of laughter. If you're in a crowded room, all the better—you'll be able to laugh at how silly it is to laugh at nothing at all while those around you wonder what's wrong with you. If you laugh long enough in this situation, the others will join you, proving that laughter, like yawning, is contagious.

Pay attention to how you feel both during and after the laughter. Notice the way you breathe. Most people inhale deeply and exhale in short bursts. This is the exact opposite of the very shallow, rapid breathing pattern which occurs during periods of anxiety.

Try this in real life situations when fear, anxiety, sadness, or any other negative emotion interferes with your ability to enjoy good mental and physical health. Move your facial muscles into the form of a smile. The pleasure sensation the brain associates with smiling serves to neutralize the negative emotion being experienced.

- Humor as a coping tool allows you to maintain distance from and control over stressors.

The emotion-arousing ability of music has intrigued researchers. Happiness appears to follow fast tempos, simple harmonies, and flowing rhythms. Melody apparently plays a very small role in arousing particular emotions. Music written in the major chords is associated with happiness, gracefulness, playfulness, and merriment. The minor chords are usually sad and sentimental. Complex, dissonant harmonies can stimulate vigor and excitement. Classical music tends to gain more pleasant emotional value with repetition than popular music. Popular works reach a rapid peak in affective value, followed by a rapid decline in pleasantness with continued repetition.

Music is capable of both inflaming as well as taming the passions. By penetrating your very core, it can cause you to experience intense pleasure or to weep. Through its ability to modulate the expression of emotions, music has its greatest impact upon your health. Most music theories are predicated upon the association between music and emotions. More than 100 years ago, Herbert Spencer observed that when speech became emotional, the corresponding sound spanned a far greater tonal range and more approximated music than syntactical language. He believed that these fluctuations of sound eventually became separated from language and then evolved into a form of music. This is quite opposite to the viewpoint of Charles Darwin, who believed that music evolved as a form of sexual invitation, a tool with which to attract the attention of a potential mate. This conclusion was based upon observations of birdsong as well as evidence that the males of many species use their vocalization capabilities far more when under the influence of sexual feelings. I suppose it could be argued that the custom of women throwing panties onto the stage when being crooned by a popular performer might be a human version of this biologically-based behavior.

A more pragmatic viewpoint is that music evolved as a means by which to communicate information. For example, the singing voice has been found to carry over a greater distance than does the spoken voice. In fact, many wind instruments probably were invented for this purpose. Related to this interpretation is the observation that, in certain aboriginal cultures, songs were used to map the borders of territories. In essence, the contours of the territory were reflected directly in the contours of the melody.

Regardless of the precise origins of music, there is absolutely no question that it is a facilitator of social interaction. The behavior of dancing as well as hand clapping is an obvious manifestation of this. Music is used in religious ceremonies as well as in rites of passage in order to prepare people for action. It is used not only to facilitate the display of a particular emotion, but also to enhance the probability that all of those in the social group will be experiencing the same emotion at approximately the same time. Music does not necessarily cause an emotion. Instead, it has the ability to intensify or to highlight the emotion which might be elicited by some other event.

Extreme forms of arousal often are perceived as being painful or unpleasant. But, we all crave to have some milder form of excitement in our lives, which is actually life-enhancing. The physiological correlates of arousal are very similar, regardless of the particular emotion that is being elicited. For example, the original Kinsey report reveals that aggressive arousal and sexual arousal share in common psysiological changes. These include increased heart rate, muscle tone, and blood pressure. Of course, not all music is intended to induce arousal. Some forms do just the opposite. Either way, music is a powerful tool that can be used to enhance the emotional state that you wish to experience.

Music has many benefits in the context of health. It has very strong mnemonic properties. Many of us are able to recall the words of songs with much greater accuracy than we are able to recall prose. This also has been demonstrated in mentally retarded children, who have been found to be capable of recalling more material after it is presented to them in the form of song than when it is read to them simply as a story. Oliver Sacks, in his book Awakenings, described a patient who exhibited excitability as well as uncontrollable movements. Sacks goes on to describe how, "By far the best treatment of her crises was music, the effects of which were almost uncanny." In his other book, The Man Who Mistook His Wife for a Hat, Sacks describes a musician who, because of a neurological condition, was unable to recognize a number of common objects, although his musical abilities were largely unimpaired. Functioning was very difficult for this individual, unless he took care of his basic needs while singing. Indeed, music was the only means by which he was able to find structure in his environment. Music also has been found to enable people who stutter to communicate more readily. Mel Tillis, the popular Country and Western performer, has a difficult time communicating in spoken language, but he has no difficulty entertaining huge audiences through song. There is good reason for this. Language is dominant in the left hemisphere of the brain, while music awareness and expression is dominant in the right hemisphere. There is no reason why a pathological condition that impairs one activity should interfere with the other.

There are instances whereby music actually can impair health. Some individuals are susceptible to a condition called musicogenic epilepsy. As a result of the physical properties of music acting directly upon the brain, certain passages of especially arousing music have been shown to induce grand mal seizures. In some very rare instances, even the recollection of music can provoke these convulsions. Another detrimental side effect of music may well occur as a result of its widespread use in hospital operating theaters. Several years ago, a research paper published in one of the leading medical journals revealed that surgeons make fewer mistakes if they are able to listen to their favorite music while in the operating room. This is all well and good for the surgeon, but it may be detrimental to the patient in other ways. Implicit memory is sometimes thought of as the subconscious memory. There are certain types of anesthesia that actually preserve implicit memory, enabling you to recall events that might have occurred while you supposedly were deeply anesthetized. At least one case has been recorded in the legal journals in which a person recalled her surgeons making disparaging remarks about her obesity. Re-exposure to certain cues enabled her to recall those remarks, and she successfully sued her physicians. The same could happen with respect to any stimulus to which you might be exposed, including music. That previously therapeutic score may now elicit anxiety, having been associated with a hospital stay.

The Greeks of Plato's era believed that training in music was essential for full development. They recognized it as a powerful tool that could, indeed, alter the character of those who studied it. They also believed that certain types of music could be detrimental. A modern era application of the use of music for evil ends occurred during the days of Nazi Germany, when music was used to heighten the emotions of the crowds, as well as a means by which to cloud their judgment. Not only did Hitler use music to manipulate the emotions of those who were listening to his speeches; he often used musical passages composed by Wagner to arouse himself. For Hitler, music was an energizing drug.

Music has been subject to censorship perhaps more than any other art form. During Stalin's Russia, American jazz was banned for many years because it was thought to be decadent. There is currently considerable debate as to whether or not certain forms of rap music should be censored because the messages conveyed are considered counter to the norms of society. Regardless of whether you agree or disagree with such censorship, these concerns do acknowledge the ability of music profoundly to influence the lives of those who listen to it.

If you are experiencing an excessive amount of anger or fear, then use music to facilitate the appearance of the emotional state you would rather be in or need to be in to achieve a state of optimal health. Whether music really induces feelings or simply evokes images and memories of feelings is debatable. Some argue that listening to music is nothing more than an escape from reality, and this may be the case under some circumstances. However, there is also overwhelming evidence that the physical properties of the sound waves are able to penetrate the inner recesses of the brain to induce very real physiological and emotional consequences. Use it.

The following guidelines were created by the performance coach, Dr. Jim Loehr, during the course of working with elite athletes:

- Make two separate music CD's of 12 to 15 minutes each. CD 1 should be music that energizes you, lifts your spirits, and puts you into a state of High Positive Energy. This is the music that pumps you up and stimulates feelings of confidence and empowerment. This is your positive fight—your warrior music. CD 2 should be music that relaxes you, slows you down, and enhances feelings of inner peace and harmony. This is your recovery— healing music.
- Sound tracks from movies and music without lyrics work best for most people. The idea is to

move physiology in targeted directions with the help of music. Select what works best for you.

- Use your CD's daily to either facilitate positive energy and arousal or relaxation and recovery.
- New CD's need to be made approximately once a month to keep the impact strong and powerful.
- Combining visualization and imagery with the music dramatizes the effects.

Winning the Physical Challenge

Every Breath You Take: A crisis has just arisen. Don't let your physiology overwhelm you. Take immediate control. One of the most effective interventions was suggested by Judge Ito when, during a particularly heated moment of the O.J. Simpson trial, he admonished Marcia Clark to "take three, deep breaths." It was excellent advice. Controlling your breathing is an indirect means by which to exert control over many physiological processes. Breathing influences your blood gasses, which, in turn, affect heart rate. Furthermore, you really are controlling the neurotransmitters in the brain, which regulate the muscles of the diaphragm. Those same neurotransmitters can impact your perception and judgment. These are just a few of the benefits of controlled breathing:

- Helps to trigger a relaxation response
- Enables you to better focus

- Establishes an optimal level of oxygen in the body
- Induces a feeling of being in control
- May cool the brain

Breathing exercises also counteract the detrimental effects of rapid, shallow breaths. If it leads to hyperventilation, this can result in vascular changes in the brain, along with feelings of dizziness.

There are certain components of emotional responses that lie outside your control. The autonomic nervous system and neuroendocrine pathways are extremely difficult, if not impossible, for the average person to exert control over. Some highly skilled practitioners of yoga have been shown to have such mastery, but it requires years of intensive practice to achieve. Still, there are particular things which can be done that are subject to your conscious control and which, in turn, transmit signals to those systems within your body over which you have minimal influence.

You cannot consciously control the proportions of oxygen and carbon dioxide in your blood, but you can regulate your breathing and, in doing so, can transmit signals throughout the body which have the ultimate effect of stabilizing various physiological systems. If you experience the very rapid and shallow breathing often associated with fear and anxiety, this can create build-up of carbon dioxide in the bloodstream. Elevated CO_2 has been correlated with attacks of anxiety. Thus, while the anxious state occurred in response to something threatening in the environment, the emotional state is continued by the physiological consequences.

Simply drawing three, long, deep breaths—inhaling through the nose, filling the lungs, distending the diaphragm, and then exhaling slowly through the mouth—has a substantial effect on altering the chemical makeup of the blood and, therefore, on alleviating fear or anxiety. You'll not only find yourself energized; you indirectly will be controlling your physiology. This type of deep breathing normally is associated with the relaxation response, not with anxiety. Signals are transmitted into the nervous system, conveying to the body that it is actually in a relaxed state.

By inhaling through the nostrils, another effect occurs—the brain experiences a very slight drop in temperature. An elevation in brain temperature is associated with negative feelings, which explains why so many clichés have grown up around the concept, such as calling someone 'hot-headed,' or suggesting they 'chill out.'

There is still another benefit to engaging in deep breathing exercises; you almost immediately will feel different because you are actively doing something. And remember, it's not the stressor, but your feeling of helplessness, that is detrimental to your health. Breathing helps you take control.

- Deep breathing helps you distance yourself from the immediate stressor through an act you control.
- The body associates deep breathing with a state of relaxation, which leads to an enhanced emotional state.
- Deep breathing actually cools the brain and stabilizes the physiology.

Abdominal Breathing

- Lie down on a comfortable surface and place a light object on your stomach. A book or small pillow will be fine. While breathing, you want your abdomen to expand in response to downward movement of the diaphragm. This is the muscle that separates the abdominal cavity from the lungs. As the diaphragm moves down, air is drawn into the lower part of the lung. At the same time, your stomach will rise. By placing an object on your stomach, you will see this happen. Inhale slowly, hold the breath for a short interval, and then slowly exhale.

- Begin by doing a set of 10 deep breathing exercises. Then, as you become more adept, do three or more such sets. Be careful that you do not become lightheaded. This can happen when you start doing this for the first time. When you reach the point where you can breathe smoothly and rhythmically for five minutes, you will have mastered a time-honored technique for reducing stress. By the way, the reason for lying down is so that you can observe your abdomen rising as a confirmation that you are doing it correctly. After you know what to do, you can practice this technique in just about any comfortable setting— standing, sitting, or lying down.

Are you really in a bind? Is the pressure overwhelming? Then try this 15 second variation for an almost instant calming effect. Inhale slowly over a period of five seconds. Remember to use the diaphragm. Then, hold your breath for another five seconds before exhaling for another five. Take two regular breaths, and repeat the cycle. Keep doing this until you begin to feel calm.

The Benefits Of Relaxation: Relaxation counters stress and so, by extension, helps to undo the damage that stress does to the body. In addition, relaxation very well may have beneficial effects independent of its ability to counteract stress. That is, you will benefit from a relaxation protocol, regardless of whether you are experiencing stress. For example, many people have reported that a regular program of relaxation helps them to:

- Increase their energy level
- Enhance memory
- Lower blood pressure
- Enhance awareness of their emotional state
- Increase the restful stage of sleep
- Increase sense of control

Relaxation can be achieved in a number of different ways. Furthermore, it does not have to begin with a state of quiescence. A very effective way to achieve relaxation is to briefly exercise and, then, to allow heart rate, respiration rate, and the other physiological changes follow a natural, downward spiral. You will experience relaxation even though you may be out of breath. Indeed, many athletes report that exercise induces a state of relaxation when it's over. Whether this is due to the release of endorphins, which commonly occurs at the conclusion of exercise, or whether it is due to the altered kinetics is debatable. What's important is the fact that it works.

Regardless of which method you choose, each will be enhanced if you limit sensory distractions. Dim the light, select a room temperature that is neither too warm nor too cold, and wear loose, comfortable clothing. You want to reduce anything that might prove to be a distraction.

Touch Me In The Morning: Most mammalian species employ touch in the context of healing. Humans rub sore and tender spots, while animals lick the abrasion. A symbolic form of this behavior is a mother kissing her child's wound in order to make it better. It makes sense that touch would play an important role in your well-being when you realize that the skin is one of the largest organ systems of the body, and that it is constantly at the interface of the environment in which you reside. It is well documented in the acupuncture literature that applying pressure to certain regions of the body can, indeed, have a profound impact upon distant sites. There may be additional benefits.

When an animal is licking a wound, not only does this serve to cleanse the area, but, in recent years, very powerful substances have been detected in saliva, which are capable of exerting anti-microbial effects. These include powerful antibiotics. There is even a chemical which interferes with the ability of HIV to attach to target cells. There are many components of the behavior of touching that impact upon your health and well-being, depending upon the precise manner in which the touch is being applied.

Massage may induce a state of relaxation, which serves to counter the adverse effects of generalized stress. Massage has been found to reduce anxiety and depression in those suffering from chronic fatigue syndrome, in adolescent mothers, and in those who are HIV positive. This may explain the correlation between massage and elevated Natural Killer Cell activity and T-cell levels in those diagnosed with HIV.

Some massage therapists assert that massage may stimulate the movement of immune system cells within lymphatic channels in the body. It is argued that by engaging in a form of deep massage, one would be able to stimulate the migration of lymphocytes. This is not an unreasonable claim. It is essential that lymphocytes constantly move around the body in order to seek out pathogens. They move through the circulatory system as well as within the lymphatic channels. The lymphatic channels can be looked upon as a series of garden hoses that link the lymph nodes and the spleen. Lymph nodes and the white pulp of the spleen are those large filters where pathogens accumulate and where they come into contact with disease-fighting lymphocytes. But the lymphatics, in contrast to the circulatory system, have no heart. There is no equivalent pump. What enables the cells to move, albeit very sluggishly, from one lymph node to another is the peristaltic movement of muscles surrounding the lymphatic channels. An argument is made that by recreating that peristaltic movement through massage, one can facilitate lymphocyte trafficking. Regardless of whether the effects are direct or indirect, massage certainly has been found to have positive effects in treating a variety of immunologic illnesses, such as asthma, chronic fatigue syndrome, pediatric dermatitis, and HIV.

No one would question the fact that massage provides a form of escape. You temporarily are removed from stressful circumstances and, if relaxing in this manner is conducive to your personality, then it's clearly going to have beneficial effects. Furthermore, you might manifest stress in the form of muscle tension, which can be directly alleviated through massage. There also is a degree of social interaction which is very beneficial to your health.

Massage And Development Of Infants: There is no question that touch and massage not only are beneficial but absolutely essential in the context of early development. Tiffany Fields, a clinical psychologist, conducted a study in which premature infants were divided into one of two groups. One group was gently touched several times a day. Their backs and the backs of their legs were stroked. The other premature infants were handled only when it was necessary to change their diapers and when it was time for them to be fed. Otherwise, they were left alone. Those children who were touched grew at a rate that was over 30 percent greater than those children who were not touched. They attained their neurologic reflexes sooner and checked out of the hospital several days prior to the children who were not touched. At eight months of age, they even had motor and cognitive advantages over those children who were not touched.

Maggot Therapy: There's another form of massage which many people find rather disgusting, but which is returning as a treatment option. It is based upon an observation that was made during World War I. It was observed that those soldiers who were severely injured and who remained on the battlefield for several days before they could be tended to by health care workers often had speedier recoveries compared with those soldiers who were transported almost immediately to the first aid areas. In other words, those soldiers whose wounds became infested with flies and maggots actually were better off than those soldiers whose wounds were kept clean and had various medicines applied. It was the latter individuals whose limbs most often required amputation.

One interpretation is that the maggots were responsible for the observed healing. While seeking out infected and decaying tissue, the maggots also were gently massaging the healthy cells that were replacing those that were damaged. When their job was done, they sprouted wings and gently flew away. No need to rip away dressings containing growth and other healing substances. It also provided an opportunity for air to surround the injury, which, in turn, promoted healing. As incredible as this may sound, maggot therapy is making a comeback. No, not in out of the way locations where people can't afford more modern techniques, but in major hospitals in large cities in the United States are maggots once again being utilized. This is because many of the antibiotics that were such powerful weapons a few decades ago now are practically useless in protecting us against the bacteria that they originally were designed to attack. This is due to the indiscriminate and inappropriate use of antibiotics in our society. Maggots, though, keep on working. In fact, deep bone infections seldom respond to antibiotics, but they always have responded reasonably well to maggot therapy.

One final interpretation of how massage might work is that it brings about harmony within energy meridians within the body. The role of energy meridians is the foundation for many forms of Oriental medicine, and this interpretation must not be excluded simply because it does not fit into the Western medical paradigm. I'm not suggesting that you embrace this interpretation with blind acceptance, but only that you keep an open mind about it.

Aromas And Aromatherapy: Some people claim that the sense of smell is a means by which to manipulate emotions. Proof of this claim is not available, although when considering how olfaction is mediated within the brain, it certainly is feasible. Most of the sensory systems course through the brain via a labyrinth of structures and pathways. For example, the sense of hearing as well as vision wends its way through the sensory apparatus, arriving initially within a structure called the thalamus. From this relay site, this information is transmitted to so-called 'higher brain centers,' where it is processed in ways that enable you to make the appropriate decision about what is happening in the environment. Eventually, all of the information arrives in the amygdala, which is the brain's emotional computer. The sense of smell is different. Olfactory information is able to short-circuit many of the higher brain areas and to plunge directly into the emotional brain. Some of the information goes into the part of the brain, which controls the autonomic nervous system as well as many of the hormonal pathways which are activated during stress. This very well may explain the well-documented association between the sense of smell and those behaviors that are linked with emotions. They would include sex as well as aggression. Many species actually recognize each other, as well as their emotional state, on the basis of smell alone.

There's a very good reason why the sense of smell is processed differently, at least in mammals. Most mammals depend upon visual information to negotiate their environments. Furthermore, the type of information coming in through the visual system is relatively complete and enables us to respond almost immediately. For example, during the Stone Age, if a meat-eating dinosaur were to see a small object scurrying across a field, it would have been able to make the immediate decision that this was something to eat. On the other hand, if it saw a very large animal, indeed one larger than itself, it probably would have enough information to know that it should flee. However, if that same animal caught the odor of something, a large amount of cognition would be required in order to make the appropriate decision. If it were the scent of a female dinosaur that a male happened to identify, he would need to recall her normal repertoire of behaviors and tap into a variety of cognitive centers in order to determine where she most likely would be. So it was very important that the memory of past experience become very closely associated with the sense of smell.

This, along with other research, clearly reveals that there is a pathway by which olfactory information is able to enter those areas of the brain that are intimately involved with the expression of emotions. That does not necessarily mean that these pathways still are being used. They could be left over from some period in our evolution which has no functional purpose at all in modern society. Let's briefly review the evidence that, in certain contexts, proves that odors can have a profound impact both upon our physiology as well as upon our behavior.

The Scent Of A Woman: It is the study of reproductive pheromones, which provides the most convincing argument that aromas can impact upon your health. Pheromones are molecules emitted into the environment by a number of species. They communicate information from one member of that specie to another. Fish, rats, dogs, and even humans rely upon them. Some evoke the emotion of fear, others anger, but those that have been most extensively studied are those that elicit the emotions associated with arousal of the reproductive system.

The most convincing documentation that pheromones do function in human society is to be found in those situations where women live together. Women who live in college dormitories with many other women have been found to have synchronized menstrual cycles. The same is true of women who live on the same floor in prisons. In addition, men and women each produce chemicals which serve as an attractant for the member of the opposite gender. Short chain fatty acids called copulins have been identified in the vaginal secretions of a variety of female primates, with the amount of copulin increasing as estrogen rises. When men are exposed to a large number of odors, they will exhibit preference for secretions containing copulin. In addition to men being attracted to copulin, which is found at highest concentrations at the time of ovulation, women are attracted to a chemical called exaltalide. It is a macrocyclic ketone which children, men, and post-menopausal women have a very difficult time detecting, unless they are given estrogen. Studies have revealed that not only will exposure to exaltalide affect the judgment of women when evaluating the written and interviewed descriptions of male job candidates, but they selectively will seek out and sit on chairs which contain a trace amount of this chemical.

This is the basis of the perfume industry. People wear fragrances primarily for the purpose of making themselves attractive to members of the opposite sex. If you question this conclusion, try to recall if you have ever seen an advertisement for a fragrance which would make the wearer smell like an engineer, a school teacher, or a nurse. Of course not. That's not why they are marketed. Not only are they marketed as sexual attractants, but it is the perfume industry that has sponsored much of the research delving into the nature of reproductive pheromones. It is noteworthy that women are 10,000 times more sensitive to aromas at the time of ovulation as compared with other intervals during the menstrual cycle. This, undoubtedly, enables them to identify a male when the probability of procreation is optimal. Of course it works in the other direction as well since men are attracted to copulin, which is produced most when women are ovulating. This may explain why oral sex has such an intimate impact. The exchange of bodily odors is forced to occur and, undoubtedly, serves as a means of social communication.

Aromatherapy: The observations made in the context of reproductive pheromone research clearly reveal that trace amounts of chemicals can make their way into key areas of our brains and arouse not only the endocrine physiology that is paramount for reproduction to occur, but also libido and other behavioral manifestations of procreation. Is it really that far fetched to propose that other types of odors might also arouse other physiological systems, including those that affect your health? This is the basis of aromatherapy. It is predicated upon the belief that essential oils found in plants are capable of imparting fragrances that are capable of affecting not only emotions but also mental and physical well-being. For example, the fragrance associated with lavender is believed to be relaxing and serves as a gentle sedative. Rosemary, on the other hand, is thought to have the opposite effect and serves to stimulate. And rose oil is said to be able to calm the emotions of anger. Claims are made about many other fragrances, as well.

There are three forms of aromatherapy. Holistic aromatherapy is the first and incorporates the use of essential oils, often in the context of massage. The second form is medical aromatherapy, in which specific fragrances are prescribed in order to counter various maladies. Finally, aesthetic aromatherapy involves the use of oils and fragrances to treat skin problems, such as stretch marks. It's also used to induce a state of relaxation. While the use of aromatherapy dates back 5,000 years to the days of the early Egyptians, the form of aromatherapy practiced in Western society dates to 16th century Germany. A large number of claims are made regarding the use of aromatherapy. Conditions ranging from arthritis and allergies, to anger and depression, are thought to be affected by different aromas. Whether these claimed benefits really are due to something associated with the chemical configuration of the odor-inducing molecule or simply the evocation of memory is hard to discern. Many people do associate fragrances with certain situations or people, and it may be the memory of that circumstance which is actually evoking the emotional state. Of course, the same odor may evoke completely different states, depending upon the nature of one's memory. When evaluating such claims against the backdrop of data collected under well-controlled circumstances in the arena of reproductive pheromones, I believe they should be given serious consideration.

At least one study conducted in mice under well-controlled laboratory conditions has revealed that, when animals are exposed to a stressor, they produce a type of pheromone that is capable of inhibiting the immune system of other mice. This included a reduction in the proliferation of antibody-producing cells as well as the proliferation of T-cells, which coordinate so many aspects of the immune system. It was concluded that the mechanism, most likely, was activation of the brain circuitry that gives rise to elevated stress chemicals. These are the same chemicals that are capable, at high concentrations, of suppressing the immune system.

Environmentalize Your Surroundings: Let's consider a very practical way in which you can utilize this information in dealing with emotions. You might start by environmentalizing your surroundings. If you had a bad experience in your office, re-exposure to some fragrances might evoke the same physiological and psychological consequences that you experienced at the time the event happened. In other words, conditioning may be occurring. If you can, reduce your exposure to those odors. On the other hand, certain fragrances may elicit memories of very pleasant emotional states. If that is the case, then seek out those fragrances in order to induce the state you wish to evoke. And who knows? Perhaps some of the claims made by aromatherapists are valid. It's unlikely that a therapy would have endured for thousands of years if there weren't some basis for it. Use your body as a laboratory, and discover which fragrances work for you in helping you to win the stress challenge.

- By circumventing pathways employed by the other senses, the sense of smell allows you to experience more rapid emotional reactions to events.
- Possibly because of past memories associated with certain scents, aromas can be used to induce positive emotional states.

It Hurts So Bad: Pain profoundly interferes with the ability to enjoy emotional or physical pleasure in life. Just as perceived control enables you better to cope with stress, control also enables you to endure greater amounts of pain.

When it was first suggested that terminal cancer patients be allowed to control the amount of pain medication they received, physicians were gravely concerned about the potential for over-medication, as this might lead to addiction or, even worse, death. Yet exactly the opposite proved to be true. Patients given control over their pain medications actually used fewer and lower dosages and reported less pain than patients who received medications on a schedule set by the health provider.

Pain is one of the less-than-pleasant facts of life, which we must all cope with at varying times in varying degrees. Here are a few suggestions for dealing with it:

- **Accept the pain rather than becoming locked into an emotional battle with it.** Accepting the pain as part (but not all) of your experience can reduce its grip on your ability to function. Pain exists to make you aware of a part of you that needs care. Consider it a byproduct of a healing process going on within your body. Work with this function rather than against it, and healing will be facilitated.

- **Create a diversion for yourself.** Use imagery to mentally transport yourself to a setting that is pleasant and painless. Note any physical and emotional circumstances that make the pain worse, and take steps to avoid those circumstances.

- **Try to relax.** Seek out a tranquil setting, get comfortable, breathe, and meditate. Just focusing on your breath as you inhale and exhale can provide an effective diversion.

- **Change your diet.** If pain is triggered by inflammation, realize that saturated fats, especially those found in meats and dairy products, can aggravate inflammatory pain. So can caffeine, which tends to increase tension. On the other hand, nutrients such as calcium and magnesium help relax muscles. Some evidence also suggests that a diet rich in carotenes and vitamins E and C can help decrease sensitivity to the pain of inflammation.

- **Pursue some social support for yourself.** Having others around can serve as a distraction from pain. Being lonely can trigger depression or make discomfort feel worse.

- **Take control of your situation.** A person who has control over events is able to endure more adversity than a person who has no control at all.

Most stress-related chemical changes are highly adaptive. They have evolved for the purpose of getting us out of short-term emergency situations. Problems arise when they persist for months or even years. For example, blood pressure will rise as a result of a stress-induced increase in heart rate. Furthermore, as a result of the metabolic changes that occur within your body, there can be a build-up of cholesterol, resulting in a reduction in the diameter of the blood vessel lumen. If blood pressure remains elevated for an extended period of time, damage to the inside lining of the blood vessels can occur and, especially in post-menopausal women, result in hypertensive stroke.

There are behavioral interventions that may help. George Engel, a famous psychologist, conducted an experiment in which he trained monkeys to either increase or decrease their heart rate in order to avoid a mild stressor. This and other types of studies provide the most convincing evidence that biofeedback works. Put on a heart rate monitor and try this simple exercise:

A Simple Biofeedback Exercise

1. Find a comfortable place to sit.
2. Measure your heart rate.

3. Inhale and exhale, all the while observing how your heart rate responds.
4. Concentrate on lowering your heart rate. Adjust the tempo of your breathing until the beats per minute start to decline.

Now try to increase your heart rate without resorting to physical activity.

Learning
Stress-Recovery

Most people know how to experience stress. That's not the problem. The problem is that very few of us know adequately how to respond to stress. As odd as it may sound, it actually is possible to train your body to withstand stress.

Every cell within the cardiovascular system, the respiratory system, and even the immune system has the ability to learn to withstand stress. It is well-documented that if the concentration of a chemical increases within the body, there will be a corresponding adjustment in the ability of the receptor to attract the chemical. It's one of the ways the body adapts to change. By bathing the body's cells in stress hormones during their episodic release, the cells learn to recover; and, then, when a major stressor arises, these cells are better able to adapt.

The best form of stress from which to train recovery is exercise, yet very few people take advantage of this powerful tool. Some studies suggest that the average person spends two and a half hours a day watching television, yet only 15 minutes per day exercising. Many people get no exercise at all. Never in the course of history have people been more inactive, and never have we been more susceptible to so many diseases. Physical activity of any kind will help protect you against coronary arterial disease, colon cancer, breast cancer, and, without question, obesity and all of its health consequences.

Cross-Stressing Through Exercise: There is a medical syndrome sweeping the United States. It is characterized by being out of breath, post-exertional exhaustion, chronic muscle tension, obesity, high blood pressure, fatigue, and difficulty falling asleep and awakening refreshed. No, it's not Chronic Fatigue Syndrome. I call it Chronic Sedentary Syndrome, and there's not a thing your doctor can do. The treatment is in your own hands, and it is 100 percent effective. The elixir is called EXERCISE!

"Before engaging in a new or different exercise program, first see your doctor."

Everyone who has opened an exercise book or door to a gym has been greeted with this ominous warning. While it is advisable, it simultaneously conveys a subtle and potentially dangerous message: exercise is dangerous.

Yes, it is true that high impact activities or misuse of some forms of equipment can be detrimental to your health. Exercise-induced joint injury, asthma, and cardiovascular ailments come to mind, along with other examples. Some forms of exercise can be dangerous, but not nearly as dangerous as the failure to exercise. Sedentary behavior stands shoulder to shoulder with smoking and high levels of cholesterol as a risk factor for coronary arterial disease. Our bodies are designed for movement, and, without it, dire consequences can occur. Therefore, my recommendation is:

"If you do not exercise, please see your doctor."

Exercise is a form of stress. No, it's not in the same category as losing a job or a loved one because, in terms of exercise, you are in control. Nonetheless, exercise and stress do have some shared features, enough of them that you can actually use exercise as a means by which to train yourself to better cope with stress. They are:

- Increased heart rate
- Increased respiration rate
- A switch from anabolism to catabolism
- Decreased salivation
- Inhibition of digestion

How does this stress training program work? While each stressful experience and your response are unique, there are some features that occur in everyone. Thus, when your body learns to adapt to one form of stress, you are able to better cope with most other forms. It's like learning to drive a car. No two automobiles are exactly the same; yet, having learned to drive one model, you readily can apply your basic driving skills to all others. You may have to search for the light switch or the hood release button, but the essential components are about where you would expect them. The same applies to stress. It's called cross-stressing. Once you learn to respond to one form of stress, you will have the basic skills to respond to most all other types. Exercise is the form of stress that you are going to use for training.

Calculate Your Maximum Heart Rate: Begin by calculating your maximum heart rate, which is the number of beats per minute (BPM) that cannot be exceeded when you increase the intensity of your exercise. In other words, if your heart were a car, it would be the highest number on your speedometer. The engine might be capable of going faster, but the needle on the gauge won't go any higher. There are several ways that you can determine your maximum BPM. I recommend that you take a stress test. Under a doctor's supervision, you exercise to the point where your heart rate levels off. Even though you run faster, your heart rate pegs out. This method will enable you to identify your precise maximum under medical supervision.

Some very fit individuals will test themselves using a heart rate monitor. Be careful. You will be pushing your heart to its maximum, which may unmask a latent heart condition. For this reason, I don't recommend this approach. A less accurate but better alternative to pushing yourself to the limit uses a simple mathematical formula. Subtract your age from 220 if you are a man, or 226 if you are a woman. Sample calculations for a 40 year old man and woman are as follows:

Woman (age 40)	Man (age 40)
226−40=186 bpm	220−40=180 bpm

Why the difference? A woman's heart tends to be smaller than a man's. Consequently, a woman's heart has to beat at a slightly faster rate to maintain a comparable blood volume. As noted previously, this very simple calculation is not very accurate. It assumes that all men and women of the same age are basically the same, and it fails to take into account medical problems, genetics, or the type of exercise being performed. A person who is very fit may have a measured maximum heart rate 10 to 20 beats per minute faster than the value calculated using the formula. Furthermore, many athletes discover that their maximum heart rate for bicycling is quite different than that for running. Swimming may yield yet another value. Despite its flaws, you, at least, will have a starting point.

Determine Your Stress Zones: Next, calculate your high, medium, and low stress zones. These are based upon some of the same guidelines that athletes use to determine their aerobic and anaerobic zones. Aerobic means oxygen is being used. Anaerobic is without oxygen. If you exercise at an intensity that leaves you short of breath, chances are your body will not have enough oxygen to maintain aerobic-based pathways to generate energy. That's when you shift to anaerobic pathways to produce the energy you need to keep pace with the physical demands that you are placing on your body. This is very important if your objective is to lose weight. That's because plenty of oxygen is needed for fat to be converted into energy. If your workout is too intense, fat will be spared while you derive energy from stored glycogen—a process that does not require oxygen.

Low Stress Zone is where you should start if you have not exercised before, or if you are recovering from an injury. When you are in this zone, your heart rate will be between 50 and 60 percent of your maximum. Completer the calculation to determine your low stress zone.

Low Stress Zone

Max HR _____ x 0.60 = _____ bpm

Max HR _____ x 0.70 = _____ bpm

Moderate Stress Zone activity will help you increase your endurance for the stress of exercise. Your heart will beat at a faster rate because it will be bathed in larger amounts of adrenaline and other stress-related chemicals that speed your heart. The number of beats per minute will be between 60 and 70 percent of your maximum. At the same time, your body will become accustomed to this change so that when similar events occur under circumstances outside of your control, your body will be able to recover more efficiently. You will be breathing rapidly, but you'll still be able to obtain enough oxygen to maintain aerobic metabolism.

Moderate Stress Zone

Max HR _____ x 0.70 = _____ bpm

Max HR _____ x 0.80 = _____ bpm

High Stress Zone is the zone within which your body will learn to recover from an even greater amount of stress. When in this zone, your heart rate will be between 80 and 90 percent of your maximum, and the average person will not be able to take in enough oxygen to sustain some of the more common processes for obtaining energy. Your body will switch to anaerobic metabolism. Calculate the limits of this zone. Once you have all the numbers, you can create your own customized cross-stressing program.

High Stress Zone

Max HR _____ x 0.80 = _____ bpm

Max HR _____ x 0.90 = _____ bpm

You now have all the information needed to train yourself to better recover from stress. And that is the key—learning to recover. It's important to realize that stress causes harm when the intensity of the stressor overwhelms your capacity to cope. In other words, you feel helpless. Exercise is a form of stress, but it is one over which you have total control. You determine the start time, the intensity, as well as when to end the regimen. Consequently, you are subjecting your body to many of the same physiological events that occur during uncontrollable stress, but without the harmful consequences. That's why exercise is going to be used to induce a form of stress so that you can practice recovery.

Set Your Limits: Identify your personal stress zones using the formulas discussed above. The table below summarizes the heart rate that corresponds to the different zones.

Low Stress	60 to 70% of maximum heart rate
Moderate Stress	70 to 80% of maximum heart rate
High Stress	80 to 90% of maximum heart rate

A Stress-Recovery Workout: There are many ways that people exercise. One is called steady-state aerobics. Typically, a person will exercise for a set period of time at the same intensity. They might run 5 miles or work out on a bicycle for 30 minutes. That certainly is a wonderful form of exercise, especially from the standpoint of building endurance or burning off fat. The following depicts the heart rate of a person engaged in steady-state aerobics.

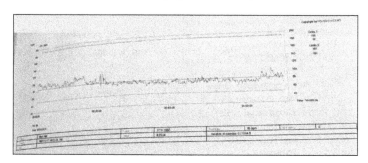

If you look closely, you'll notice that there is no opportunity for recovery until the end of the regimen, and then only a single period of recovery. In other words, this person is getting a good work-out, but he is not providing the body with an opportunity to recover. Compare the steady-state workout with the following cross-stressing regimen.

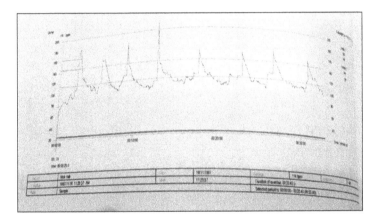

Notice how the heart rate is pushed to the upper levels of the high stress zone and then is allowed to recover. This person is exercising in a manner that incorporates no less than 8 recovery cycles into the program. Each time heart rate is elevated, the body is learning to adjust to greater amounts of stress. Each episode of stress is then followed by a period of recovery. Why is this beneficial for your health? It's beneficial because many of the same chemical events that occur during the stress of exercise occur during stressors over which you may have little control. There's little difference between a rise in heart rate when you are cut off by an eighteen-wheeler, and the increase that occurs when you voluntarily put demands on your body for more oxygen. However, since exercise is taking place on your terms, it's comparatively harmless.

Plan on spending approximately 80 percent of your workout within the moderate stress zone. This corresponds to the aerobic zone and will improve your cardiovascular fitness. The remaining time should be spent oscillating between the low and high stress zones as you create a wave-like pattern of heart rate change. When your heart rate reaches 90 percent of your maximum, slow down until it gradually descends to 60 percent. Then repeat the cycle, perhaps reaching 85 percent. Allow your heart rate to drop to about 65 percent. In doing this, you are incorporating a universal principle into your workout:

"For every action, there should be an equal and opposite reaction."

Or, for every episode of stress (increased heart rate), there needs to occur an equal amount of recovery (a decline in heart rate).

Choosing A Form Of Exercise: It really doesn't matter what form of exercise you choose. What is important is that you do something you enjoy. However, it is important to recognize that some exercise regimens enable you to attain a higher heart rate than others do.

The following table lists common aerobic activities, comparing them to running, which is the most common. Therefore, running is arbitrarily assigned a factor of 1. Lower numbers mean it is easier to attain a higher heart rate, while a higher number means more effort will need to be expended. For example, compared with running, a bicyclist would have to work between 10 and 20 percent harder in order to achieve the same heart rate. This is because cycling is a non-weight bearing exercise.

Running	1.0
Aerobics	0.9–1.1
Cycling	1.1–1.2
Mountain Biking	1.0–1.1
Stepping	1.0–1.2
Canoeing	1.2–1.3
Rowing	0.9–1.2
Walking	1.1
Swimming	1.2–1.3
Tennis	1.0
Badminton	1.1–1.2
Squash	1.0–1.1
Soccer	1.0
Skating	1.1–1.2
Cross-country Skiing	0.9

(From *The Heart Monitor Book*, Polar Electro, Inc.)

The Conversation Rule: Some people prefer a simpler approach to life. Heart rate monitors, formulas for calculating maximum heart rate, and worrying about the upper and lower limits of different zones of activity may be all the incentive you need to reject totally the recommendations to be found in this section. If this applies to you, then forget the monitors and calculations. Use the following rules to determine in which zone you are:

Low Stress	Converse with ease
Moderate Stress	Converse with difficulty
High Stress	Unable to converse

You Are What You Eat

What You Eat May Be What's Eating You: The foods you eat can influence the chemicals within the brain that are so important to achieving certain emotional states. Just as there are different types of fuels for machines, different foods can have a profound impact on the machine that is the human body. Athletes are highly aware of this and tend to be very finicky about what they put into their bodies prior to competition. They know that food can affect their performance, as well as their emotional well-being. Some people call this concept psychodietetics. The name doesn't really matter. What does is the fact that foods can and do have a profound effect on your mood.

It's ironic that nutrition is, without question, the most important component of your health, yet we know so little about it. We know what starving children in Third World countries need, and we know a great deal about what to feed our dogs, cats, birds, and fish. We also know what specific nutrients and vitamins can do to cells in tissue structure. Nevertheless, how much of what form of what food and when it should be consumed are questions that continue to perplex us.

Have you ever felt sluggish a couple of hours after lunch, finding it difficult to concentrate and even to keep your eyes open? This is a perfectly natural occurrence, especially in our culture, which revolves around three square meals a day. And it happens for a number of reasons. First is how rapidly the food is converted into blood sugar, which triggers insulin production. Insulin maintains blood sugar at a fairly constant level. If the blood sugar rises rapidly, the body may release a little too much insulin, causing an overcompensation, which then sends the blood sugar plummeting. It's all part of the natural fluctuation, and it is nature's way of ensuring a balance of energy in the body between meals.

Also prompting that mid-afternoon sluggishness is another natural occurrence: body temperature actually drops during this time of day, just enough to facilitate the induction of sleep. Unfortunately, our historically-based Puritan work ethic tells us that taking an afternoon nap is a sign of laziness. If the boss catches you catching 40 winks around 3 p.m., you'll likely be passed over for the next promotion, if not shown the door. However, if the boss were really smart, she'd be following the example of so many other countries, where the afternoon siesta is an accepted part of the day, and productivity doesn't suffer.

So what can you do to control these fluctuations in your
body?

- Eat more often, but eat less. Instead of three large
  meals each day, consume the food over five or
  even eight smaller feedings. This will maintain
  your blood sugar at a more constant level.

- Stay away from candy. There's no question a
  candy bar provides energy—but only for a few
  minutes. All that refined sugar sends the blood
  sugar soaring; but, ultimately, it drops even lower
  than before the candy bar was eaten, and you feel
  even more lethargic.

- Snack on a piece of fruit or whole grain breads.
  Their complex carbohydrates allow the body to
  maintain a steadier blood sugar level. Choosing
  foods wisely can help you more easily accomplish
  your tasks and goals. If you're working on a project
  that requires sharp focus and mental alertness, eat
  a meal rich in proteins, which energize you. After
  a hectic day, eat a dinner high in carbohydrates,
  such as pasta, to help you unwind and get a good
  night's sleep.

Are you aware that chocolate is both a food and a drug?
Along with a small amount of caffeine, chocolate contains another chemical with effects similar to caffeine.
Research has linked chocolate to an increase in adrenaline level by almost 10-fold. As a consequence, chocolate
has an impact upon both the body and the mind, and it
can truly be addictive.

Interestingly, many chocoholics are women, many of whom crave chocolate most intensely just prior to the onset of menstruation. Because of the cyclical timing of the craving, some nutritionists believe chocolate may alleviate symptoms associated with premenstrual syndrome. Many women claim that chocolate acts as an antidepressant for them. Unfortunately, the large amount of sugar in chocolate may predispose some people, especially women, to yeast infections, as well as to arthritis and asthma. It also may be correlated with hyperactivity, irritability, aggression, and other assertive-type behaviors in children.

Cheeseburger In Paradise—Not! As a nation, we have become obsessed with fat, both the amount we carry on our bodies and the amount we consume. And well we should be concerned about that fat. Dietary fat has been linked with obesity, cancer, and heart disease. In 1980, one out of four people was obese. Now, it's one out of three and getting worse. The rates of breast, colon, and prostate cancers are on the rise, and heart disease is the No. 1 killer of both men and women. All of these diseases directly are linked to fat consumption. Despite the constant bombardment of information through the media, from health-care providers and even from food labels, Americans are heavier than ever before. Since people claim to be eating less fat, why does this paradox exist? It exists probably for a variety of reasons. The average person doesn't have a clue about what they actually are consuming because food labels are misleading. Fat content may be expressed as a total percentage of the food, as a percentage of the daily minimum requirement, or in grams, all of which require an educated, analytical ability held by few people, other than dietitians and nutritionists.

Frankly, the information we receive is terribly confusing. For example, not all fat is the same. Monounsaturated and polyunsaturated fats are less harmful to the arteries than highly saturated fats found in meat, dairy products, and coconut oil. So, to interpret the effect on the body of that fat noted on the food label, it's also important to be aware of what type of fat it actually is.

Compounding the issue is that, while polyunsaturated fats found in corn, sunflower, and other oils are less harmful than saturated fats, polyunsaturates are not nearly as effective in lowering the so-called bad cholesterol as are the monounsaturated fats in olive and canola oils. In fact, there is evidence that monounsaturated fats not only reduce the bad cholesterol, but that they also augment levels of the good cholesterol by helping transport artery-clogging factors from the bloodstream.

Even the term fat-free does not mean that. FDA regulations dictate that for a product to make such a claim, it only must contain less than one-half gram of fat per serving. Reduced-fat means the product contains 25% less fat than its regular version. The term low-fat, with the exception of milk, means that the product has no more than three grams of fat per serving.

Milk labeling really adds to the confusion. When you see 2% low-fat % on the milk label, you're likely to assume that means it has a 2% fat content. No. Two percent milk derives about 36% of its calories from fat. That's better than the 50% of calories from fat in whole milk, but it is certainly a far cry from the perception inferred from the large print on the label. So be wary of labeling claims, and be careful to read all the fine print.

As confusing as the fat issue is, the solution is simple. We should consume no more than 20% of our calories in fat, no matter what its source. Even the beef industry endorses no more than a three-and-a-half-ounce serving of meat per meal. How can you gauge the correct portion? It's just about the same size as a deck of cards. You won't often see that size serving on a plate in a fancy restaurant.

As important as it is to limit dietary intake of fats, some research indicates that by adulthood, it may be too late to alter any link to correlated cancers. Two variables have been correlated with breast cancer—increased height and age of menstruation onset, both of which are determined, in part, by the intake of dietary fat. It's important to instill healthy nutritional habits early and to keep dietary fat intake at the recommended 20% level for children above the age of two. Extra fat is called for, though, during the initial phase of growth. The best way for parents to do this is by setting a good example through their own eating habits.

When it comes to adding vitamin and mineral supplements to the diet, do so wisely. It is far better to receive the proper nutrients through the foods which naturally deliver them. Research has yet to prove that supplements in capsule or pill form work in the same protective manner that natural sources provide. Most of these supplements, when present in larger amounts than are necessary, simply are flushed from the body by the kidneys. And some, like vitamin A, can build up to toxic levels.

As a society, Americans are known to have the most expensive urine in the world. In the United States, we spend an average of $13.30 per person on vitamins each year. The Germans spend $9.81; the French $7.40; in Britain, it's $6.01, and in Spain, only 48¢. And there's no conclusive evidence that links the amount spent with the health of people.

- What you eat and when you eat can have a direct impact upon your emotional states.
- Eating habits developed as children may have greater impact on adult health and well-being than changing those dietary habits as adults.
- Nutrients provided through their natural food sources are more valuable to the body and mind than dietary supplements.

Getting Started: Let's keep the priorities straight. It's not the stressor about which you are concerned. Instead, your concern is the impact it will have on your body. Your response to the stressor will determine if your capacity for productivity, pleasure, or health will be affected. No two people will respond in the same manner to a stressor. However, your unique way of responding can be optimized provided you take certain steps. Create a nutritional stage upon which every reaction within your body will be able to function with maximum efficiency. These guidelines will be the same for everyone. And don't allow stress to interfere with this extremely important component of your health.

All the recommendations in this section are guidelines. Use them as a starting point, and then experiment. Vary both the amounts of food as well as their proportions while simultaneously monitoring your mental, physical, and emotional states. Begin with the USDA guidelines. Obviously, they will not work for everyone, but it's a well thought out starting point.

Milk products are important because they provide protein, vitamins, and minerals. Milk, yogurt, and cheese are the best sources of calcium. The Food Guide Pyramid suggests 2 to 3 servings of milk, yogurt, and cheese a day—2 for most people, and 3 for women who are pregnant or breastfeeding, teenagers, and young adults to age 24. Meat, poultry, and fish are important because they supply protein, B vitamins, iron, and zinc. The other foods in this group—dry beans, eggs, and nuts—are similar to meats in providing protein and most vitamins and minerals. The Food Guide Pyramid suggests 2 to 3 servings each day of foods from this group. The total amount of these servings should be the equivalent of 5 to 7 ounces of cooked lean meat, poultry, or fish per day. Fruits and fruit juices are important because they provide large amounts of vitamins A and C and potassium. They are low in fat and sodium. The Food Guide Pyramid suggests 2 to 4 servings of fruits a day. Vegetables are important because they provide vitamins (such as vitamins A and C and folate) and minerals (such as iron and magnesium). They are naturally low in fat and also provide fiber. The Food Guide Pyramid suggests 3 to 5 servings of these foods a day. Breads, cereals, rice, and pasta are important because they provide complex carbohydrates (starches), which are an important source of energy, especially in low-fat diets. They also provide vitamins, minerals, and fiber. The Food Guide Pyramid suggests 6 to 11 servings of these foods a day. The small tip of the Pyramid shows fats, oils, and sweets. These are foods such as salad dressings and oils, cream, butter, margarine, sugars, soft drinks, candies, and sweet desserts. These foods provide calories and little else nutritionally. Most people should use them sparingly. The tip of the pyramid consists of added fat and sugar that do not naturally occur in the food item. (From 1997 ESHA Research)

The total number of calories you need will vary depending upon how active you are. A very active, middle-aged male may well require in excess of 3,000 calories per day, while a comparatively inactive individual will be better off with less than 2,000 calories.

- Slow down when eating. As food fills your stomach, messages are transmitted to the brain signaling that you are full and don't need any more. However, this takes time. If you eat too quickly, you may eat more than you need because by the time the signals arrive in the brain, you already have started on seconds.

- Separate needs from wants. When you have eaten enough to want more, but you don't really need it, push your plate away. That point will vary, depending upon how active you are. Not only will you achieve balance between energy replenishment and expenditure, but research reveals that you probably will live longer as well.

How Many Calories Do I Need? How do you know how many calories you actually need? Here are three easy steps to help you approximate the number of calories you need.

1. Start by multiplying your body weight by 11. The number you write down will be the number of calories that you need in order to make sure that your body works. After all, you do need calories in order to operate the muscles of the heart and lungs, as well as to fuel all of the other vital activities that are going on within your body. This number is your required amount of base calories.

2. In step two, determine your activity level. You actually might need help with this, so ask a couple of your friends or family members to give their opinion, too, as this is rather subjective. Your perception of high activity may not agree with somebody else's, and the guidelines are really just average determinations. As you go from sedentary to strenuous, write down the following percents. If you are sedentary, your percent is 30 to 50. If your activities are light, 55 to 65. Moderate, 65 to 70, and strenuous, 75 to 100. Now multiply

your base number of calories by the two percentages corresponding to your activity level. If you are a moderate exerciser, then you will multiply your minimal level of calories by 65 percent and also by 70 percent. The lower number will be the minimal number of extra calories that you will need, while the higher number represents the maximum number of extra calories needed.

Activity	Description	Percent
Sedentary	No planned activity	30 to 50
Light	Occassional slow walk/stroll	55 to 65
Moderate	Brisk walking or bicycling	65 to 70
Strenuous	Out of breath exercise	75 to 100

3. The third step really is quite easy. Simply add the low and high percentage values to your minimal base calories, and this will give you the approximate range of calories that you need on a weekly basis. Keep track of the amount of fat, carbohydrate, and protein in the foods you eat. Remember, these are the percentages you should have in your diet on a weekly basis. That's right—weekly. You have to be realistic. When your boss is hosting a dinner, it would be rude to pull out a calorie guide. Furthermore, there are times when starvation may be the only alternative to fast food or pizza, so you occasionally will consume foods which, by all rights, should turn your cardiovascular system

into a Jiffy Lube. However, every seven days, this is what you should be close to:

Carbohydrates	55%
Protein	25%
Fat	20%

Healthy Choices: If you are not careful, you may well fall victim to an advertising blitz which has the fast food industry spending more than any other industry. They are offering larger portions along with added value packages. In other words, buy the deluxe burger, and they'll throw in the large fries and an extra large drink. Let's not even consider the add-ons. Hardee's Monster Burger, draped in cheese and bacon, will, by itself, provide you with 970 calories. Stop at Long John Silver's, and order the Blazin' Cajun Shrimp Wrap, and you'll walk out with 1,419 additional calories. You probably already have reached or exceeded your daily quota with just two meals. It really isn't difficult to reduce your caloric intake. You don't always have to decrease the amount you eat, just the types of food.

Q. Why am I telling you to watch calories as part of a stress-management program?
A. It's because you are what you eat. Your immune system, cardiovascular system, endocrine system, and nervous system—the major systems that have to work optimally under stress—depend upon the foods you eat.

If you want them to work on demand, you have to take care of them. That means being aware of every aspect of your nutrition program.

Is It Working? Everywhere you turn, someone is anxious to provide you with definitive nutrition advice in exchange for your hard-earned dollars. This section will teach you how to evaluate what is best for you. From now on, whenever you are presented with a new and improved version of dietary advice, you will have a definitive test at your disposal. Before you begin, you'll need a heart rate monitor, a watch, and access to either a stationery bicycle or a treadmill with an odometer attached. The routine will always be the same. Warm up until your heart rate reaches 75 percent of the maximum. This is the moderate stress range. Then, note the time and maintain that heart rate as closely as you can for exactly five minutes. You are going to measure two variables: 1) the distance traveled during the five minute test, and 2) the time it takes for your heart rate to return to 50 percent of the maximum. Make every attempt to keep the conditions exactly the same each time you take this test. This is especially important with respect to the warm up and cool down phase of the regimen. You also should note your fluid consumption and medications. You could use virtually any exercise for this test. The reason stationary fitness equipment is recommended is because weather conditions are no longer a variable.

First, take this test after eating your favorite foods. Then, follow the food guidelines suggested in this sec-

tion, if they are different. As a result of eating healthier foods and smaller portions, your entire body should
function at a greater level of efficiency. At the same heart
rate, you will be able to cover a greater distance, and
your heart will recover faster. Use this test to evaluate
your performance at different times of the day or after a
variety of different foods. It's also a great way to check
out the claims made by those selling supplements.

Remember, exercise is a form of physical stress. Consequently, you actually are testing the effects of specific
foods upon your ability to perform and recover from
stress. What works during exercise also will serve you
well in the corporate boardroom, negotiating with your
teenager, or dealing with the myriad of daily stressors
that simply are unavoidable. No, the test is not perfect.
Each time you do this brief work-out, there will be a
modest training effect, which might confound your measures. So vary the sequence, and then repeat certain
dietary regimens to control for circadian, monthly, or
seasonal effects.

You'll be amazed when you discover what a profound
impact food can have upon your body. In all likelihood,
you will see a greater magnitude of effect with increasing amounts of stress. So, repeat the evaluation keeping
your heart rate in the low as well as high stress ranges.
Keep track of the results.

Red, Red Wine: The consumption of alcohol has been
controversial since the first fermented berry juice was

ingested. While a bit of a nip creates a physical effect that may allow you to be more openly emotional in social situations, too much leads to the short-term misery of a hangover, or the long-term embarrassment when you realize you really did dance naked on a table.

A lot of media attention has been given lately to the connection between alcohol and the reduction of coronary arterial disease. At first, the theory was that the alcohol itself flushed out the arteries, but research now shows that the effective element is something called flavonoids, which are found in red wine and dark beer. In general, the more intense the color of the beverage, the more flavonoids it contains. Red wine, for example, provides more flavonoids than white because the skins, seeds, and stems of the grapes are left in during the wine-making process. It's these elements of the grape, which contain the highest concentrations of flavonoids. A similar accumulation of flavonoids occurs in the processing of dark beer—the longer the hops, barley, and malt are left in the liquid, the more flavonoids are present. This is neither a license nor a recommendation to increase consumption of alcoholic beverages. Consuming more than two ounces of alcohol a day has serious, detrimental effects on the brain and liver. The benefits of flavonoids in the diet can be obtained from a variety of other sources. Purple grape juice has about one-third of the anticlotting capability of red wine. Broccoli, onions, apples, and garlic, plus the skins of fruit and green and black teas also contain large concentrations of flavonoids.

Winning The Daily Challenge Using Food

1. **7:00 A.M.** Everyone's heard that they should drink at least eight glasses of water daily. Actually, that's wrong. If you exercise on a regular basis, you need at least two or three times that on a daily basis. Mild dehydration is probably the single most common cause of feeling weak and tired. So before you even think about getting dressed, grab that big plastic cup you got at the gas station, fill it up with water, and chug it down.

2. **8:15 A.M.** Eat a breakfast that contains complex carbohydrates and a small amount of protein. These more rapidly will be converted into blood glucose than will be protein and fat. Realize as you eat your breakfast that you are putting fuel into your body to enable you to make it through lunch. Your options would include a bagel, fruit, or a bowl of cereal. Oatmeal, grits, and even a stack of three pancakes will work as well, provided that you ease up on the butter and syrup. As much as 76 percent of the calories in pancakes, are in the form of carbohydrates. If you wash it down with a glass of orange juice, you'll be in good shape.

3. **10:00 A.M.** It's time for a break, and you're feeling a little hungry. Stay away from the vending machine, which dispenses junk food. instead, walk down to the cafeteria, and get a container of non-fat yogurt. This will provide you with protein to

help build muscle. You don't want too much protein, or else it will be converted into fat. A cup of
yogurt is just about what you need.

4. **11:00 A.M.** That protein you consumed an hour
earlier needs water in order for it properly to be
utilized by the body. If you eat protein without
water, it could put a bit of a strain on your kidneys and liver. Not only that, but the fluid will
help prevent dehydration, which is a primary
cause of weakness and fatigue. This also would
be a good time to eat a banana, which not only
is a very good source of carbohydrate, but also of
potassium, which helps keep your body fluids in a
state of good balance.

5. **11:30 A.M.** Time for a coffee break. Remember that
caffeine is a stimulant, and high dosages potentially can be harmful. But some research findings
do indicate that the amount of caffeine in two
strong cups of coffee (which, by the way, would be
about 200 mg. of caffeine) actually may help you
burn more fat when you exercise. This is based
upon data from Wichita State University. It does
this by stimulating an increase in the levels of
fatty acids circulating in the blood. There's also
evidence from McMaster University in Ontario
that a little caffeine may make you work a bit
harder in the gym, enabling you to get more benefit from your workouts. By decreasing fatigue,
you're able to last longer. But realize that excessive caffeine also can affect your cardiovascular

system in adverse ways. But forget this regimen if you already are consuming six to eight cups of coffee each day just to survive. That extra caffeine that you're putting into your body isn't going to do any good at all.

6. **Noon.** Time for a workout. But remember that for every 20 minutes of exercise, you need between four to six ounces of water. And remember that if the water is cool, it will be absorbed much faster than if it's warm.

7. **1:30 P.M.** Time for a 30 minute lunch. You need at least 100 calories in the form of carbohydrate, which is precisely what your body is screaming for right now. Especially after a workout, which is when you need to replenish the glycogen stores that you have been using up. So look for a pasta salad or baked potato or rice. If you order a sandwich, make sure it's made with whole wheat bread. Remember that my philosophy is predicated upon energy expenditure followed by recovery. You need that carbohydrate in order to get maximal recovery. And don't forget to mix a little protein in your lunch as well. This will help to build up new muscle as well as keep you alert. That means some low-fat cottage cheese or, perhaps, a slice of turkey or chicken in that sandwich.

8. **4:00 P.M.** There's a natural biological rhythm in the body that causes your blood sugar to drop in the afternoon. If your work situation allows it, try to get a little exercise. Climb a flight of stairs

or, even better, walk outside and expose yourself to a little sunlight. The sunlight will help with the production of vitamin D, which your body needs in order to strengthen bone. You'll also rev up your cortisol, which will provide you with a source of energy because this is the steroid that converts stored energy into usable glucose. Then have a small snack—low-fat yogurt, a slice of cheddar cheese, or, perhaps, some skim milk. This will provide you with some protein again to help build up your muscles.

9. **6:30 P.M.** It's now time for a well-earned dinner. Start with a salad. Spinach is good, and, while you're at it, add a few sunflower seeds or walnuts and then pour a little olive oil vinaigrette on. You are adding a little fat to your diet, but you're also giving yourself a pretty good dose of vitamin E. This natural antioxidant not only helps to neutralize free radicals, but it helps the body to better utilize oxygen. There are lots of options for healthy eating, but you might want to consider some stir-fried beef with broccoli and green peppers. Beef is an excellent source of protein, and a three-ounce serving will give you more than 40 percent of the RDA of vitamin B12. This vitamin helps to burn off fat and gives rise to red blood cells, which will help with your endurance. The broccoli will provide 120 percent of the RDA for vitamin C, while a single green pepper will provide another 90 percent. That vitamin C not

only will help neutralize free radicals, it will help reduce the inflammation that often occurs if you exercise excessively. Finally, add a potato. It's an excellent source of complex carbohydrate, and it also contains more vitamin C, as well as potassium and iron. If it happens to be a sweet potato, it will give you a pretty good dose of beta-carotene, which is another antioxidant.

10. **9:00 P.M.** It's time for a snack or, if you prefer, you might just want to call it dessert. Frozen yogurt might work, or have a fruit bar. These are good sources of carbohydrate, which, ultimately, will help facilitate your falling asleep.

Coping With Stress In Relationships

S tress can induce changes in behavior that can have an adverse effect upon your relationships. Relationships at work, with family, or just casual acquaintances can be threatened. By making just a few adjustments, the same information can be applied to the relationships you have with a business partner, a co-worker, or a child. Here is a listing of some of the stress-induced behaviors that can affect your relationships:

Isolation	Distrust
Lower sex drive	Lashing out
Intolerance	Less contact with friends
Nagging	Hiding
Resentment	Lack of intimacy
Blaming	Clamming up
Loneliness	Using people

To Thine Own Self Be True: Unfortunately, relationships sometimes can be a major source of stress. Some people are manipulative, deceptive, or overly controlling. Such relationships can take a serious toll on your health if you find yourself on the receiving end of these tactics.

If your answer to any of the following questions is 'yes,' you may need to take steps to modify your response.

1. Have you ever purchased something you didn't really want?
2. Have you ever accepted a food or beverage item when you didn't want to?
3. Have you ever agreed to do something that was counter to your value System?
4. Have you ever regretted not taking action?

Now reflect upon why you responded the way you did:
What emotions allowed you to be manipulated?

What kept you from holding your ground or speaking your mind?

If someone wanted you to do something against your will, how best would that person accomplish this goal?

Reflecting upon the answers to these questions will enable you to identify the problem. Now, set about to fix it. A very simple strategy is to employ acting skills. Recall that occasion when you did speak your mind, and you achieved your objective. Recall when, under similar circumstances, you were able to do what you believed was right. Create a screenplay, and practice. Before entering a situation, practice, practice, and practice. You will become what you believe you are. And by recreating the behaviors associated with success, you will drive the physiology of success. It will happen. But this is something that has to be learned. And learning requires practice.

The rules for dealing with such problems are quite involved and have to be tailored for each situation. Nonetheless, here are some general guidelines:

- Do what you believe is right, not what is expected.
- Your choices are always yes, no, or none of the above.
- You do not have to give a reason for your choice.
- You do not have to apologize for your choice.
- Sleep on it before deciding.
- Read between the lines, but be careful of making inappropriate assumptions.
- Watch for signs of deception.
- Recognize your vulnerability.

It's a Mad, Mad World: Before you start working on the problem, get your anger under control. Realize that anger is a normal and healthy emotion. It is when there's a mismatch between your anger (or its expression) and the circumstances that a problem will arise. For example, you have been wronged by a co-worker, and you misdirect your wrath at a family member.

There are some interesting differences between men and women with respect to the expression of emotions, especially anger. Both get angry with about the same frequency usually six or seven times a week, and the reasons behind the anger and its intensity are about the same. The differences lie in the manner in which anger is expressed.

Men are more inclined to shout and pound their fists. Women are more likely to cry or keep their anger to themselves. Also, women are more likely to express their anger in private and to someone who is not the source of the anger. And the greater the intensity of anger within the woman, the longer it takes her to recover. This isn't so with men. However, regardless of how anger is expressed, the toll this emotion takes on the body is the same.

- Inappropriate expression of anger is emotionally harmful, while justifiably expressed anger can be beneficial.
- Whether appropriate or not, anger unleashes chemical changes that place stress on the coronary system.
- The number and type of situations that cause you to feel angry can indicate your risk for coronary disease.
- You can train yourself to respond to situations with emotional responses other than anger.

The following questionnaire has been devised by Redford Williams, the author of Anger Kills, as a means by which a person can measure his level of hostility.

Count the number of times you answer yes:

1. Have you ever been so angry at someone that you've thrown things or slammed a door?
2. Do you tend to remember irritating incidents?
3. Do little annoyances have a way of adding up during the day, leaving you frustrated?
4. In the express line in the grocery store, do you count to see if anyone has more than 10 items?
5. If a person who cuts your hair trims off too much, do you fume about it for days afterwards?
6. When a driver cuts you off, do you honk your horn?
7. Have you dropped any friends because they just didn't live up to your expectations?
8. Do you find yourself getting annoyed at little things your spouse does that get under your skin?
9. Do you feel your pulse climb during an argument?
10. Are you often irritated by incompetence?
11. If the cashier gives you the wrong change, do you assume he's probably trying to cheat you?
12. If someone doesn't show up on time, do you plan the angry words you're going to say later?

If you scored three or less, then you probably do not have a problem. But a score of four to eight is an indication that your level of anger may very well be in the range that can cause coronary arterial disease. A score of nine or more puts you at very high risk.

Reducing Anger: The next time you find yourself becoming very angry, ask yourself each of the following questions:

1. Is this really worth getting worked up over?
2. Is my anger justified?
3. Will an angry outburst make any positive difference?

Only if you answer 'yes' to all three of these questions should you go ahead and have an angry outburst. But if your answer to any one of those questions is 'no,' then chill out. Actually, you already will have started to do it. Pausing long enough to ask yourself those questions takes the emotional edge off. If you still find yourself fuming, then find a distraction. Read a book, go for a walk, or do some meditation exercises. Here's another option. Get it out of your system physically. Hit golf or tennis balls, chop wood. Hit a punching bag, or pound a pillow with your fists. Scream if that will help, but to avoid triggering a panic attack in those nearby, bury your face in a pillow, or do it in some isolated location. Do remember, however, that carrying this approach too far can result in an actual increase in your anger. Monitor yourself carefully.

Sometimes, people have difficulty expressing anger. In many instances, expression of anger in the past has resulted in dire consequences: punishment as a child, loss of a job, break up of a relationship, or criminal charges. The stakes can be considerably higher than expressing happiness. First,you must overcome barriers to express-

ing anger, and then identify healthy outlets and appropriate means of expression.

- Realize that you don't always have to be pleasant,
  although despite the conventional wisdom, there
  are ways of expressing anger without necessarily
  causing offense.
- Maintain a realistic perspective about possibly
  upsetting those you care about. Failure to communicate your feelings shows an attitude of indifference, which can be destructive to any relationship.
- When expressing anger, be assertive, but not
  aggressive. Stay focused on the issues, but avoid
  being accusatory.
- Stop projecting into the future and imagining
  worst case consequences. If your anger is justified,
  the issue important, and speaking out may well
  help to rectify the problems, then the cost benefit
  ratio definitely will be in your favor.
- Calm yourself so that you can move into a higher
  level of processing, and carefully weigh the
  options. You're at the top of the food chain because
  you have a large, well-developed brain. Use it.
- Sometimes it's ok to do nothing.
- Accept responsibility for your actions.

Prepare For Your Defense: Sometimes, life is not fair, and,
despite playing by the rules, you fall victim to those
deliberately trying to undermine you. Here's what you
do when all else fails, and you encounter a vindictive
person.

Make sure you document everything that happens when your efforts are being undermined by a co-worker or supervisor. You need to include the date and time and, as best as you can recollect, exactly what was said. It is also a good idea to make a notation of other individuals who might have witnessed the event.

By writing things down, you will have a record that you can more objectively analyze in your attempt to seek a solution to the problem. Furthermore, you will realize that you are not going crazy—there really is something seriously wrong in the workplace. If the worst-case scenario occurs, and you are forced out of your job, by having things documented, you may be able to convince someone in the administration to respond. If you do decide upon legal action, then that record will be worth its weight in gold should you need to back up some of your claims. Hopefully, by following the recommended advice, this ultimate step will not be necessary.

There are some people who will not respond to even the most constructive intervention. But it is still important to do something; and, by using some of the recommended approaches, at the very least, you are putting yourself in the driver's seat. You are not shrugging your shoulders, walking away from the situation, and adopting the attitude, "Well, there's nothing I can do. If I say anything, if I do anything, I'll lose my job." Instead, you are engaging in behaviors that put you in control. To do otherwise will reinforce a feeling of helplessness.

Avoid These Pitfalls

- **Bill of Rights:** You do not have the right to always have your way. Conflicts should be resolved so everyone has at least some of their needs met.

- **Generalizations:** Avoid labels. Personality is a function of the environment. Yes, a person may act like an idiot when serving on a committee with you, but such labels zero in on only a limited part of that person.

- **Dichotomous Thinking:** Everything is black or white. People are angels or devils. It may seem that way, but that's because of the way you filter the information available to you. People really are different shades of gray. Parts may be good; parts may be bad.

- **Embellishment:** The more bizarre your behavior, the more you may have to justify your actions. The result is a tendency to collect only that information which will support your point of view and, if you are unsuccessful, will exaggerate the other person's actions.

- **Assigning Blame:** It is quite likely that the other person did not intentionally make you angry. In fact, they didn't make you angry at all. You made yourself angry through your interpretation of their behavior. So stay with the issues. Criticize their behavior, if warranted, but avoid criticizing them.

Burnout in Marriage

Burnout in marriage should be the rule, not the exception. I can't imagine a more incompatible relationship than that which exists between a man and a woman. Boys and girls grow up with different emphases on what they should be doing with their lives; we look different; we act different; and perhaps most importantly, we think in quite different ways. Yet, for some bizarre reason, marriages do persist, despite the fact that the person you may be living with on your 40th anniversary is not the same person you courted. That's because we change, which, in turn, alters the dynamics of the entire relationship. You start off being married to a lover and friend. When the children arrive, you find yourself being married to a father or a mother. The children may become the focus of attention for the next 20 to 30 years.

Humans are one of the few species that even attempt to endure the constant change that occurs in marriage and enter into a life-long, monogamous relationship. Of course, not all marriages do endure, so let's look at some of the reasons why some do, and some don't. I don't wish to imply that marriage should or should not be a goal. Some people have personality traits that are not suited for this kind of relationship. Others are better off single, and there is nothing wrong with the 'single' lifestyle. Assuming you have decided that you do want to be married—and for the right reasons—or that you want your current marriage to be successful, beware of potential pitfalls and how best to minimize stress in the relationship.

Types Of Partnerships: There are three general types of partnerships.

1. One type is typified by two members who work outside the home. Both the husband and the wife share in earning money; they share the household chores, the child-rearing tasks, and making friends, as well. In other words, their lives are very closely intertwined at just about every level.

2. The second type of relationship is one in which responsibilities are divided on the basis of particular tasks. The common denominator is the home and family unit, but one individual goes out and earns the money while the other takes care of the home. They may even have different friends.

3. The third type of relationship is made up of two very independent individuals where each partner lives his or her own life, keeping separate bank ac-

counts, and having separate circles of friends. They share only what happens to be convenient, and, for some individuals, this might be just the home.

There is no right or wrong type of relationship. Each of these distinct types works very well for some couples. Problems occur when the relationship changes, and what started out as a relationship where everything was shared now becomes a relationship where one partner seeks a greater degree of independence. The same is true where couples started out being more independent, and then one begins to desire more sharing. If that occurs, then the best solution might be separation. But before reaching that stage, I would like to discuss the process whereby loving relationships are established and their progression to a state of co-habitation.

Almost Like Being In Love: Infatuation is usually the first step in a love relationship because it is important to have some spark to ignite such a relationship. Unfortunately, some people never move past this first step. They thrive on the excitement of the new person in their life, feeling whole, believing that they have met the perfect person, that they will never be lonely or disappointed again, or that they will experience never-ending bliss. When this feeling ends, they assume it simply was not the right person and look for someone else, neglecting the steps that might lead to a long term relationship. For others, once the infatuation dims, they settle for a numb, stagnant existence with their partner, remaining disappointed and cheated, believing love is an illusion or that they simply will not experience lasting love in their lifetime.

While meeting a special person can and should be a joyous time, it is important to realize that a deeper sense of intimacy is required to sustain most relationships for the long term. As you move beyond infatuation toward true love, couples often find that a new type of connection unfolds. Complete trust and unconditional love for your partner allows this process to happen. The trust and security that come with love open the door to new spontaneity, creativity, and excitement.

Looking For Love In All The Right/Wrong Places: The choice of partner for a long-term relationship is one of the most important decisions that you will make in your lifetime. While meeting a potential partner is rarely a planned or deliberate event, it is important to have an idea of what you are looking for in a mate before you start looking. Then, when you do meet someone, you can make some informed choices. This is not to say that reason is the only consideration. What we term as chemistry, attraction, and a spiritual connection between two people are equally important. But you do need to temper emotion with reason. Unfortunately, it is often difficult to truly know another person until you are strongly attached to them. Given this fact, it is helpful to make informed decisions early in the relationship, making it more likely that you and your partner are prepared for a committed relationship.

Asking certain questions and making careful observations are very useful when assessing a partner's capacity for a long-term relationship. Remember that people do change over time, and there is no way to know for certain without spending a large amount of time with the person. People typically present their most favorable side in the early stages of a relationship, so making observations about a person's actions on a day to day basis, along with what you can glean about their past, may be the most effective way to size up a partner. Remember, too, if you are looking only for positive traits in a person, you will find them; and if you are looking only for negative traits, that is what you will find. You must strive toward a balanced and reasonable perspective. Take some time, and make a list of what characteristics your partner must have, those that you would like them to have, but which are not essential, and those that you absolutely cannot accept.

Troubled Waters: There are many barometers of a troubled relationship. In general, a relationship is in trouble when two people are no longer a support for each other, when communication stops, or when two people become stuck in repeated cycles of conflict over which they feel powerless to change. Often people find themselves caught in a vicious cycle, where trying harder and harder works less and less. The end result may be anger and hurt feelings, or apathy and numbness. When you reach the point where nothing you do seems to work anymore, it is time to begin learning some new tools, possibly with the help of a trained therapist.

It is important to keep in mind that any long-term, committed relationship will confront people with parts of themselves and their partner that will challenge coping skills. Just because difficulties arise in a relationship does not necessarily mean it is unhealthy. Rather, a couple's willingness and ability to deal with the important issues are far more important factors. The following are some signs that a relationship is in trouble:

- **You Prefer To Spend Time Away from Your Spouse.** When you find yourself persistently building walls in your relationship by isolating yourself from your partner with work, hobbies, or children, your relationship is in trouble. While it is healthy to spend some time away from your partner, when you begin to avoid sharing time to avoid conflict or to meet too many needs not met in your relationship, there is a problem.

- **You Are Caught in Endless Cycles of Silent or Active Conflict.** When you find that all disagreements end in angry outbursts, hurt feelings, miscommunication, or a feeling of hopelessness, you need to be concerned. Most relationships cannot tolerate this pattern for extended periods of time.

- **Effective Communication Has Ceased.** When you stop sharing, listening, and discussing your emotions, thoughts, or interests with your partner, closeness will suffer.

- **Emotional Alienation Has Set In.** When you feel completely disconnected from your partner, you are essentially living together alone. If you don't feel you know what is going on emotionally in each other's lives, intimacy will suffer.

- **There Is Lack of Trust.** Basic trust and a belief that your partner has your interests at heart are crucial in a relationship. When trust suffers, closeness suffers. Honesty and genuineness are essential to any meaningful relationship.

- **A Climate of 'Me Versus You' Is Present.** When it is no longer 'us' and becomes 'me versus you,' the commitment of a long-term relationship begins to fade. In order for a healthy relationship to last, each partner's separate interests must somehow be balanced with what is in the best interest of the relationship. Remember, you are both on the same team. Competitiveness can greatly divide relationships.

If these circumstances apply to your relationship, you may be suffering from marital burnout. If you are not sure, take this quick test:

1. Are you tired of your marriage?
2. Does the relationship you have with your spouse make you feel depressed?
3. If not depressed, do you often feel run down?
4. Do you feel trapped in your relationship?
5. Do you feel worthless in your marriage?
6. Do you feel resentment towards your spouse?
7. Do you believe the marriage creates for you a hope less situation?
8. Do you believe that you are helpless in dealing with the problems associated with your marriage?
9. Have you reached the point where you think you just can't handle things anymore?

If you answered yes to three or more of these questions, you and your partner have your work cut out for you.

If your partner is unwilling to be involved in resolving the conflicts, you will need to make a choice whether or not you can accept the relationship as it is or whether you need to terminate it. Going outside the relationship to meet unfulfilled needs is a choice for some, but serious consequences can follow this decision, even if you believe you have done it for the right reasons.

First, focus on the positive. No individual and no relationship, even a long-lasting marriage, are perfect, no matter what you have convinced yourself of or how it might appear to the outside observer. The reason that some couples are happy and others are not is largely because the happy couples focus on the positive aspects of the relationship. For example, you might be very frustrated because your spouse is disorganized. But when you start to reflect upon your spouse's warmth and sensitivity, that perspective may enable you to diffuse your anger.

Another important ingredient in a happy relationship is the willingness to express appreciation. It is not enough to assume that your partner knows how you feel. It is important to show the appreciation, as well. Do it verbally and through actions. Too often, we tend to voice criticism and express anger. Positive reinforcement always is more effective.

Talking to each other cannot be overemphasized. There has to be communication, and without it, the emotional and physical intimacy that a relationship needs to be based upon is going to disappear. Talking has to be a priority. Don't wait until there is simply a convenient time. Make the time available. Set aside 20, 30, or 60 minutes, whatever it takes. By simply doing this, you are communicating to each other that this aspect of the relationship is at least as important, if not more important, than those things you are taking the time away from.

Talk to your spouse and not a confidante. Or at least don't exclude your spouse from discussions. A lot of people, when they find themselves in a troubled relationship, will turn to a friend, partly because the friend is more likely to side with them and to offer sympathy. But all that individual is going to be able to do is speculate about why your partner has engaged in a particular pattern of behavior. The only person who can provide the critical information to resolve the problem is the one who is directly involved. When you do talk, don't attack the other person. Avoid criticism. Your goal is to help the relationship. Identify what it is that each of you wants, and then focus on what it is that needs to be done in order to achieve that objective. Avoid reminding the other person of past behaviors that may date back years or decades. The focus must be on the relationship, not personalities. This is not about assigning blame or taking credit. The objective is to build a solid relationship. Focusing upon individual issues increases the probability that the discussion will evolve into a debate.

The adage "variety is the spice of life" is absolutely true. Too many people get into a rut. I don't mean variety in the number of partners you have. I'm talking about varying the way you do things within the relationship. It might be breaking the routine of what you usually do on weekends, or the place you go on vacation. It might be the types of food you eat, or even where and when you have sex. Everyone needs a certain amount of emotional excitement in their life to counterbalance boredom and tedium. And don't forget to have fun. Seek out ways to make your marriage fun, adventuresome, and exciting. While there are times when you need a certain amount of excitement, there are also times when you may need tranquility. The same applies to a relationship. The marriage needs to have a solid foundation with each partner secure in the knowledge that the other person is going to be there. At the same time, each one needs to build on that foundation. They need to build together, and they need to build individually. Each person needs a certain amount of personal growth as well as spiritual growth. In order to achieve this growth, it may be necessary to take different courses. Successful marriages work because there is a balance. There is a solid foundation, and there is opportunity within the marriage for each person to spread their wings and to develop their own interests, leisure activities, and, perhaps, even friends. A marriage that is founded only on security may stifle growth and development. At the same time, too much growth and development, especially on an individual basis, may make it difficult to keep the marital bond strong. There needs to be a foundation of commitment as well as the energy to grow.

After reviewing all of the difficulties and attempting to resolve them, you and your partner may conclude that the relationship is a lost cause. Divorce may be the best course of action.

He Got the Goldmine; I Got the Shaft: Divorce is a very difficult transition. Even when a divorce eventually makes life better for a person, there are a number of losses that must be dealt with. People lose much more than a partner. Divorce may lead to a reduction in your standard of living, the loss of a home, important routines, and time with children or friends. As a result, feelings of shock, confusion, sadness, fear, and anger typically arise. Often the adjustment period following divorce can be much different, depending on whether you were the person who made the decision to end the marriage or whether your partner decided. For many, divorce is the beginning of an emotional roller coaster. The key to getting through this time is to deal with emotions directly. You also need to maintain or even expand your social support system in order to fill the void left by divorce. Moreover, seek out people to help you talk about the emotions you are feeling, and avoid overly distracting yourself with work, another relationship, or unhealthy coping mechanisms. Recognize that the first year following a divorce is a period of reorganization. While many decisions can't wait, major job, family, and lifestyle decisions are best postponed during this period.

Although time alone may be very difficult at first, it is important to take time to reflect upon your life and your priorities. This is particularly important if you have never been on your own. Learning to be comfortable with your 'alone time' is an important goal. You will be surprised at what comes up when you simply slow down and focus on what you feel.

In order to assist with the process of grief, it can be helpful to arrange one or more rituals to symbolize and to make real the loss. Like a funeral ceremony for the dead, a ritual makes the experience real and provides a concrete way of saying good-bye. You could take a hike to a favorite view point and recite a poem or a note you've written about the relationship ending, or you could schedule a ceremony to dispose of some pictures or mementos from the relationship. Be creative, do what works for you, and allow this to be an emotionally significant, ceremonious event. If it doesn't seem real the first time you try it, you may want to repeat the ritual a few more times. The timing for your ritual may vary, but many people find it useful to schedule a ritual on the day the divorce is finalized. Rituals such as this can provide an opportunity to feel important emotions, to say good-bye, and to move on.

Divorce will often get people thinking about who they were before the marriage. Indeed, it may be a good time to think about what you used to do for fun, what subjects you were passionate about, or what used to be meaningful in your life. Reflect on what you did to survive other tough times in your life. Most importantly, trust that things will improve. Remember that every loss in life involves the letting go of something old and the birth of something new. Did you used to enjoy exercising, reading, painting, music, or hiking? During this time of transition, you will need to fill the void left by the divorce with an increased awareness of who you are and what makes you happy. Look inward and use your support system to navigate through a new phase in life.

Managing Depression

A t various times, we all experience what is usually described as 'the blues.' The treatment of these minor, sub-clinical depressions should focus initially upon determining to what degree environmental factors are responsible for the symptoms. The initial approach could be, then, to respond to the stimulus in a different way.

Often, the symptoms cause us to be distracted and unable to properly perceive what may appear to others as an obvious solution to our problem. That's why an attentive listener, such as a friend, can be very helpful in guiding us along the most appropriate course, as well as in improving our sense of self-worth.

A subject of dispute is whether women experience more emotion than men or whether they simply are more aware of their emotions because they've not been taught to repress them. Whatever the cause, it is true that women seek more treatment related to their feelings than men, and certain emotional states are more likely to present in women.

PMS: Premenstrual Syndrome or PMS is not a disease but a collection of symptoms which may have multiple causes. It's unlikely that any one intervention effectively will deal with all of the symptoms, but here are several interventions which may help alleviate some of them:

- **Breathe deeply.** This can help alleviate depression and anxiety, two of the major symptoms associated with PMS.
- **Reduce caffeine and alcohol use,** both of which can trigger everything from headaches to irritability, anxiety, and even depression.
- **Reduce your salt intake** to help alleviate fluid retention and the bloated feeling that often accompanies PMS.
- **Eat calcium-rich foods** to reduce both fluid retention and **moodiness.**
- **Undertake moderate exercise,** which helps relieve cramps and has a definite effect on mood improvement through endorphins being released into the blood.
- **Eliminate refined sugars,** which have been linked to the onset of PMS-induced irritability, fatigue, and even depression.
- **Try chocolate.** Some nutritionists suspect that chemicals in chocolate directly can alleviate some symptoms of PMS. Don't overdo it, though. Too much refined sugar will offset the potential benefits.

- **Eat a baked potato,** but hold the butter and sour cream. The carbohydrates will help boost serotonin, which can alleviate symptoms of depression.

There Is A Season, Turn, Turn, Turn: Just as there are seasons to the annual cycle of our world, there are seasons of the emotional cycle. When an event launches us into an emotional high—the summer of emotion, full of lushness and excitement—that high eventually passes. Our feelings about the event fade like the passing of summer into autumn. Eventually, we move into the emotional equivalent of winter, when our feelings lie fallow before entering the season of spring, when other emotions may grow and create a new dimension. From this seasonal cycle of emotions, we develop memories and a perspective that lead to wisdom as the years pass. Emotional states have long been thought to be brought on by the physical changes of the annual seasons themselves. This has been confirmed by the recognition of Seasonal Affective Disorder (SAD), thought to involve, at least in part, changes in the body's production of melatonin. Normally inhibited by sunlight, the levels of this neurotransmitter increase within the brain during darker, winter months. SAD, which is an apt acronym for the syndrome, is characterized by:

- a feeling of sadness.
- a decrease in libido.
- social withdrawal.
- decreased concentration.
- greater daytime drowsiness.
- overall fatigue.

Often, the syndrome is accompanied by appetite increase, weight gain, and hyper-insomnia. Some studies have found that the symptoms can be alleviated through exposure to full-spectrum lighting, which readjusts melatonin levels within the body. However, neither light therapy nor drug manipulation of melatonin levels is always effective, indicating an interplay of various neurotransmitters.

Seeking Counseling Or Psychotherapy. Psychotherapy or counseling may be helpful for individuals suffering from an array of emotional difficulties. Individuals suffering from depression, anxiety, relationship problems, eating disorders, panic attacks, phobias, or addictions may benefit from the many treatment approaches that psychologists, social workers, religious leaders, and counselors offer. In addition, therapy can be of great benefit in dealing with stressful events and major life transitions. These may include, for example, job or relationship loss, parenting issues, stress-related illness and physical symptoms, or death and grief. Therapy often can help people adjust more quickly and effectively to adverse events.

In general, when emotional issues begin to interfere with individual, family, work, or social functioning, therapy is indicated. In addition, treatment clearly is indicated for those who are experiencing recurrent thoughts of harming themselves or others, and/or become unable to care for their basic needs. Individuals who need therapy are often caught in a vicious cycle in which their efforts to bring about personal change on their own are increasingly ineffective. In spite of their many attempts to change, people often find that they lack the tools to make changes. In essence, they need the objective perspective of a trained professional. While there are many different treatment approaches, most therapies provide an opportunity to identify ineffective coping patterns and assistance in learning new, more effective methods of responding in a safe, accepting, and supportive environment. Ultimately, a more objective perspective of oneself is gained, and important decisions in life are made more consciously. In short, therapy can help you help yourself.

Seven Ways To Deal With Depression And Anxiety

1. **Translate your emotions into language.** Talk out loud or simply write the problem down. This will enable you to view the problem through a different sensory modality, for example, the auditory or visual system, giving you a different perspective from which to identify causes and/or solutions.

2. **Identify the emotion you are experiencing.** Are you feeling sad, angry, fearful, guilty, embarrassed, or a combination of these or others?

3. **Identify the source of the problematic emotion.** Are you angry at yourself for not accomplishing a goal? Are you fearful or sad about the consequences for not having done so? Are you feeling guilty because you failed? And remember that what really causes you to blow up at the end of the day may

very well be some event you've been mulling over all day long.

4. **Identify the negative thoughts you might be experiencing and hold them up to reality.**

5. **Identify those thoughts, which are grossly exaggerated** and replace them with more rational thoughts. For example, if you happen to be late for a family gathering, don't assume that your family will think that you don't love them. Recognize that they will probably accept that your tardiness was due to reasons outside of your control.

6. **Re-think the entire scenario.** Just as a result of going through these steps at this point, you probably have already avoided a major emotional crisis.

7. **Once you figure out what went wrong, take corrective action.** Learn from your mistakes, and set about to make sure that it doesn't happen again. Remember that even your biggest blunder can always serve as a bad example for future choices.

Excuses To Do Nothing

You know what you need to do, but you just don't seem to get around to doing it. The following are some of the more common excuses along with counter-arguments:

It's boring. It certainly will be with that attitude. It doesn't have to be. Exercise, for example, can be done with a friend. Make it a learning experience, and keep detailed notes on how you progress. That's why I encourage you to use a heart rate monitor. Still boring? Even if it is, is that worse than the toll unmanaged stress is going to take?

People will think I'm weak if I can't handle stress without this program. If they do, chances are they are transferring their attributes to you. It's a common ploy called 'projection.' Don't fall for it. The world has changed so rapidly that your body hasn't had a chance to adapt. Human minds have created the Information Age, along with all the pitfalls. Use yours to make sure your journey is as smooth as possible. It's your choice.

I don't need this program. Then why are you reading this? If you think you might need it, you probably do.

I don't have enough time. That's the worst excuse of all. Fatigue is a common symptom of stress. Anything you can do to counter it will enable you to use your time more efficiently. By employing the exercise and nutritional guidelines recommended in this program, you will fall asleep faster and obtain more restful sleep. After a few weeks, you will need less sleep. Yes, the program described in this book will help you create time.

Surviving the
Medical System

The medical paradigm embraced by the established medical authorities in the United States is simultaneously a spectacular success and a dismal failure. It has produced the best medical care to be found anywhere in the world, yet infant mortality rates in this nation are comparable to those of Third World countries.

The successes are to be found in trauma centers where physicians have acquired the skills to repair everything from broken bones to damaged hearts. And we are increasingly successful in diagnosing disease and predicting, through gene technology, the probability that certain illnesses might occur. But little success has been achieved in devising treatments for chronic illnesses, especially those that involve multiple organ systems and which appear to be associated with emotional distress.

Ironically, the successes of Western medicine stem from the same approaches that account for its failures. By focusing on the separation of mind and body, the result has led to the body being dissected into well-defined, component parts. The endocrine system, the immune system, the nervous system, and the cardiovascular system are not only designations which carve our bodies into parts; they also define the boundaries of common medical specialties, as well. This reductionistic approach has enabled medicine to unravel the molecular mysteries of a variety of diseases and to devise intervention strategies based upon these discoveries. But in focusing solely upon isolated systems and their corresponding parts, we have lost sight of the fact that each of us is considerably more than the sum of our biological parts.

Consequently, many practitioners of modern medicine who take great pride in adhering to the rigors of this approach cannot incorporate the notion that a disease may be triggered by a twisted soul or by spiritual bankruptcy. These are terms that simply cannot be defined and for which no chemical or biological markers exist. Today, disease is attributed to the invasion of the body by pathogens, which, during previous eras, might have been labeled as 'evil spirits' or a 'curse.' The focus is upon the external causes of disease, both during the diagnosis and the treatment of the illness. While pathogens are certainly important triggers, the powerful healing system that lies within each of us is largely ignored.

The discovery of pathways that bind the brain and the immune system rescues the behavioral approach to disease from the shadowy practices of witch doctors and places it squarely within the rational tradition of Western medicine. We are witnessing the birth of a new integrative science—psychoneuroimmunology—which begins with the premise that neither the brain nor the immune system can be excluded from any scheme accounting for the onset and course of disease. The first, and, in the long run, the most valuable, clinical spin-offs of Psychoneuroimmunology will be in disease prevention—initially, in the development of ways to manage stress.

I do not advocate that behavioral interventions simply replace traditional treatments, especially those of proven efficacy. What I am advocating is that you engage in activities which enable you to maintain an optimal state of health. Healing should be like an investment portfolio—diversified. Rely upon your physicians, but invest in your own health by strengthening your mental and physical assets through exercise, nutrition, and the resources that best inspire your emotional forces with hope and guidance.

Ideally, you and your doctor will function in a balanced partnership striving to achieve the same goal—your health and well-being. To this relationship, the doctor brings years of learning and experience in working with the human body. But this is no more valuable than the knowledge of your own body that you have acquired. Your doctor can serve you based only upon what he or she can learn from you—and your healing directly is enhanced by your involvement in the treatment.

Pay attention to the questions the doctor asks you. The answers you give will provide vital information and valuable clues to your health. And make sure you get all of the information you need. During physical exams and consultations, anxiety can cause you to forget questions you want to ask or the answers to those you do. Take along a list of what you want to discuss, and take notes on the answers. Better yet, let a tape recorder act as your back-up memory.

Don't depend on your doctor as your sole source of information. Accept responsibility, and do some detective work so you can ask intelligent questions and better understand treatment alternatives.

Reward your doctor with gratitude. Unfortunately, doctors too rarely hear from patients when things are going well. Let your doctor know what is improving for you, as well as what still needs attention. Thank him for helping you get better. Acknowledge her insight. Small tokens of appreciation can pay huge dividends in the emotional bond which may develop and the extra attention you're likely to receive.

Pertinent References

Ader, R., (Ed.) (2007). Psychoneuroimmunology IV. New York: Academic Press.

Alexopoulos, G.S. 2001. New concepts for prevention and treatment of late-life depression. American Journal of Psychiatry 158 (June): 835.

Andrews G, Sanderson K, Slade T, Issakidis C 2000. Why does the burden of disease persist? Relating the burden of anxiety and depression to effectiveness of treatment. Bull World Health Organ;78(4): 446-54.

Antonijevic, I. 2006. Depressive disorders—is it time to endorse different pathophysiologies? Psychoneuroendocrinology 31: 76.

Archer, J.C. 2005. An integrated review of indirect, relational, and social aggression. Personality and Social Psychology Review 9: 212.

Aron, A. et al. 2005. Reward, motivation, and emotion systems associated with early-stage intense romantic love. J. Neurophysiol 94:327.

Black, A., et al. 2000. Calorie restriction reduces the incidence of proliferative disease: Preliminary data from the NIA CR in nonhuman primate study. Gerontological Society of America annual meeting. Nov. 17. Washington, D.C. Black, P.H., and Garbutt, L.D. 2002. Stress, inflammation and cardiovascular disease. J. Psychosom. Res. 52: 1-23.

Boren, E. and Gershwin, M.E. 2004. Inflamm-aging: Autoimmunity, and the immune-risk phenotype. Autoimmunity Reviews, 3: 401-406.

Brown, A.S., et al. 2000. Maternal exposure to respiratory infections and adult schizophrenia spectrum disorders: A prospective birth cohort study. Schizophrenia Bulletin 26 (No. 2): 287-295.

Brown, S.L., et al. 2003. Providing social support may be more beneficial than receiving it: Results from a prospective study of mortality. Psychological Science 14 (July): 320-327.

Butler, T. et al. 2005. Fear related activity in subgenual anterior cingulated differs between men and women. Neuroreport 16:1233-36.

Cohen, S., et al. 2006. Positive emotional style predicts resistance to illness after experimental exposure to rhinovirus or influenza A virus. Psychosomatic Medicine 68 (November/December): 809-815.

Cavigelli, S.A., and M.K. McClintock. 2003. Fear of novelty in infant rats predicts adult corticosterone dynamics and an early death. Proceedings of the National Academy of Sciences 100 (Dec. 23): 16131-16136.

Coe, C. 2004. Biological and social predictors of immune senescence in the aged primate. Mechanisms of Ageing and Development. 135:95-98.

Collins, S.M. 2001. Stress and the gastrointestinal tract. Modulation of intestinal inflammation by stress: basic mechanisms and clinical relevance. Am. J. Physiol Gastrointest Liver Physiol 280, G315-318.

Cordle, C.T., et al. 2002. Immune status of infants fed soy based formulas with or without added nuclotides for 1 year: Part 2: Immune cell populations. Journal of Pediatric Gastroenterology and Nutrition 34 (February): 145-153.

Damasio, A.R., et al. 2000. Subcortical and cortical brain activity during the feeling of self-generated emotions. Nature Neuroscience 3 (October): 1049-1056.

Danner, D.D., D.A. Snowdon, and W.V. Friesen. 2001. Positive emotions in early life and longevity: Findings from the nun study. Journal of Personality and Social Psychology 80 (May): 804.

Dantzer, R. et. al. 2007. Cytokines, sickness behavior, and depression. In: Psychoneuroimmunology, 4th editions, Academic Press, NY. 281.

Davidson, R.J., et al. 2003. Alterations in brain and immune function produced by mindfulness meditation. Psychosomatic Medicine 65 (July/August): 564-570.

de Kloet, E.R. et al. 2005. Stress, genes and the mechanism of programming the brain for later life. Neurosci Biobehav Rev. 29: 271-81.

De Rubeis, R.J. et al. 2005. Cognitive therapy vs. medications in the treatment of moderate to severe depression. Arch Gen Psychiatry 62: 409-16.

Debiec, J. 2005. Peptides of love and fear: vasopressin and oxytocin modulate the integration of information in the amygdala. Bioessays 27: 869-73.

Doyle, W.J., D.A. Gentile, and S. Cohen. 2006. Emotional style, nasal cytokines, and illness expression after experimental rhinovirus exposure. Brain, Behavior, and Immunity 20 (March): 175-181.

Elavsky, S. et al. 2005. Physical activity enhances long-term quality of life in older adults: efficacy, esteem, and affective influences. Ann Behav Med 30: 138-45.

Franklin, T. 2006 Sex and ovarian steroids modulate brain derived neurotrophic factor (BDNF) protein levels in rat hippocampus und stressful and non-stressful conditions. Psychoneuroendocrinology 31: 38-53.

Freidman, H. 2008. The multiple linkages of personality and disease. Brain, Behavior, and Immunity, 22: 647.

Gilbertson, M.W., et al. 2002. Smaller hippocampal volume predicts pathologic vulnerability to psychological trauma. Nature Neuroscience 5 (November): 1242-1247.

Grant, I., et al. 2002. Health consequences of Alzheimer's caregiving transitions: Effects of placement and bereavement. Psychosomatic Medicine 64 (May/June): 477-486.

Gretan, F.R. and M. Karin. 2004. IKK links inflammation and tumorigenesis in a mouse model of colitis-associated cancer. Cell 118 (Aug. 6): 285-296.

Halbreich, U. 2006. Major depression is not a diagnosis, it is a departure point to differential diagnosis—clinical and hormonal considerations. Psychoneuroendocrinology 31: 16-22.

Hall, N. R. 2008. Understanding Stress and Immunity. Nursing Spectrum Press.

Hawkley, L.C. and Cacioppo, J.T. 2003. Stress and the aging immune system. Brain, Behavior and Immunity, 18: 114-119.

Kiechl, S., et al.2002. Toll-like receptor 4 polymorphisms and atherogenesis. New England Journal of Medicine 347 (July 18): 185-192.

Kiecolt-Glaser, J.K et al. 2003. Chronic stress and age-related increases in the proinflammatory cytokine IL-6.Proceedings of the National Academy of Sciences 100 (July 22): 9090-9095.

Kiecolt-Glaser, J.K. et al. 2005. Hostile marital interactions, proinflammatory cytokine production, and wound healing. Arch Gen Psychiatry 62: 1377-84.

Kubzansky, L.D., et al. 2007. Prospective study of post-traumatic stress disorder symptoms and coronary heart disease in the normative aging study. Archives of General Psychiatry 64 (January): 109-116.

Madden, K.S. 2003. Catecholamines, sympathetic innervation, and immunity. Brain, Behav. Immun. 17:5.

Marsland, A. et al. 2008. Antagonistic characteristics are positively associated with inflammatory markers independently of trait negative emotionality. Brain, Behavior, and Immunity. 22:753.

Meaney, M.J. 2001. Maternal care, gene expression, and the transmission of individual differences in stress reactivity across generations. Annu Rev Neurosci 24: 1161–92.

Meerlo, P., et al. 2002. Sleep restriction alters the hypothalmic-pituitary-adrenal response to stress. Journal of Neuroendocrinology 14 (May): 397–402.

Merrill, J.E. 2001. Production and influence of inflammatory cytokines in diseases of the adult central nervous system. In Psychoneuroimmunology, 3rd Edition. (R. Ader, D. Felten, N. Cohen, eds). Academic Press, New York.

Moldoveanu AI, Shephard RJ, Shek PN 2001. The cytokine response to physical activity and training. Sports Med. Feb; 31:115

Onard, J., M. Schoneveld, and A. Kavelaars. 2007. Glucocorticoids and immunity. In: Psychoneuroimmunology, 4th edition, Academic Press, NY. 281

Ostir GV, Markides KS, Black SA, Goodwin JS. 2000. Emotional well-being predicts subsequent functional independence and survival. J Am Geriatr Soc; 48 (5): 473–8.

Ownby, D.R., and C.C. Johnson. 2002. Exposure to dogs and cats in the first year of life and risk of allergic sensitization at 6 to 7 years of age. Journal of the American Medical Association 288 (Aug. 28): 963-972.

Peters, E.M. et al. 1993. Vitamin C supplementation reduces the incidence of post race symptoms of upper respiratory tract infection in ultra marathon runners. American Journal of Clinical Nutrition 57, 170.

Phelps, E.A. 2004. Human emotion and memory: inter-actions of the amygdala and hippocampal complex. Curr Opin Neurobiol 14: 198-202.

Phillips, D.P., et al. 2001. The Hound of the Basker-villes effect: A natural experiment on the influence of psychological stress on the timing of death. British Medical Journal 323 (Dec. 22): 1443.

Postolache, T, Komarow, H. and Tonelli, L. 2008. Allergy: A risk factor for suicide? Current Treatment Options in Neurology. 10:363.

Quirk, G.J., et al. 2003. Stimulation of medial prefron-tal cortex decreases the responsiveness of central amygdala output neurons. Journal of Neuroscience 23 (Sept. 24): 8800-8807.

Sapolsky, R. M. 2004. Why Zebras Don't Get Ulcers: A Guide to Stress, Stress-Related Diseases, and Cop-ing. W.H. Freeman and Co., New York.

Seligman, M. 1998. Learned optimism. Simon and Schuster, New York.

Shi, Y., J.E. Evans, and K.L. Rock. 2003. Molecular iden-tification of a danger signal that alerts the immune system to dying cells. Nature 425 (Oct. 2): 516-521

Singer, T. et al. 2006. Empathic neural responses are modulated by the perceived fairness of others. Nature 439: 466-69.

Stoltz, P.G. 1997. The Adversity Quotient: Turning Obstacles Into Opportunity. John Wiley & Sons, New York.

Temoshok, L et. Al. 2008. Type C coping, alexithymia, and heart rate reactivity are associated independently and differentially with specific immune mechanisms linked to HIV progression. Brain, Behavior and Immunity. 22: 781.

Tucker, P.M., et al. 2007. Physiologic reactivity despite emotional resilience several years after direct exposure to terrorism. American Journal of Psychiatry 164 (February): 230-235. Wallenstein, G. 2003. Mind, Stress and Emotions. Commonwealth Press, Washington DC.

Wan, R., S. Camandola, and M.P. Mattson. 2003. Intermittent food deprivation improves cardiovascular and neuroendocrine responses to stress in rats. Journal of Nutrition 133 (June): 1921-1929.

Watkins, L. et al. 2007. Neuroimmune interactions and pain: The role of immune and glial cells. In: Psychoneuroimmunology, 4th editions, Academic Press, NY. 281.

Weisler, R.H., J.G. Barbee, and M.H. Townsend. 2006. Mental health and recovery in the Gulf Coast after hurricanes Katrina and Rita. Journal of the American Medical Association 296 (Aug. 2): 585-588.

Wetherell, M. and K. Vedhara. 2007. Stress-associated immune dysregulation can affect antibody and T-cell responses to vaccines. In: Psychoneuroimmunology, 4th editions, Academic Press, NY. 281.

Weuve, J., et al. 2004. Physical activity, including walking, and cognitive function in older Women. Journal of the American Medical Association 292 (Sept. 22/29) 1454-1461.

Williams, L.M., et al. 2006. The mellow years? Neural basis of improving emotional stability over age. Journal of Neuroscience 26 (June 14): 6422-6430.

Zak, P.J. et al. 2005. Oxytocin is associated with human trust-worthiness. Horm Behav 48: 522-27.

Zald, D.H. 2003. The human amygdala and the emotional evaluation of sensory stimuli. Brain Res Rev 41: 88-123.

Ziv, Y. and Schwartz. 2008. Immune-based regulation of adult neurogenesis: Implications for learning and memory. Brain, Behavior, and Immunity. 22: 167.

About the Author

N ick Hall, Ph.D. is a medical scientist and professional speaker, who for over 30 years has conducted groundbreaking studies linking the mind and body. This research has been published in over 150 periodicals and featured by the national and international media, including CBS' 60 Minutes, the BBC's Nova series, and the Emmy Award-winning program Healing and the Mind, aired by PBS. He also has been the recipient of two prestigious Research Scientist Development Awards, which the National Institutes of Health grants only to the top scientists in the United States. Nick is no stranger, as well, to the more pragmatic aspects of dealing with change and with making difficult choices. After earning his way through college wrestling alligators and milking rattlesnakes, he worked as an intelligence-operative for the U.S. Government. He also led a National Geographic-sponsored expedition to the West Indies, where he studied mass-stranding behavior in whales. While working in the islands, he

endured the Marxist revolution in Grenada and the La
Soufriere volcano eruption in St. Vincent. His practical
insights for coping with change and adversity have been
shaped over a span of nearly four decades. For example,
in 1968, he became the first person to complete the grueling Baja 1,000 mile off-road race on a bicycle; while in
2006, he completed WaterTribe's Ultimate Florida Challenge in a Kayak. This 1200 mile nautical race, which
included a 40-mile portage, has been described by Times
of London as, "the most dangerous small boat race in
the world." At his Saddlebrook Resort headquarters in
Florida, Dr. Hall presents highly successful workshops
and motivational programs for some of America's leading corporations. Nick Hall, Ph.D. is a medical scientist
and professional speaker, who for over 30 years has conducted groundbreaking studies linking the mind and
body. This research has been published in over 150 periodicals and featured by the national and international
media, including CBS' 60 Minutes, the BBC's Nova
series, and the Emmy Award-winning program Healing
and the Mind, aired by PBS. He also has been the recipient of two prestigious Research Scientist Development
Awards, which the National Institutes of Health grants
only to the top scientists in the United States. Nick is
no stranger, as well, to the more pragmatic aspects of
dealing with change and with making difficult choices.
After earning his way through college wrestling alligators and milking rattlesnakes, he worked as an
intelligence-operative for the U.S. Government. He also
led a National Geographic-sponsored expedition to the

West Indies, where he studied mass-stranding behavior in whales. While working in the islands, he endured the Marxist revolution in Grenada and the La Soufriere volcano eruption in St. Vincent. His practical insights for coping with change and adversity have been shaped over a span of nearly four decades. For example, in 1968, he became the first person to complete the grueling Baja 1,000 mile off-road race on a bicycle; while in 2006, he completed WaterTribe's Ultimate Florida Challenge in a kayak. This 1200 mile nautical race, which included a 40-mile portage, has been described by Times of London as, "the most dangerous small boat race in the world." At his Saddlebrook Resort headquarters in Florida, Dr. Hall presents highly successful workshops and motivational programs for some of America's leading corporations.

Visit www.drnickhall.com for information about his programs, books, and audio series.

Printed in the USA
CPSIA information can be obtained
at www.ICGtesting.com
JSHW012030140824
68134JS00033B/2981

xo

Second Chance Contract

WALL STREET JOURNAL & USA TODAY BESTSELLING AUTHOR

M. ROBINSON

To all my angst readers!

I wrote this for you!

Second Chance Contract

Prologue

Autumn

"I'm sorry, Autumn."

Three little words that left a gaping hole in my heart. I should've listened to my brother. I should've known this man would break me. He didn't just tear me open, no... He shattered me into a million tiny pieces.

"You're sorry?" I countered in a condescending tone. "What exactly are you sorry for, Julian? The fact that you not only pushed me away but also led me on all these years? Or is it the fact that you took my virginity, and now you're telling me you're sorry for it? Which is it? Because I honestly don't know."

"Kid, you know that's not true. I've been back inside of you since I took your virginity months ago."

I scoffed out, shaking my head in disgust. "That's all you've ever seen me as. I'm just a kid to you."

"You think I see you as a child?" He jerked back. Offended was an understatement. "For fuck's sake! Your mouth's been wrapped around my cock, Autumn, so your statement is full of shit."

I couldn't help but remember the first time he'd called me kid. I was six years old, and he was almost thirteen. Even back then I knew I loved him. There we were, almost thirteen years later, and I was no longer a little girl with a crush on her older brother's best friend.

Now I was a woman who was madly in love with him instead.

"I can't do this anymore. *We* can't do this anymore."

It pained me to hear him say that. He sounded so unbelievably defeated which wasn't in his nature. Julian was always determined in whatever he wanted, and he never backed down from a challenge.

"So what? Are we just supposed to pretend like you don't love me?"

With the utmost sincere expression on his face, he argued, "I don't love you, Autumn."

I stumbled back, almost falling to the ground from his cruel response. "You don't mean that."

Our relationship wasn't supposed to be this hard. Today was supposed to be Christian's day. My brother was getting married, and I was in the wedding. We both were. Julian was the best man, standing tall beside my brother who was marrying the love of his life that he'd known since childhood. They were high school sweethearts.

Throughout the entire ceremony Julian and I cautiously locked eyes, and I wondered if his thoughts mirrored mine. Was he was envisioning us standing in front of all our family and friends, sharing our vows to one another?

Our love for each other?

I'd known Julian for as long as I could remember. He was always there, through thick and thin, my brother's best friend. I should have been celebrating with everyone else at the reception, not wallowing in the illusions I'd made up in my mind of a future that existed only in my mind.

"I've never meant anything more in all my life."

I didn't know what to say or how to act. All I could do was feel this powerful pain spiraling inside of me. I closed my eyes as a single tear fell down the side of my face, reminding me of all the times I'd spent crying over him.

Over us.

"Why are you doing this? Is it because I told you I loved you?"

"Autumn, you've been telling me you love me since you were almost seventeen years old."

"Then why are you doing this? You at least owe me that."

I would never forget the expression on his face when he confessed, "At Christian's bachelor party last weekend, I fucked someone else, kid."

Julian

"You're lying!"

"Do I ever lie to you?"

She wrapped her arms around her torso in a comforting gesture while I waited to finally end us once and for all.

"Who?"

"It doesn't matter."

"Then why are you telling me?"

"I'm not good for you. I've never been good enough for you."

"That didn't stop you from sleeping with me, did it?"

"If anything, kid, you should be thankful it was me and not some boy in the back of his car who doesn't even know how to make you come."

"Oh, because you did?"

"Yeah, just ask my soaking wet sheets."

"You arrogant asshole!"

"What do you want from me? You want me to lie and tell you I love you when I don't? You want me to hurt you more than I already am? More than I already have?"

"You know what I want. It's what I've always wanted. It hasn't changed, it never changes. You know it as much as I do. All I've ever wanted is you."

I hated that she was speaking the truth.

"I want you to look me in the eyes and swear to me that you cheated on me, and you're not just telling me that to push me away again."

"We're not together, kid. I didn't cheat on you."

I debated for the last week if I was going to do this. If I truly had the strength to tell her this. I thought about it for hours on end, driving myself fucking insane with what the right or wrong thing to do was when it came to us.

We never had a future.

We barely had a present.

After seeing the look in her eyes during the ceremony, I knew what she was envisioning, and it was the cold, hard reality I needed to witness in order to tell her it was over. The sneaking around and lying to her brother, to her family. The only family I'd ever known. They took me in when I didn't have anyone, and this was how I repaid them.

By fucking over their daughter.

What kind of man was I?

I was hurting her in the worst possible ways, and I had to live with knowing I did that. My hands were firmly placed in the pockets of my slacks, resisting the urge to pull her into my arms and comfort her the only way I knew how.

The second I walked into the church this afternoon, I stopped dead in my tracks just to take her in. She was a vision in her lavender gown. Her red hair was down, framing her beautiful freckled face and her bright green eyes that I lost myself in night after night.

She looked breathtaking, smiling at everyone. Always the center of attention in any room without having to try. I couldn't take my eyes off her. It took everything inside me not to claim her right then and there. In front of her family, her friends, her brother...

My best friend.

There was no controlling the internal battle that surfaced in the forefront of my mind—it was such a wave of emotions.

It wasn't fair.

None of this was fucking fair.

Especially to her.

When she suddenly caught my stare like she'd felt me from across the church, I didn't look away. She was the first to break our connection, gazing at the ground instead of my eyes. Fully aware she couldn't hide her feelings for me.

Her love.

It seared off of her, burning into my skin. Inflicting scars that would never heal—I wouldn't let them. I didn't know if she'd adverted her gaze for my benefit or hers, but I didn't give it too much thought.

I shoved it away as I did with everything when it came to her. Out of respect for her overprotective brother, it was easier to pretend she was just my best friend's little sister and not the woman who had the power to bring me to my knees if I'd let her.

Since she'd turned eighteen almost a year ago, there was no holding back anymore, and I indulged in the sweetest sin that was Autumn Troy. The little girl who used to follow me around with pigtails and her baby doll in her arms was long gone, and in her place stood an adult, a woman.

My feet moved of their own accord as I followed her out to the cove. We exchanged words that would eternally haunt me, only adding to the pile of endless secrets and betrayals I'd let happen to the family that raised me as if I was their own.

For a few seconds, I inhaled the sweet and enticing smell of Autumn. Remembering that the scent of her strawberry shampoo and coconut lotion still lingered on my pillow and sheets was the only comforting thing I had to go home to.

Stepping toward her, I swept the hair away from her face as a few tears slid down the sides of her cheeks. I wiped those away too. Her tears were the only thing I'd ever be worthy of. Our emotions were running wild, fighting a battle I knew I could never win.

The emotional turmoil ate away at me the closer I got to telling her this would be the last time she would see me. It would be the last time anyone in her family would see me. Including her brother.

I had to leave.

If I stayed, I'd make her mine, and I couldn't do that to them. Not after everything they had done for me.

Gripping onto the back of her neck, I tugged her toward me, and she caught herself on my chest. Her lips were now mere inches away from my mouth.

Leaning in, I rasped, "I'm leaving town."

Autumn's doe eyes widened, and her breathing hitched. "Leaving?" She choked back a sob. "What do you mean leaving? Where are you going?"

"Away from you."

She sucked in a breath. "Julian…" Softly, she pecked my lips, beckoning my mouth to open for her.

"But before I go…" I hesitated for a moment, wanting to remember the feel of her lips against mine. "I just need you to know."

There was no coming back from this.

What I'd say next would break her heart. She'd hate me, but in the end, I did what I had to do.

Looking deep into her eyes, I viciously spewed, "You were nothing more than a fuck to me, kid."

Those were the last words I'd ever said to her before I turned around and left her there.

With nothing but the man she once knew.

One

Autumn

Ten years later

"WELCOME, MISS TROY. WE CAN'T TELL YOU HOW EXCITED we are to finally have you here in Miami with us."

I smiled, nodding at the women who'd just welcomed me. "Thank you. I'm excited to be here and working with everyone."

She nervously chuckled, quickly playing it off. "Right… We've spoken on the phone several times in the last couple of weeks, and I've given you a brief overview, but I figured it would be best for us to discuss all the details in person and with everyone present."

"Everyone except the most important person," an older man sitting to the right of her informed.

She didn't pay him any mind. "Now that you've signed your nondisclosure, it's best if we begin with introductions before we proceed." She touched her chest. "As you know, I'm Claire, the head of human resources, and I've been with Mr. Locke for the last four years. This is Mr. Locke's assistant, Erin." She gestured to the younger woman sitting beside her who appeared anxious and a bit shy.

"Erin will be citing our entire meeting, so please don't be alarmed as she types away on her computer. Mr. Locke prefers all meetings to be noted for future reference and, of course, to avoid any indiscretions that may arise."

"I understand."

Claire nodded toward the older man who had just spoken. "This is Carl, and he is the Vice President here at Locke Enterprises. He's been with Mr. Locke the longest out of everyone in this board meeting."

"And because I've been with him the longest, I know we're all wasting our time. He's never going to go for this."

"He doesn't have a choice in the matter. We're announcing and going public in ten days, Carl."

"I understand the severity, Claire, but we both know he's a private person."

She ignored his statement, gesturing toward the man who sat in front of her at the rectangular mahogany table where we were all sitting at.

"That's Robert. He's our chief financial officer." She pointed to the woman next to him. "This is Julia. She's our senior marketing officer, and the man sitting to her right is Adam. He's the head of our public relations department. The woman sitting beside him is Sylvia, and she's one of our board members who is accompanied by James and Andrew, who are also board members. Last, but certainly not least is Marcus." She nodded toward the man sitting parallel to her. "He's one of our chief executives."

I smiled at the room. "Nice to meet everyone."

"Great, now that we have that out of the way, I can share some history on Locke Enterprises with you. I'm sure you Googled the company, but even the internet doesn't know much about our CEO. As Carl stated, Mr. Locke is an extremely private man and is adamant about staying so. However, we're in the process of transitioning from a private business to a public one as we discussed on the phone. We've all come to the mutual agreement that Mr. Locke must remain the face of the company, and with that, there are a few concerns."

"There aren't a few concerns," Carl interrupted, only looking at me. "There's only one, Miss Troy, and it's why you're here."

She glared at him. "We're not trying to scare her away, Carl. She's the best at what she does. It's why she's here."

"I am the best at what I do, and I'm fully aware of the reputation that precedes Mr. Locke. The whole world is, but trust me, if I can change Life of Debauchery's (LOD) rock star image to golden boys, then I can handle your CEO."

"I know." Claire beamed, sitting up in her chair. "It took me months to get a phone call with you. You're a very busy woman, and your resume speaks for itself."

"Thank you." I smiled, gazing around the table before I confidently added, "I've worked for High Society Public Relations for the last five years, and after my success with softening Life of Debauchery's image about two years ago, my phone hasn't stopped ringing with new clientele. LOD had endless stints in rehab and problems with authority, not to mention the law didn't hold well with their record label. When news got out that I was the woman responsible for their rebranding, things most certainly took a turn in my career. By the time I was through with them, they landed the cover of *The New York Times* and went from bad boy rockers to misunderstood musicians. I was in charge of their interviews, live appearances, and everything in between. Most importantly, I established and maintained cooperative relationships with industry representatives across a broad spectrum of media outlets which we're going to need now more than ever on our side."

I could tell by the expression on their faces they were eating up every word of what I was sharing. I wasn't exaggerating by any means. I'd graduated college early, top of my class in my master's program of Marketing and Public Relations. I wasn't just good at what I did—I was the best.

"Those are only a couple of things that I can personally handle," I continued on. "But rest assured that my entire team was handpicked by yours truly. Each person brings their own level of expertise, from writing press releases and any other media communications on promoting our clients, and in some cases, even monitoring their social media accounts. Their ideas are fresh, and they understand how this industry works. It can eat you up and spit you out in a matter of a few hours, and my job is to make sure our T's are crossed and our I's are dotted. We act as a safety net for our clients and the rest of the consumer world. We're a powerhouse and a force to be reckoned with. I am the best. Therefore, I only work with clients who are in desperate need of my services. The bigger the challenge, the more I accel." I paused to let my words sink in, loving the energy I was creating through the boardroom.

It was such a high.

Success was as addicting as any drug could be, and it was the only reason I agreed to this position in the first place. If I took Mr. Locke on as a client, I could make partner in my agency. My hands were tied, and I had no choice if I wanted to advance my career to the next level, Mr. Locke would be the man to make that possible. Everyone would want to work with me, and there would be no competition. I'd be at the top of my game, the peak of my career, and there was no turning that down.

Even if it meant I had to swallow my pride and work with the son of a bitch who deemed me nothing more than a fuck. I had to do what was in the best interest of my future.

I didn't tell them any of that. They didn't need to know my personal agenda for taking Mr. Locke on as a client.

It was no one's business.

Ignoring the thoughts in my mind, I proceeded with my pitch. "People love to feel like they're a part of something, and given the fact your CEO doesn't even participate in interviews makes it very hard for people to trust him with their hard-earned money. Especially when it comes to stock trade which is what you're transitioning from a private enterprise to a public one. No one is going to want to trade with someone who seems unstable. It's all about stability and image. Low risk, high reward. Mr. Locke may have a lot of money, but he needs to gain the notoriety and respect of his possible consumers. The media portrays him as a ... well, please excuse my language, but he's nothing more than an arrogant, controlling, and demanding asshole. Although that may work in the boardroom, business deals, and running a multibillion-dollar corporation, it doesn't work for the average Joe Schmo."

"Yes," Claire agreed, smiling wide. "That's exactly it. You nailed it, Miss Troy. Mr. Locke has built this company from the ground up. He spent years overseas in Italy, France, and Japan. Truly learning his craft and the ins and outs of sports cars. He's always had a passion for cars being from Fort Worth, Texas, and he took that passion and built an empire. Being the first person to create an ultra-efficient motor with a high RPM without having to run down battery power has made him a very influential man. There was no electronic sports car before him, and it has most definitely piqued the world's interest in who he is and what he's capable of. It doesn't hurt that he's easy on the eyes and was voted most eligible bachelor by not only People magazine but Forbes three consecutive years in a row now."

"All that may look great on paper, Claire, but it doesn't mean a damn thing to him." It was obvious Carl spoke his mind, and I, for one, appreciated his honesty.

"He couldn't care less about the glorified titles from the media. He's a businessman through and through and has no interest in being Locke Enterprises' mascot. Regardless of the outcome."

Carl didn't know I was aware of what I was taking on, of *who* I was taking on.

He couldn't say anything I didn't already know just from personal experience and my history with him. I knew the son of a bitch better than anyone in this room did.

Or, at least, I used to.

With a curt nod, I countered, "You're going to have to give him no other choice in the matter. If he refuses, then you need to make decisions based on what will benefit the company as a whole. Not Mr. Locke's ego. Going public is a whole different ballgame. One you need to be prepared for if you're going to dominate and succeed, and we have very little time."

Claire agreed. "Locke wouldn't have it any other way. When it comes to cars and business, Miss Troy, he's an expert. Now, when it comes to people… well, as you said, his bedside manner needs some work."

"Some work?" Carl chimed in again. "Jesus, Claire. The man never smiles. In the years I've known him, I've never once seen him smile. Not even when we grossed our first million within the first two weeks that Locke Enterprises was established."

"I'm hitting the ground running, and I already have an itinerary full of press for him in the next week. Beginning tomorrow, his days and nights will be jam-packed with editorial interviews, photoshoots, live interviews, dinners, luncheons, and those are just to name a few. I have one week to make the world fall in love with Mr. Locke."

"The media doesn't even address him by that name. They've branded him as the Alpha CEO. I don't know about you, but that doesn't sound like a family man to me."

I was about to open my mouth to respond to Carl when I felt *him…*

The double glass doors opened, and the atmosphere instantly changed. It didn't surprise me, he always had the ability to govern a room, even way before his net worth was 3.2 billion.

Without taking a look around, Mr. Locke merely announced, "I have no interest in becoming a family man, Carl."

The man walked into the boardroom exuding dominance, heading straight for his seat at the head of the table. Parallel to me. His confident stride was as demanding as his reputation. No longer the man I remembered, he'd come a long way from a Texas junkyard, wearing grease-smeared jeans, to now dressed in custom three-piece suits that were worth thousands.

Once he was sitting down in his black leather chair, he leaned forward with his elbows on the table, and without so much as a "good morning" to his colleagues and staff, he simply got down to business, locking eyes with Claire then Carl.

Although, she was the first to speak to him. "We called this board meeting on your behalf."

"What exactly are we discussing on my behalf, Claire?"

"Before we get into that…" She smiled, nodding over to me. "I'd like to introduce you to the woman who is about to change your life."

Locke's inquisitive stare followed her gaze until his eyes landed right on me. For the first time in over ten years, I looked into his icy, bright, blue eyes.

And felt absolutely nothing.

Two

Julian

I WAS A MAN WHO PRIDED HIMSELF ON CONTROL, AND FOR A BRIEF moment, it felt like I didn't have any. My mind suddenly raged war with itself thinking about the last time I saw her bright green eyes connecting with mine. It didn't help that the aloof expression on her face was consuming and punishing me all at the same time.

It wasn't until she greeted, "Nice to meet you, Mr. Locke," that I mocked in a condescending tone, "Nice to meet me? It's Mr. Locke, is it?"

She nodded, her composure steady and unwavering, but it didn't matter how poised she appeared sitting there staring only at me, I knew what was beneath her designer dress and fuck-me heels.

Is she even wearing a bra?

As if reading my mind, she casually leaned forward emphasizing her chest to show me she was indeed not wearing a damn thing underneath her dress, and I couldn't tear my eyes away from her. She'd always been a beautiful girl, but now—as a woman—there was this alluring confidence and sexy demeanor that wasn't there when I'd left her.

She'd grown up and come into her own skin, only triggering the memory of her body naked beneath mine and making my cock twitch at the thought.

"Julian, Miss Troy is—"

"I know who Autumn is, Claire."

"Oh… I wasn't aware you knew who she was. Then you've heard of

Autumn didn't show any emotion over my presence or response. She was too busy portraying a woman I no longer recognized.

Coldly replying, "I would prefer you address me as Miss. Troy, Mr. Locke. You have to earn the right to call me by my first name."

I leaned back in my chair, narrowing my captivated stare at her. "Is that right?"

The sudden tension in the boardroom was so fucking thick you could choke on it.

"I'm not your friend, Mr. Locke, and if this relationship is going to work between us, then you're going to have to treat me like the professional I am."

She was right.

We weren't friends.

We were so much more than that.

She could pretend all she wanted, but I knew what she felt like riding me. The way she screamed my name when she wanted more, and the tiny purrs she'd make right before she'd come on my cock.

"Relationships aren't really my thing," I reminded her. Watching and gauging her reaction, I added, "But you already knew that."

Her eyes lit with anger.

Good. Two could play this game, sweetheart.

"Our *working* relationship, Mr. Locke."

"I wasn't aware we were in any type of relationship, *Miss Troy,* but by all means do enlighten me."

"Julian, she's here because you need her."

Claire brought my attention to her statement.

"We're going public."

"I'm fully aware, Claire."

"Of course you are. I didn't mean to imply—"

"Time is money, so stop wasting mine and get down to business. Why is she here?"

"Your team is concerned about your image, Mr. Locke."

My gaze shifted back to Autumn. "My image?"

"Yes. Your personality doesn't exactly speak highly for itself. Especially in the media's eyes."

"And why is this my problem? I've made everyone in this room a very rich individual, and that speaks for itself."

"It does for their bank accounts but not for the general public, which is who you are catering toward to invest in your company."

"My profits are public knowledge, Miss Troy. It's a Google search away. Knowing my favorite color isn't going to decipher if or how much money someone should invest in our shares."

"You'd be surprised how influential knowing someone's favorite color can be when it comes down to giving you their money."

"I have no interest in performing for the public like I'm some teenage boy who needs to have his dick stroked, Miss Troy."

Her cheeks slightly flushed, and I'd be lying if I said it didn't thoroughly please me that I still affected her, despite the game she was trying to play in front of everyone.

"I'm a businessman, Miss Troy. I make money, and that's all anyone needs to know."

"I'm not asking you to perform for anyone. It's actually quite the opposite, so check your ego at the door, Mr. Locke. I believe your best approach in this situation is to show the public how far you've come. Let them into your world. Show them there's more to you than just cars, business, and money. You came from nothing and made something of yourself. You're the American dream, and we need to capitalize on that."

"Julian, it's a necessary evil," Carl intervened. "It's what's best for the company."

"Carl, we both know how Wall Street works. I know people. The *right* people. I don't need to change my image any more than you need to kiss my ass."

"Julian—"

I interrupted him, "We need to clear the room, Claire. I'd like to talk to Miss Troy alone."

"I don't think that's the best idea."

I cocked my head to the side, stating the truth, "Whose name is on the building, Claire?"

She cleared her throat, nodding for everyone to leave.

After they were gone, I crossed my arms over my chest and focused solely on the woman who thought she could change me.

Again.

"Now that they're gone, let's cut the bullshit, Autumn."

"Mr. Locke, I won't remind you again to address me as Miss Troy."

"How long do you plan on playing this little game?"

"I don't know what you're referring to, but let me inform you that your team reached out to me. Not the other way around. I'm just here to do my job."

"Your job? Which is what? Wear a tight dress with no bra so your tits get you employed."

Her eyes widened. "That's not—"

I put my finger up in the air, silencing her. "That wasn't a question."

She glared at me. "I could report you to HR for that, Mr. Locke. Do you always sexually harass women in your office who are dressed professionally?"

"I'm simply stating facts, and I never mix business with pleasure."

"I find that hard to believe considering you are referred to as Alpha CEO and the world's most eligible bachelor. What is it now? Three years in a row?"

I grinned. "Kept tabs on me, have you?"

"I researched you. It's what makes me damn good at my job."

"And what did this research inform you of, kid?"

She glared at me again, clenching out, "I won't be disrespected by you, Mr. Locke. You need to address me as Miss Troy—end of conversation."

"Sweetheart, we're just getting started."

"I'm not one of your employees you can treat like shit. Am I making myself clear?"

"You're on my payroll, are you not?"

"*You're* paying *me* to change your image—that makes me your boss."

I let out a throaty laugh, unable to remember the last time I'd done so. "The only thing you're the boss of, kid, is being a royal pain in my ass."

She abruptly stood, sliding documents across the table before strutting her way to the door. "Get used to it, Mr. Locke. Take a look at your itinerary for the next week because beginning tomorrow morning, I control you."

I resisted the urge to argue, realizing all too quickly that my sweet, innocent girl had changed, and in her place stood a confident and sophisticated woman dressed to impress. Her tight cream dress stopped just below her knees, accentuating every curve of her body.

Was she wearing a garter belt?

HR would have a fucking field day if they knew I was admiring her luscious ass that swayed with each step she walked. She knew exactly what she was doing and what I was thinking, only fueling the fire raging inside of me.

Her narrow hips.

Her ample breasts.

She was sporting diamond earrings, a gold bracelet, a solitaire diamond necklace, and a gold watch with an oversized designer bag tucked in the nook of her arm. Topping her outfit off with red, sky-high fuck-me heels just as I presumed when she was sitting down. She had more makeup on than I'd ever seen on her before.

She was a goddess.

An angel.

Making me realize this was what Hell looked like.

Despite her temper tantrum, our connection was still alive and thriving all around us. It felt like forever had passed, waiting for her to walk by me. I contemplated if she must have felt the same way when it came to me all those years ago.

She was constantly waiting for me to admit I had feelings for her. Never understanding how it didn't matter if I had. We couldn't be together.

Not then.

Not now?

Too many emotions and questions tore through my mind in those brief seconds, one right after the other with no end in sight. I couldn't believe she was there with me, in my building, and with this unexpected ambush by my team of all places.

The clicking sound of her heels vibrated deep within my core with each step she took. One by one it added to all the chaos erupting in my mind. I had questions, and I wasn't going to stop until she answered each one of them to my satisfaction.

My head was already throbbing, a migraine was looming, and I was surprised I could still fucking see straight with the uncertainty racing through my body.

All I wanted to do was pull her into my arms and have her stop with the games she was trying to play. The wall she'd built against me was so thick, so high, so solid that for the first time in I didn't know how long, I feared I might lose this sudden battle between us.

I'd never lost at anything, except maybe her…

When she walked past me, I growled at my impulsive thought and grabbed her hand, tugging her back toward me. She instantly misplaced her footing and fell into my lap, catching herself on my chest.

As soon as she realized her lips were now inches away from mine, she gasped. The scent of her surrounded us, and for a moment, I almost lost control.

Almost.

Instead I rasped, "You can play this game all you want, but we both know it's only a matter of time until you're in my bed *again*, sweetheart."

She pushed off my chest, standing tall in front of me. "If you ever speak to me like that again, Mr. Locke, I won't just report you to Human Resources—I'll sue you for everything you're worth."

I smiled, unable to remember the last time I'd done that either. Eyeing her up and down, I didn't hesitate.

Speaking with conviction, I boldly stated, "As you know, kid, I never back down from a challenge." Before she could shove me away again, I leaned forward and gripped onto the back of her neck, roughly bringing her to me.

When our lips were centimeters apart, I declared, "Consider this war, Miss Troy."

Meaning every last word.

Three

Autumn

Then

"WHY IS THIS JUNKYARD SO FAR AWAY?" I ASKED, SITTING in the backseat of Christian's truck while he drove.

Our parents had just bought it for his sixteenth birthday last week, saying he deserved it for being such a great son, friend, and big brother.

Christian wasn't like other brothers, not like most of my friends' siblings anyway. He was always nice to me and enjoyed having me around. Even though we were six years apart, he didn't make me feel like I was a little girl who couldn't hang around with him. He usually let me tag along with them wherever they went.

It was only the four of us, well, five of us because Julian never went home. He stayed at our house almost every night, and he even had his own room. Mom turned one of our guest bedrooms into his own space for his tenth birthday.

I didn't remember since I was only four years old at the time, but it was one of her favorite memories to share with us. Saying he never looked happier than he did the moment she'd surprised him with what she did for only him.

He was part of our family—always had been, always would be.

Julian didn't know his real parents. He was raised in the system, going from foster home to foster home. I didn't really understand what that meant, but I guessed the state-owned him until he was eighteen—a legal adult.

Julian always acted older than he actually was, though. Our parents said it was from him having to grow up fast.

Sitting in the passenger seat, he turned around to look at me. "When you see my new baby, you'll know why we drove so far away, kid."

I smiled.

I loved it when he called me kid. It was his nickname for me. No one else called me that, only him.

It was our thing.

"Is it like Christian's baby?"

I'd learned at an early age what cars and trucks meant to boys and how they called them their babies. Both of them loved vehicles since we lived in Fort Worth, Texas. Near NASCAR and street races, but Julian really loved them.

Cars were his everything.

He worked at a junkyard by our house, close enough he could ride his dirt bike through the woods before he got his driver's license a month ago. He'd been working there for the last four years helping Big Ben with all his classic cars.

Most of the time he wore a black cowboy hat or some sort of backward hat with a white t-shirt and jeans. His clothes were usually covered in oil or grease, and his hands and nails were normally stained with it too.

He smelled like gasoline and motor oil, and it was one of my favorite smells because it reminded me of him. I even stole one of his hoodies, and he never asked for it back.

Julian didn't like to feel like a burden on our parents, so he always tried to help out whenever he could. Buying random things at the grocery store or ordering food for us for lunch and dinner.

One time he tried to help out with the water bill, and it made our mom very sad. She started crying, telling him he didn't have to worry about adult responsibilities, and it was their job to provide for us.

A couple of years ago my parents wanted to adopt him, but Julian said no. Saying what they already did for him was enough. I still had nightmares about the time he'd shown up at our house with bruises on his face and body. I thought he'd been in a fight at school. Sometimes that happened. He had a short fuse and bad temper which got him into trouble a lot.

Especially with his foster parents.

In this situation, his foster dad beat him up pretty badly, and Daddy got really mad.

Since he was a super important and successful district attorney, he was able to pull strings and get him out of that placement. They put him in a home closer to ours, and that made us all very happy.

Christian met Julian in preschool, and from the moment they exchanged fist bumps they were best friends.

All my friends were in love with my brother *and* his best friend. But Julian was mine; he just didn't know it yet. The thought alone made my belly flutter and my face flush. I had to look out the window so Christian wouldn't see. He was very protective over me, even when it came down to his best friend.

Julian was the most handsome boy I'd ever seen. He had bright blue eyes that spoke for themselves. I could always tell his mood through his eyes. They would change to all different shades of blue depending on his feelings. His eyes were my mood ring.

He was tall, way taller than me. Big and with lots of muscles because he worked out a lot. His hair was dark, and he had the most perfect nose and teeth. They were straight and super white.

I thought he looked like Eric from the Little Mermaid—my favorite Disney movie. I wanted him to be my Prince Charming, and right now I was too little, but one day I wouldn't be little anymore, and we could be together forever and ever.

My brother's good looks had girls falling all over him since the day he was born too, but it didn't matter. He already had a girlfriend, Kinley. They'd officially been together since last year. Whatever that meant.

They'd known each other since middle school, though. She was pretty and nice to me, and I liked her; the whole family did.

"Julian, can I use your cell phone?"

He handed it over to me. I wasn't allowed to have one. Daddy said maybe next year when I was eleven.

Swiping over his locked screen, a text message appeared from Katie.

Who's Katie?

I can't wait to see your new car. Maybe you could take me for a drive… I mean, I'd love to ride you too.

"Julian, some girl named Katie wants you to take her for a ride in your new car and she said she'd love to ride you too."

He choked on his drink, and Christian's eyes widened. I could see the expression on his face through the rearview mirror.

"Are you okay?" I patted Julian's back to help.

He cleared his throat and coughed a few more times, snatching the phone out of my hands.

"Hey! I wasn't done."

"Yeah, you were up to no good."

"I was not! She texted you as I unlocked your phone."

He texted her back, and I glared.

What did he reply?

"Are you going to give her a piggyback ride?"

He chuckled, and Christian smacked him on the chest. I was the only girl he ever gave piggyback rides to, and I couldn't help but feel jealous.

"This conversation is over, Autumn. Hey, dickwad!" Christian smacked him on the chest again, harder that time. "Don't let her use your phone anymore."

"I didn't know she'd be texting me."

"Since when did you start talking to her?"

He grinned. "Talking isn't exactly what I'd say we were doing."

Before I could ask if she was his girlfriend, my brother pulled into a gas station and got out of his truck to fill his tank.

"Kid."

"What?"

Julian laughed. "What do you mean what?" He rustled up my hair with his fingers, making me giggle. "What's your problem?"

"Nothing."

"Then why aren't you looking at me?"

I shrugged. "I don't know."

"You mad?"

"No. Why would I be mad?"

"Do you want my phone?"

"No. Katie might text again, and Christian will be mad that I'm reading messages I don't understand."

"Autumn."

I deeply sighed, hating when he used that low tone with me.

"I'm not giving her any piggyback rides, okay? Those are only reserved for you."

I looked up at him. "Promise?"

He made a cross over his heart.

"Then what is she riding?"

"I'll tell you what…" He smiled. "One day you're going to know the answer to that question, but today isn't that day, kid."

"So then what? Is she your girlfriend now or something?"

"Or something."

"What does that mean?"

"Why does it matter?"

I shrugged again. "I'm just curious."

"You, curious? Never," he sarcastically joked.

This wasn't the time to make fun. This was serious. I needed to know about my competition.

What if he loves her?

Before I could ask, Julian added, winking, "You'll always be my number one girl, kid."

I smiled. He always knew what to say to make me feel better, but I wasn't naive, knowing he only saw me as a little girl.

Right now.

Christian jumped back into his seat, and for the rest of the drive, I didn't say anything while they talked about Julian's new baby.

I couldn't believe my eyes when I saw the car they were speaking about. It was…

Well, it was a piece of crap.

The outside looked like someone scratched off all the paint, the doors and windows were missing, the interior had been removed, the tires were flat, and the front windshield was cracked. You couldn't see through it. Those were just the obvious things. He hadn't popped open the hood yet.

I knew a lot about cars because Julian had taught me. Sometimes I'd go with him to the junkyard. I'd seen him work on lots of vehicles, but none of them looked this bad.

"Uh, Julian." My gaze found his. "I don't think this car is going to work. I think it died."

He smiled, I loved seeing him smile. It lit up his eyes.

"All the more reason to bring her back to life."

"Do you think you're going to be able to, though? I mean, she looks pretty dead to me."

"Kid." He tugged on the end of my pigtail, and for the next eight years, almost nine, he proved his next words to me on a daily basis.

Stating, "I never back down from a challenge."

Four

Autumn

Now

THE ABSOLUTE NERVE OF THAT MAN.

I couldn't believe the way he'd talked to me like he had a right to. If he thought I was going to forget everything he'd put me through, then he had another thing coming.

He was a job.

He was just another client.

Nothing more, nothing less.

I'd earned a shot at that partnership at High Society, I deserved it, and I'd be damned if he was going to mess it up for me.

By the time I stepped into my hotel room I was beyond exhausted, having back-to-back meetings here in Miami with other clients after what could only be identified as a power struggle between client and publicist.

It wasn't like I hadn't experienced this before. Sometimes influential men had to be knocked down a few notches. Their egos were as big as their bank accounts.

Mr. Locke wasn't any different.

I could handle him.

I was a professional.

I wouldn't let him get to me—not his words, not his devastatingly handsome good looks, not even the bullshit I was aware he was going to fight me on simply to stay in control. He'd always had an issue with authority, especially when it came down to telling him what he could and couldn't do. I

"Hmm…" I groaned, sinking into the hot bubble bath of my suite.

This was how I usually ended most of my days. It didn't matter where I was.

Part of my job required a ton of travel, particularly press tours. We were always flying from New York to LA, anywhere really. For the next week, my ass was stuck beside Locke's. Where he went, I went. Submerging myself into his life was the only way I was going to guarantee he didn't fuck this up.

For the both of us.

He was already proving to be everything the media had made him out to be. I had seven days to change him into the man I used to know.

Before he'd broken my heart.

I could do this.

"You can do anything," I reassured myself, sinking further into the jacuzzi tub made for several people while sipping the wine I had delivered from room service.

Out of nowhere, the hotel phone rang, and I answered from the tub. "This is Autumn."

"How did it go with our Alpha CEO?" my boss inquired, catching me off guard.

I replied, "It went great," with my voice steady and calm.

"Really?"

"Yes."

"He agreed to your week-long press tour?"

"Not in so many words, but we're getting there."

"You're getting there? His first editorial interview with *The New York Times* is tomorrow afternoon, Autumn."

"He will be there." *Even if I have to drag him by his balls.*

"Has he signed your contract?"

"Laurel, I know what I'm doing."

"I don't need to remind you what's at stake here."

She usually wasn't on my ass with any of my clients, but *he* wasn't just anyone. The notoriety we'd get from changing his image would take High Society to the ultimate level. We'd be number one, and that was a spot Laurel wanted more than anything.

We both did.

"You don't need to remind me. Once I'm made partner we'll be unstoppable."

I could tell by her silence she was smiling on the other end of the line.

"Keep me posted on how tomorrow goes."

"Will do."

"Try to get some sleep, alright? You have a busy and demanding schedule ahead of you."

Yeah, and that was only his press tour.

"Of course."

"Goodnight."

"Night."

I hung up, about to breathe a huge sigh of relief when the phone rang again.

I answered, "Laurel, I can deal with Julian, I promise."

"So when you're talking about me to other people I'm suddenly Julian?"

I jerked back, staring at the phone as if it had suddenly grown a head. "How did you get this number? Wait, how did you know where I was?"

"I asked you a question, and I expect an answer."

I rolled my eyes.

"Don't roll your eyes at me, Miss Troy."

"What the hell? How did you—" I looked around the bathroom. "Are there cameras in here? Are you watching me?"

"Would you like me to be watching you while you're naked in your bubble bath?"

"Juli—" I caught myself, fully aware he was grinning that I'd almost said his name to him. "Mr. Locke, how do you know what I'm doing?"

"Unlike you, I'm not pretending to not know everything about you."

"You don't know anything about me."

"I know your hair is held back by an ink pen right now, and you're drinking Merlot while you're soaking in a warm bath, contemplating how you're going to get me to agree to your little press tour."

My mouth dropped open. "How do you—" I sat up, peering around the bathroom again, covering my chest that time.

"You don't have to hide your breasts, Miss Troy. I've seen them."

Through a clenched jaw, I threatened, "If I find out you set up cameras in my suite, I swear to God, Mr. Locke, I will—"

"You'll what? Play with your perfect pink pussy so I can watch?"

"You're unbelievable!" I gasped. "How dare—"

"Relax, kid. My company set up your accommodations."

"Oh yeah … right. But how do you know—"

"I don't have to watch you through cameras if I want to see you naked. All I have to do is think about all the times—"

"Enough!" I roared, losing the last bit of patience I had with him. "You cannot talk to me like this. I won't stand for it."

"You used to love the way I talked to you. Especially when my face was buried in between your—"

I hung up on him. "The fucking nerve of that man!"

Of course, the phone immediately rang again, but I didn't answer.

Instead, I heard his rough, husky tone on the voicemail of the hotel suite as it echoed off the walls.

"If you don't pick up, I'll walk right into your suite. I don't even need to knock, Autumn. I have a key. You're staying in one of my hotels."

Tired of his bullshit, I picked up the phone and dialed his number. "Are you fucking insane?" I seethed into the phone as soon as he answered.

"No, but I won't go ignored either."

"You own hotels?" This was news to me. I had immersed myself into Julian's world without realizing just how deep I was in.

"I own a lot of things, kid. Locke Enterprises is just one of them."

"Oh my God." I rubbed my face. My head was suddenly pounding. "If you come here, I'll have you arrested for trespassing."

"Too late. Open your door." With that, he hung up.

And I lost my shit.

Julian

She answered the door like she was ready to beat my face in. Considering I was the one who taught her how to throw a mean right hook, I was prepared to block any advances.

Except for the one where she threw herself at me, but we weren't there *yet.*

"You cannot be here! This is not appropriate!"

"Since when have we ever been appropriate, kid?"

"You're not even listening to me! This is like ten years ago all over again!"

"But look what it's done for your perspective. At least you're recognizing our past."

"Oh. My. God."

While she threw yet another temper tantrum in the span of a few hours, my eyes raked in her wet body. She was wearing a light blue silk robe that left very little to the imagination. Her nipples were hard, they were pointing right at me.

When she realized where my stare had drifted, she gazed down and instantly covered herself.

"You're violating so many HR rules, I don't even know where to begin to report you."

"You and I both know you're not going to report me, Miss Troy." I shoved open the door and walked inside. Heading straight toward the rectangular dining table.

She slammed the door shut behind me, turning around to lean against it. Her arms crossed over her chest. "You know most people wait until they're invited inside."

"I'm not most people."

"Right, you're Alpha CEO," she mocked in a condescending tone I wanted to spank right out of her. "You don't ask for anything."

"You're right, I don't." Sitting down at the head of the table, I met her pissed off stare. "I simply take, Miss Troy."

"Oh, trust me, Mr. Locke, I, understand better than anyone, how much you take from people."

"Are you referring to your virginity?"

Her eyes widened. "No! I'm referring to your asshole ways! How do you know I wasn't here with my husband tonight?"

"You're not married."

"How do you know I'm not married?"

"You're not wearing a ring and I know how much you love jewelry."

"That doesn't mean I don't have a boyfriend."

"I'm calling your bluff on the boyfriend," I confidently countered.

"Given your reoccurring attitude, I'm going to bet you haven't been fucked in a very long time."

She connivingly smiled, cocking her head to the side. "Just for that comment, Mr. Locke, I'm going to go down to the bar and find a real man who can satisfy my needs."

"Try to leave, sweetheart. You don't need a random fuck when I'm sitting right here."

"I said a real man who can satisfy my needs, not some pretentious, arrogant asshole who breaks into my hotel room."

"It's not breaking and entering when you own the whole damn building. As far as satisfying your needs, we both know how many times I can make you come without trying. This pretentious, arrogant asshole gave you your first orgasm, and that was just with my mouth sucking your greedy little clit. Would you like me to elaborate on how many times I made you come with my fingers, tongue, and cock, Miss Troy?"

"No! I don't need to be reminded about all the regrets and mistakes in my life."

"Great, because I'm not here for a trip down memory lane. I'm here to talk business." I nodded toward the chair next to me. "Sit down."

"I'm not a dog, Mr. Locke."

I resisted the urge to call her out on her bitch attitude, knowing it wouldn't get me anywhere other than proving my point and pissing her off further. Although the desire was there, I firmly nodded to the chair again instead.

Mumbling under her breath, she walked toward the table and sat in the seat parallel to me. "Why are you here? What do you want?"

"I'm here to make you an offer you can't refuse." I opened my suit jacket to grab my own contract before sliding it across the table.

"What is this?" she asked without looking at it.

"This ... is *our* contract."

"Our contract? Our contract for what?"

"For your little press tour."

"Stop calling your itinerary a little press tour. You make it sound insignificant when it's far from that."

"Well, Miss Troy, I have yet to see anything worthwhile other than it bringing you back into my life."

"I'm immune to your bullshit charm. You said we were discussing business, and all you've done is piss me off."

"I'll do your press tour, but it's going to be on my terms."

"Your terms?" She jerked back. "Is that supposed to make me happy? I think you're sadly mistaken on who is in control, Mr. Locke."

"Quite the contrary, kid. I remain at the head of the table. Now turn to page two."

She did, reading out loud, "Publicist, Autumn Troy, agrees to spend personal time with the client, Julian Locke, that isn't considered working hours." Her eyes snapped to mine. "What the hell is this?"

"I'm a businessman, and these are my negotiations."

She slammed the contract shut, roughly sliding it toward me. "I don't need to read the rest to know I'm not signing that."

"You'll sign it, Miss Troy. If you refuse, I won't do the tour, and you won't make partner."

All the color drained from her face when she realized I knew more than she'd wanted me to.

"Let's face it, kid. You need me. I'm the key to your promotion."

She scoffed out in disgust, shaking her head, "You're unbelievable."

"So you've said."

"How did you find out?"

"You're not the only one who knows the right people."

"Get out! Now!"

I gave in to her demands. It was the least I could do. Before I left, I placed the contract on the table, where it would undoubtedly mock her, and then made my way to the door.

I'd won.

Game over.

She knew it too.

But I stopped dead in my tracks when I heard her exclaim, "I fucking hate you, Julian."

Without turning around, I simply stated the truth. "It's not the first or last time I'm going to hear those words out of your mouth, kid. You still haven't read the rest of my terms, and I'm certain it's only going to make you hate me that much more. Especially page three."

"Is that where it says I have to have sex with you?"

"This isn't about sex, Miss Troy. It's much deeper than that."

"Don't use words you don't understand, Mr. Locke. I was nothing more than a fuck, remember?"

Having her throw my own vicious statement back at me from all those years ago wasn't a surprise. I just didn't think it would happen this soon. Pretending as if it didn't kill me to hear her say those words, I regained my composure and opened the door.

"I'll be in my office by seven. Sleep well, kid."

Shutting the door behind me, I left, and as soon as I did, a loud banging shattered against it.

I grinned and walked away.

Autumn shouldn't have played with fire if she didn't want to get burned.

Five

Day 1 of Press Tour

I WAS ALREADY SITTING IN FRONT OF HIS DESK IN HIS OFFICE WHEN he walked in the next morning with the contract in my lap.

"Good morning, Mr. Locke."

"I see we're back to Mr. Locke." His dubious stare went from me to his assistant, Erin, who was sitting beside me, recording what we were saying by typing away on her laptop.

I smiled when I noticed the sudden smoldering expression on his face as he took in my dress. It wasn't what I would normally wear to a meeting, more like what I would wear for a night out on the town with my girlfriends if we were looking for men.

His gaze lingered on my cleavage. My nipples were hard from the cold air in his office, and I might have rubbed them a little bit before he walked in to ensure they were extra alert.

"We never left, sir."

"Sir?" He arched an eyebrow, sitting behind his desk. His eyes were firmly locked with mine. "Now that I could get used to you calling me."

Of course, you could, you cocky dick.

"I just want to start this meeting by saying thank you for the push I needed to finally get thoroughly satisfied last night. The random fuck I met in the bar that I brought back after you'd left excelled each and every one of my desires and fantasies. It truly was the attitude adjustment I needed. I'm bright-eyed and bushy-tailed for you this morning."

Despite him trying to remain calm and unfazed, I could still see the slight clench of his jaw and the vein on his neck protruding as his gaze shifted back to Erin.

I imagined her eyes were wide as saucers as she continued to type away.

"You can go to your office, Erin."

"No, no, no…" I intervened in a high-pitched tone. "I prefer she stay and cite our entire conversation. I would hate for anything to be taken out of context, especially when we're discussing the negotiations of your contract."

"There are no negotiations. You either take it or leave it."

"I think you should follow your own advice," I snidely baited. "I forgot how good it felt to have orgasms. I came over and over again. And trust me, Mr. Locke, there was no mistaking my orgasms this time. My soaking wet sheets speak for themselves. Please do apologize to your cleaning crew for me."

His jaw tightened again. "I'll relay the message, Miss Troy."

"Great."

"Well, given your night of satisfaction, did you have time to go over my contract?"

"Of course, Mr. Locke. Unlike you, I love mixing business with pleasure," I lied. I never did. I just wanted to get a rise out of him. "I guess you could say it's how I've gotten this far. Ask around since you know all the right people. Yet, you probably don't have to since you've had a taste of me yourself."

"I've had more than a taste, sweetheart."

"Did you get that, Erin?" I looked at her. "Make sure you accentuate 'more than a taste.' I believe it's against company policy to fuck an employee."

"Autumn, that's enough."

"But, Julian…" I leaned against his desk and pressed my breasts together, giving him one hell of a view. I wasn't wearing a bra. "We're just getting started, *sweetheart.*"

"Leave us," he demanded, his eyes now cold and calculated. "Now."

Erin didn't have to be told twice. She practically hauled ass toward the door and out of his office.

"Just out of curiosity, how many assistants do you go through in a month? I'm going to assume maybe one a week?"

"Erin has been with me for three years."

"She seems awfully shy and submissive. Huh, I guess that would work well for you, though. I imagine she's always ready on her knees for you."

"My assistant doesn't get on her knees for me, kid, but you sure as fuck can."

"I thought you don't mix business with pleasure, Mr. Locke?"

"For you…" He paused to let his words sink in. "I would."

"Is that supposed to make me swoon? I'm immune to your bullshit lines. I've heard them all before."

"Autumn—"

I threw the contract on his desk in front of him. "I highlighted what I agree to, scratched out what I don't, and added my own terms. If you don't like it, I'll walk right out of this office and never look back. I may need you, but you need me too. Unlike the eighteen-year-old girl you fucked over, I know my worth now. I won't let you use me again. I shouldn't have let it happen the first place, but I was young and stupid."

Every time I thought about how I'd let him use me the anger seared throughout my entire body. After years of trying to get over him, I finally did, and now all those painful emotions were tearing into me once again.

I hated that I was letting him get to me, but he knew how to push all of my buttons. Determined to not allow him to win, I went in for the kill, knowing how to use his ambition to my advantage.

"You want to be number one on the market, and I'm the woman to get you there. Because mark my words, Julian, without me, you'll fail."

It was my turn to pause. I wanted him to really listen to what I was saying. He needed to understand this was a two-way street—we needed each other to advance in our careers.

I gave it a few more seconds before adding, "If we're going to make our working relationship succeed and flourish, then you're going to have to give me an inch."

"If I give you an inch, you'll take a mile."

"Everything I have planned for you in the next week is solely for the benefit of your company. I know you didn't come this far to stop now. You're going to have to trust me on this. This has to be a team effort if we're going to work together effectively."

For a moment he just sat there staring at me, and if I wasn't already sitting down, I probably would have fallen on my ass when he declared, "You want the man I was ten years ago, and he's not here anymore, Autumn. He died the day I left you."

"You're wrong," I countered, trying like hell not to let his words get to me. "He's just lying dormant inside of you. But this isn't about us. We were never an *us,* and it took me a long time to realize that. You were my brother's best friend, and I was just a stupid kid who thought her life began and ended with you. I don't hate you, Julian. At least not anymore. The truth is… I feel absolutely nothing for you."

He winced. It was quick, but I saw it.

"But from one successful person to another, I do respect the hell out of what you've built, and the world needs to know how far you've truly come. You know firsthand what it's like to grow up in the system, and there are still millions of kids who need to know that being dealt a shitty hand in life doesn't determine who they are and what they're capable of. It doesn't define them like it didn't define you. You had my father as a role model, and now here's your chance to pay it forward."

"How is your father?"

"I'm not here to discuss my family with you. If you want to know about them, their phone numbers haven't changed."

He didn't just leave me behind—he abandoned my entire family.

Including my brother.

The only difference between me and them was that he actually said goodbye to me. My family had spent years grieving the loss of a best friend and a son.

I could see the remorse on his face—he didn't try to hide it. He wanted me to see there was still a part of the man I used to know living inside of him.

For the first time since we saw one another again, I felt as if I was finally getting through to him. Making my emotions run wild with feelings I thought were gone when it came to him.

I shoved them aside, refusing to go down that road again.

"Did you practice that pitch, kid?"

"No," I simply stated. "I spoke from my heart."

Which scared me more than anything.

Julian

The times when I'd let my mind contemplate the past and what I must have put her family through were some of the darkest moments of my life. To hear her confirm how much I'd hurt her wasn't something I was prepared for, and I'd be full of shit if I said I didn't want to continue talking about us.

But this wasn't the time or place.

The new contract I had drawn up would allow me to have the time I wanted with her where we could do exactly that.

Instead of insisting that this conversation was far from over, I peered down at the contract, looking through each page to see what she had in mind.

Publicist, Autumn Troy, agrees to spend personal time with Client, Julian Locke, which isn't considered working hours. No more than two hours a day.

There was a lot I could do with two hours…

For every interview that client, Julian Locke, has agreed to, Publicist, Autumn Troy, must have dinner with him. Only if I can choose the restaurant.

I guess she was still the picky eater she was as a child. She basically had an interview scheduled every day, which meant we'd be eating dinner together every night. On top of the two hours she was giving me. I could work with that.

My eyes shifted toward the next clause, and I couldn't help but chuckle at her response.

~~When the Publicist, Autumn Troy, is ready to throw herself at Client, Julian Locke, he will be willing and able to perform up to his full potential.~~ Keep fucking dreaming. It's never going to happen.

Publicist, Autumn Troy, is NOT ALLOWED to have contact and/or private encounters with other men for the duration of the client, Julian Locke's, press tour. That goes both ways with you and women, asshole.

I grinned. She felt nothing for my ass.

Six

Julian

MOVING ONTO THE NEXT CLAUSE, I READ...

~~During travel, Publicist, Autumn Troy, must sleep in the same suite as Client, Julian Locke.~~ ABSOLUTELY NOT.

I glanced up. "Are you worried you won't be able to keep yourself from crawling into my bed, Miss Troy?"

She glared at me. "Of course not."

"Then what's the problem with us sharing a suite? Unless you've forgotten, I was the first man to see you naked. I'd be happy to refresh your memory. I'm sure some things have changed since the last time you were in my bed, except for how many times I can make you come and scream my name."

Her eyes widened. "And that's exactly why! You think you're still allowed to see me naked, when you're not. You're never going to see me naked again, Mr. Locke. You don't have that effect on me anymore. I don't even find you attractive."

I deviously grinned, leaning back against my seat. I didn't say one word, allowing my predatory regard to do all the work for me. It went from her tantalizing green eyes to her pouty lips. Slowly, I sensually started rubbing my thumb over my mouth. Obviously, she was uncomfortable, squirming as my eyes wandered over her body.

I didn't give a fuck.

I wanted to look at her, so I did.

Reminding me of all the times she'd captivated my senses when she shouldn't have. I never stopped rubbing my callused fingers over my mouth, as her gaze followed the movement of my hand, causing her luscious lips to purse as she watched my every move. Only triggering the memories of how many times I'd bit her bottom lip.

She liked it.

A lot.

My heady gaze trailed down her neck toward her tits, which were on full display, just waiting to be freed from her tight fucking dress, right down to her narrow, tiny waist. I immediately envisioned all the times I'd gripped onto her hips, guiding her down my cock, or when I fucked her from behind.

She liked that even more.

Miss Autumn Troy was a dirty little girl.

Narrowing my eyes, I continued my visual assault down to her slender thighs, wanting to bury my face between them. My cock twitched at the thought of her riding my face, still remembering the first time I sat her on my mouth, on my bed. It was the second worst day of my life—the first was leaving her. However, she made that day better for me. The second I tasted of her, and fucked her virgin hole with my tongue, I knew there was no going back for me.

For us.

I seductively licked my lips, practically tasting her against my tongue.

Her skin flushed.

Her legs squirmed.

Her body completely reacted to my greedy perusal.

Autumn might claim she didn't feel anything for me, but her body and pussy were telling a different story.

"Stop looking at me like that."

"I thought I didn't affect you?"

"You don't."

"So if I slid my fingers into your panties, you wouldn't be wet for me right now?"

"Not that it's any of your business, but I'm not wearing any."

I laughed, throwing my head back.

The little fucking minx.

"And who's benefit was that for, Miss Troy?"

She ignored my question. "This isn't a slumber party, Mr. Locke. We don't need to share a suite."

"Well, I have no intention of sleeping."

"Which is exactly why we're not sharing a suite."

I smiled. "Don't trust yourself to be alone with me?"

"I'm alone with you right now."

"You had Erin sitting here when I walked in."

"That doesn't mean anything."

"You need to trust me when I say my intentions are pure."

"You literally just said you had no plans of sleeping."

"When you have hundreds of people relying on you to make a living, you don't sleep much. You took my words out of context. What I was insinuating was that we could go over our daily game plan for the tour. You know, get me ready for the world to fall in love with me."

She beamed. "We could absolutely do that."

"Great." I grabbed a highlighter to approve the same suite clause, and she yanked the contract from my hands.

"I can easily walk to my *own* suite from yours, Mr. Locke."

"I usually rent the penthouse floor when I'm traveling."

"Why? You're only one person."

"I enjoy my privacy, and if people see you leaving my suite at all hours of the late nights, they're going to assume we're doing much more than debriefing."

"Not happening."

"What about the paparazzi? You see how much they follow me around. You want to deal with the press?"

She thought about it for a minute before she reluctantly resigned. "Fine. But I want my own room and bathroom, and they need to be the furthest away from yours."

Pretending like I wasn't pleased I'd persuaded her to change her mind, I grabbed the highlighter out of her hand and added in her terms.

Reading on…

Publicist must be present during travel, car rides, and flights from one press juncture to the next. She also agrees to be present for all the itineraries she has scheduled for the client.

Do you honestly think I trust you to say the right things? I have to be there just to cover your ass and make sure I can do damage control when you fuck it up.

I smiled—she knew me well.

The next clauses weren't anything of importance, at least not to me. The ones I wanted her to approve, she did.

Closing the contract, I hit the intercom on my phone.

"Yes, Mr. Locke?"

"Erin, come to my office."

Moments later, she walked in, and I handed her the contract.

"Have HR re-draft this immediately and return it to me once it's finalized."

"Yes, Mr. Locke." She nodded and left.

It didn't take long for her to reappear with our new contract, and we both signed.

Except Autumn didn't realize she'd just signed...

Her future with me.

Seven

Autumn

WE WALKED INTO THE BUILDING WHERE *The New York Times* interview was being held.

Julian strode in like he owned the damn place, each stride more commanding than the last. With the confidence he exuded from head to toe, no one would assume this was his first official interview.

The man had a way about him. He never wore his emotions on his sleeve, and I wish I could tell you this was something he'd developed after he'd left me, but it wasn't.

He always had the ability to hold everything in. No one saw what he didn't want them to see, and the only times I ever did were the moments he'd let me in.

When I was a little girl, I thought I had the power to read him through his bright, blue eyes. But as I got older, he realized what I could see in his gaze, and that was when he stopped showing me his emotions. Somewhere along the way he deemed me unworthy to know what he was feeling, and it not only crushed my heart, but it destroyed my soul.

Keeping up with his stride, I matched his calm demeanor, fully aware of what we were about to encounter. I was beyond thankful I'd once dated the columnist who was conducting Julian's interview. I met him in graduate school. At the time, he was just starting at a lucrative magazine.

Now, he was what dreams were made of, being able to make or break anyone's career with the influence he held as the top journalist in the industry.

"You ready?" I questioned, holding onto the door.

"I'm always ready." He walked inside, and to his back, I rolled my eyes.

"Don't roll your eyes at me, kid."

What the hell? How does he keep doing that?

"Cherry!" Charles greeted, bringing my attention over to him.

The last time I'd seen him was a little over a year ago. He'd interviewed one of my other clients.

"Charlie." I smiled, walking into his arms. "How are you?"

"I'm better now that I'm seeing your gorgeous face."

I giggled. "Always such a charmer."

"When are you going to let me take you out to dinner? I owe you a baseball game."

"You do. Maybe next time I'm in town."

My eyes connected with Julian who was standing behind me, staring at us like he recognized we'd once dated.

"This is Julian Locke. Julian, this is Charles Gordan."

"Do I get to call him Charlie too?"

I nervously chuckled. "That's just an old nickname I have for him."

"Cherry?"

"Another old nickname."

"I see."

"Nice to meet you, Julian." Charles extended his hand and Julian shook it.

"It's Mr. Locke, Charlie."

Jesus, we just got here, and he's already being an abrasive asshole.

I intervened, "Why don't you go get everything ready for Mr. Locke, and we'll be right over."

Charles nodded, feeling the sudden tension in the room.

Once he was gone, I turned to Julian. "Can you not be a snarky dick to the journalist who's about to run one of the most important interviews of your career?"

He tugged on the end of my hair. "He better be referring to the color of this, *Cherry.*"

"Oh, don't worry. He totally is. I'm fully lasered. Brazilian to be exact."

Julian groaned, making me smile big and wide.

"Did he fuck you?"

"Uh, hello, none of your business."

"When was the last time he fucked you?"

"Again, none of your damn business. Now get your head in the game, Locke. You need to be nice."

"I'm not nice."

"I'm fully aware, but you need to try."

Charles announced, "I'm ready when you are."

We made our way over to him.

Julian, of course, sat at the head of the table, while I sat behind him, and Charlie was sitting in front of both of us with a recorder and notepad in his hands.

During the interview, I lost count of how many times I had to tell Charlie he couldn't use that.

"Tell me about your childhood, Mr. Locke."

"There's nothing to tell."

I kicked him under the table. "What he's trying to say is he doesn't know where to start."

"Would you like to do the interview for me, kid? Considering you haven't allowed me to answer one question."

"Kid?" Charlie chimed in. "What's that about?"

"It's nothing."

"Oh, so that's nothing?" Julian mocked. Using my own words against me, he added, "What she's trying to say is that Cherry and I go way back."

"Now this just got good. How far back?"

"The interview is about Julian, Charles. Not Julian and me."

"Julian? Are you usually on a first-name basis with your clients, Cherry? I don't think so. Besides, this is what people want to know. Trust me." He peered back at Locke. "You were saying?"

"I used to be her Prince Charming."

"This is not—"

Julian interrupted me, "I can handle it from here, Miss Troy. I'm sure your other clients need tending to."

"Lucky for you, I cleared my entire schedule this week, just for you."

"Now this is getting really good. She never clears her schedule for only one client."

"Charles!"

Locke grinned. "Is that right?"

I was about to explain myself, but my phone rang. "This is Autumn."

Laurel was on the other line, and I had to excuse myself from the table. By the time I was done with our conversation, Julian was walking out of the interview into the lobby where I was talking to my boss with the same confident stride he had going in.

"Should I ask how that went? Or should I assume?"

"You know what they say about people who assume, kid."

"Yeah, yeah, yeah."

I didn't give it too much thought. Charlie and I had an arrangement—nothing was published without my approval first. I'd go over his article once he emailed it to me. For the rest of the day, we went from one thing to the next until it was way past dinnertime, and I was starving. I wanted to try the restaurant at my hotel, well Julian's hotel.

He held the door open for me.

"Today started a little rough—"

"You used to love it rough."

"Oh my God," I exclaimed, stepping into the restaurant. "You cannot say stuff like that to me anymore."

"Try to stop me, sweetheart."

"Damn. I should have added a clause about your inappropriate behavior."

"It wouldn't have done you any good. I wouldn't have signed it."

"On that note…" I stopped at the bar, nodding to the bartender. "I'll take a martini with four stuffed olives, please."

"And you, Mr. Locke?"

"I'll just take a water, Sam."

"A water? What are you twelve? Order a drink."

"I don't drink."

"Since when?"

The stern expression on his face answered my question. "You really need to relax on the control. It's a drink, not heroin." I glanced at the bartender. "Do you have TX Straight Bourbon Whiskey?"

"Yes."

"Great, he'll take one of those, no ice."

The bartender turned, getting our drinks ready.

"What?" I asked, taking in the same stern expression. "You used to love that liquor."

"So we're back to you knowing who I am? How long is it going to last this time?"

"Why do you have to ruin every moment?"

He leaned in close to my face, and my stomach fluttered. The strong smell of his cologne assaulted my senses.

"I used to love a lot of this. Some I still do."

"What do you mean—"

"Oi!" a familiar voice hollered from across the room.

While another familiar voice called out, "There's our girl!"

Julian stared from them to me. "Their girl?"

"Look at you, Autumn Bum Bum." Jude, the bass guitarist from Life of Debauchery, looked me up and down.

It was his silly name for me, meaning my ass was nice.

"She's mine first," Beck, the rhythm guitarist from their band stated, standing in my face.

"Hey there," I greeted, amused.

They were by far my most entertaining clients.

Beck didn't hesitate, instantly picking me up off the ground in a warm, tight embrace.

"Mate, don't bloody hog her."

As soon as Beck put me down, Jude did the same. Except he twirled me around in a circle and then kissed both my cheeks.

"Fancy seeing you here in Miami."

He set me down. "Likewise."

"We're on tour, and I'm fucking knackered."

"You're always fucking knackered."

They went back and forth for a second, and out of the corner of my eye, I could see Julian's intense stare narrowed in on them before he leaned into my ear.

Murmuring, "Is that just an old nickname too?"

"And who's this?" Beck asked, bringing our attention back to him. "Are you fucking our girl?"

"Jude!" I shouted, glancing over at Julian. Knowing he wouldn't appreciate their crude personalities, but what did he expect?

They're rock stars.

"This is my client, Julian Locke." I swallowed hard, silently wishing I knew what he was thinking.

Feeling.

Wanting…

Truth was, the more I was around him, the more I realized how much I still couldn't read him. Before yesterday, the last time I'd seen him I was crying over him. Pouring my heart out and falling apart in his arms. Telling him I loved him.

Now, there he was, with me. And after all this time, all these years, he was still so damn hard to decipher. Giving me mixed signals left and right like he did when I was younger.

Our connection.

Our friendship.

His indifference when we were in public versus private.

It all came barreling down on me, and I wasn't anticipating it to.

Eight

Autumn

I NEVER KNEW WHAT HE WAS THINKING, ESPECIALLY WHEN HE WAS around the guys I dated. He didn't stop denying his attraction to me until I was almost seventeen, and that was only because I'd made him. Thinking about that night made me pissed at him all over again.

The pushing me away, only to lead me on was definitely one of the worst games he'd played with me. Always blaming it on my brother.

Wait… Why am I thinking about this? Why do I care?

"Julian Locke." Jude looked at Beck, pulling me away from my reckless thoughts. "Where have we heard that name?"

"Fuck if I know."

"Oh! I know! Alpha CEO! You invented the eco-friendly sports car, right?"

"The engine."

"Yes! I fucking own three of those cars. Fucking spectacular, Mate! Let me buy you a drink."

"I don't need you to buy me anything."

"Julian…" I rasped under my breath, not used to this side of him.

Was he just being possessive and controlling, or was he jealous?

Jealousy wasn't something I was used to from him either. He was always so fucking confident and cocky when it came to me. It was such a turn-on and as much as I hated to admit it, it still was.

Goddamn it.

"Don't get your knickers in a bunch. We didn't fuck your girl, if that's

"Not that we didn't try," Beck commented.

"Autumn Bum Bum is a fucking peach. She turned our entire lives around. Even partied with us. This girl can drink some fucking whiskey."

"I had to keep up with you."

"Yeah, babe, you did. But our singer has turned into a fucking pussy since he got married, and our drummer is sticking it to his assistant." Jude threw his arm around Beck. "It's just me and this fucking wanker now."

I giggled, missing these guys.

"Her girly squeal is absolutely delicious, isn't it? You sticking it to her? I give it a week before you're balls deep inside of her."

My face turned fifty shades of red—Jude had no filter.

Ever.

Beck joined in. "I want in on that bet."

"Five k on him sinking into her before the week is over."

"A week?" Jude scolded. "Her ass has gotten bigger. I give it two days. Max."

This was a reoccurring thing between them. They were always betting each other on stupid shit.

In less than two strides, Julian tugged me into his side.

My heart pounded so hard, I prayed he couldn't feel it against his abrupt, dominating hold. The simple touch of his arms around me had me weak in the knees and my body stiffening. I wasn't expecting him to do that in front of them.

What is he doing?

"If she'd give me half the chance, I'd make her mine tonight."

My breath hitched. Not only could he feel my hesitation, but he could also read my mind.

I tried to step away from him, but he wouldn't let me. Holding onto me tighter. Thinking quick on my feet, I turned around in his arms and set my hand on his chest, trying to make it look like there wasn't anything going on between us.

There wasn't.

Was there?

The last thing I wanted was for Jude and Beck to start rumors and people thinking we were anything besides professional with each other.

Using the best enthusiasm I could muster in the awkward situation,

I announced, "Boys, get ready to invest in a sure thing. Someone is going to be making a huge announcement next week." I winked at them while Julian tensed, abruptly letting me go, and I instantly felt the loss of his touch.

Autumn, stop.

After I said goodbye to the guys, Julian wasn't happy.

When was he ever happy?

In a stern tone, he ordered everyone at the bar to leave us. Thank God it was only his employees and not his guests.

Why was he pissed? Was it because of how they'd treated me or—

"Why would you share that private information with them?"

I guess that answered my question. Why was I disappointed?

Before I could give it too much thought, he sneered, "I don't like to be kept waiting."

My eyes snapped to his. "Stop treating me like I'm an employee. I don't answer to you."

"Actually, you do."

"Listen, you condescending asshole. I didn't say anything. I hinted. So before you go crazy, I'm fully aware insider trading is illegal, but I'm simply doing my job, and they're going to be the best marketing you can get. Jude and Beck are going to tell people, those people are going to tell other people, and so on and so on. We want people talking, rumors like this are your best friend. By the time you actually announce, thousands of people are going to be chomping at the bit for you. What you should be saying is thank you."

Everything happened so fast. One second we were arguing, the next he roughly gripped onto the back of my neck and tugged me close to his mouth.

My breathing hitched.

"I don't like to be taken by surprise. Everything and anything gets approved by me first, understood?"

I tried to shove him away, but it was no use. He didn't budge.

In a dark, heady tone, he rasped, "Next time you're a bad girl, you'll give me your panties and face the wall with your legs spread, or I could throw you over my lap instead."

"Julian!"

"Yeah, sweetheart, you'll scream my name just like that, except it's going to be from me spanking your ass raw to teach you a lesson you won't soon forget."

I shoved him again. "Fuck you."

The next thing I knew, he spun my body and pinned my chest to the bar where I couldn't move. I huffed out a breath, instantly realizing I was at his mercy, and for a brief second, I thought there was no way he was going to do this. I was a grown-ass woman for fuck's sake.

"What the—"

He didn't hesitate.

SLAP.

Walloping my ass so hard, I instantaneously stood on the tips of my toes in my already six-inch stiletto heels.

"You rat bastard! Don't you fucking dar—"

"Talk back to me one more time, and I'll lift your dress, pull down your panties, and slap your bare ass instead."

My ass burned, and my pussy throbbed. I wanted to raise hell, although I wasn't an idiot. He'd follow through on his threat.

"Now," he bit. "Am I making myself clear?"

Going against all my instincts, I reluctantly agreed, "Yes."

"Great." He let me go, and there was no wavering on my part. I spun around with my hand shooting straight toward his face, but he caught it mid-air.

Holding onto my wrist, he yanked me toward him. "While we're on the topic of you being a very bad girl, I also highly suggest you make damn sure your future encounters with men don't provoke me again. You won't like me when I'm angry."

I jerked my hand away. "I don't like you right now."

"Prove it," he challenged all in one breath. "Spread your legs and show me you're not wet."

I glared at him. "You'd love that, wouldn't you? Tell me, Julian, what are you trying to accomplish here? What do you want from me?"

He stepped toward me, and I stepped back, putting my hand up.

"I thought you wanted to know what I wanted. I was just about to show you."

"I won't sleep with you. If this is about sex, I'm not fucking you."

"Don't worry, sweetheart, I have no problem doing all the fucking."

I pushed him as hard as I could, and he didn't move an inch. He was a cement block, fueling my fury like he was nothing more than the gasoline to my flames.

"So this is about sex? We're long past that. I'm here as your publicist—nothing more, nothing less. You need to get that through your thick, stubborn skull. I'll tell you this, though... I find it hilarious I spent most of my teenage years trying to get you to notice me, and I've gone from the girl you didn't want, to the one you can't have. How's that for irony?"

"I always wanted you, kid."

"You had a shitty way of showing it. But come on, you can't be that hard up for someone to ride your cock, Julian. Just call Katie or whatever bimbo you have on speed dial. You never had a problem parading your hookups around me before, so why stop now?"

"If you're going to bring up the past, then I insist we talk about you and me and forget about the rest."

"How convenient. There is no you and me, and there never was."

"That's bullshit, and you know it. I'm not playing your little games, Autumn."

"You're not playing my little games?" I repeated, offended. "Holy shit! You're the king of playing games!"

"I'm not that man anymore."

"And I'm just supposed to believe you? After everything you did to me?"

"If I could go back, I wouldn't change a damn thing. I made something of myself. I wasn't the man you needed then, but I am now."

"Now? After all this time? Do you actually think I'm just going to jump into your arms like nothing ever happened? You have no idea what I went through after you left! It took me years to mend my broken heart and the damage you did to my brother and parents. My family and I were devastated, not to mention worried sick about you for years! We didn't know where you were or what you were doing. You didn't call, write, or text—fucking nothing! You didn't do anything but disappear on us! After everything they did for you, that's how you repaid them?! You're nothing but a selfish prick with control issues, Mr. Locke, so get off your high horse. You're not getting a damn thing from me!" I sidestepped him to leave. "We're done here!"

He grabbed my arm, making me face him again. "We're not done until I say we are." Looking deep into my eyes, he reminded, "You're my number one girl, remember?"

"How could I forget? It was just another lie you told me."

"No." He shook his head. "You know that's not true. I never lied to you. It's why I pushed you away to begin with. I couldn't lie to you."

"You could bold-face lie to me right now, and I wouldn't be able to tell the difference. You're a businessman. You have people believe what you want them to. It's why you're so successful. Trust me, you spent years practicing on me."

"You want a confession?" he challenged, getting close to my face. His eyes were in a craze. "I'll give you a fucking confession. The only times I ever lied to you was when I told you I fucked someone else."

I didn't just jerk back, I stumbled. "What?"

"You heard me. I didn't fuck anyone at Christian's bachelor party."

"But … Christian… No way. He said you did, and everyone that was there said you went into the bedroom with the stripper."

"I let them believe that."

"Why?"

"Your brother was getting suspicious of us, kid."

He was?

I opened my mouth to reply, but I couldn't get my lips to move.

"You were never just a fuck. I told you that to make you hate me."

"Well, mission accomplished. Why would you want me to hate you?"

"It was the only way I could leave you."

I promised myself I wouldn't go down this road with him. Bringing up the past wouldn't change what he did, what he put me through.

Our memories became nightmares.

My love that became hate.

It. Ruined. Me.

He ruined me.

That fateful day he shattered my heart and then walked away, leaving me to pick up the pieces of what was left in his wake. I desperately tried to focus on all the pain he'd caused, not wanting to care about his lies and truths. Yet there I was hanging on by a thread, anxiously awaiting his next words.

"And the only other time I've ever lied to you…"

I never expected what he admitted next, and it felt as though I was holding my breath.

With the utmost sincere expression on his face, he declared, "Was when I told you I didn't love you."

Nine

WE WALKED INTO THE HAND-IN-HAND WHILE I LOOKED FOR my brother in the stands. Daniel and I had been hanging out for the last few weeks, and we were meeting him there. He was a senior, and I was a junior in high school. I was almost seventeen, and my parents had finally started allowing me to date.

But if it were up to Christian, I'd be a nun. He was more overbearing than our parents, saying guys only wanted one thing. Which didn't make any sense. He'd been with the same girl on and off for the last seven years. They were the perfect couple, and at times I envied what they had.

"I think I see him over there." I pointed to the far left side of the open arena, leading the way.

At least I had a bit more freedom now that Christian was in his senior year of college and wasn't around a lot. He was studying for his MCATs, deciding to be a doctor. Although he hadn't chosen which field yet. He was living in his own place with Julian. They were both almost done with college. Julian was majoring in finance with a minor in business.

He still loved cars, and since he'd turned sixteen, I swear I'd seen him with a new ride each year.

"Baby." Daniel pulled me against his chest while he walked behind me. "Have I told you how great your ass and legs look in that skirt?"

I beamed, listening to him.

We drove here after the football game tonight, and I was still in my cheerleading uniform. I was the only girl to make varsity my freshman year, but my excitement toward Daniel's words was cut shorter than my bloomers when I noticed Julian wasn't alone.

Shocker.

He was always with a girl. I couldn't remember the last time I'd seen him without a chick. Especially in the last four years. The man was never with the same woman. Julian didn't really have a type, he seemed to be an equal opportunist with all the different types of girls he'd bring around.

Julian made up for the fact that Christian only had Kinley, by pretty much sleeping with every hot girl from here to Dallas.

And I hated every single one of them.

Not that my brother couldn't have any woman he wanted, girls flocked to him like bees to honey. Often making his girlfriend jealous. Christian was covered in tattoos, inked sleeves down both arms, along with his chest and back. He was addicted to them.

To say I was head over heels in love with his best friend was an understatement. I think I was born loving him. My crush didn't ever go away, it didn't wear off, and I didn't grow out of it…

If anything, it became stronger.

My feelings for him became something I couldn't control or even begin to understand. I just knew I wanted him.

Then.

Now.

Forever.

I wanted him so bad it made my heart hurt and my chest ache.

Despite seeing him with several women throughout my life, he'd never seen me with a guy before, and I secretly hoped this would be what he needed to get his head out of his ass.

I had absolutely no problem picking up guys, inheriting my mom's big boobs, slender waist, and curvy ass. I began developing at a younger age than most of my friends, and not one time did Julian recognize that.

My brother did.

My parents did.

Most guys in town and at my school did.

Julian, nope. Nothing. Not so much as a, "Hey, you're looking beautiful today."

I was at my wit's end. It wasn't fair that he looked at every single girl other than me. I even saw him checking out some of the girls on my varsity cheerleading squad during practice one day when he unexpectedly picked me up.

I didn't have a car. My parents wanted me to wait until I was seventeen, and I relied on my friends, Daniel, and my good ol' bicycle for transportation. Making me feel like I was still a little girl, when in fact, I wasn't.

I was a young woman, and I was determined to have Julian see me as something more than just his best friend's little sister. How he couldn't see I was madly in love with him only proved to me that men were stupid.

Or if he knew, he never showed it—always seeming unfazed by my presence.

The older he got, the more distant he became. Maybe it was because he was busy with school and other adult things, but the guy who used to take me to his shop didn't anymore.

Out of the blue one day, he started pushing me away. At least it felt like that to me, and I hated it more than anything.

"You'll always be my number one girl."

Those seven words haunted me, hanging over my head like a freaking avalanche. Ready to pile on top of me at a moment's notice.

Why did he say it if he didn't mean it?

Those were the types of questions I constantly asked myself.

Over and over again.

Pushing away those thoughts, I walked up the stairs and smiled at Julian. He smiled back, and my stomach catapulted into somersaults, waiting for him to say something about my uniform.

Please notice me.

"Autumn, what the hell are you wearing?" Christian asked, his tone clipped.

"Oh my God. Leave her alone," Kinley reprimanded him like she often did. "Babe, she'll be seventeen in two weeks. You've met Daniel, so have your parents. Let her be." She winked at me, and I smiled.

She was always on my side, knowing how overprotective my brother was. My gaze shifted toward Julian, praying he'd heard Christian commenting about my outfit.

He didn't.

71

He was too busy sucking face with the blonde he'd brought with him. I rolled my eyes again; he was the king of oblivion.

"Daniel, let's sit over here." I popped a squat near Julian, closest to him—not the girl he was with. Enough to where he could see me and Daniel.

For the next hour, I fawned over Daniel, desperately trying to make Julian jealous, and not once he did bat an eye.

Not one ounce of emotion.

Reaction.

What do I need to do to get his attention?

Nothing ever worked.

Not my cute outfits.

Not my makeup.

Not my bikinis.

Not even the guy I'd brought around him for the first time.

It was as if he was immune to anything related to me and the more I thought about it, the further it pissed me off.

"There's Rob and Dave," Daniel murmured in my ear, bringing my attention back to him. "They have booze. Let's go over there with them."

"My brother... You know what? Fuck it. Let's go." I called out Christian's name. "We're going to hang out with some friends who just got here, okay?"

"No—"

Kinley covered his mouth. "Okay. Have fun."

I mouthed, "Thank you," to her.

"Don't go too far," Christian called out behind us as we walked away.

"Babe! Just leave her alone. She's a big girl."

My eyes wandered toward Julian's direction.

Did you hear what Kinley said? I'm a big girl!

Nope. He was still sucking face with the blonde.

Why even come to the rodeo if you're not going to watch the show?

We made our way to Daniel's friends, and I didn't think twice about it, when he handed me the bottle of Jack, taking it down like a fucking champ. It burned all the way down my chest, warming my body in the process.

I wasn't much of a drinker, but tonight would fix that.

One chug, three chugs, five chugs ... shit, I'd lost count.

Giggling up a storm, I swayed my hips to the music Daniel was playing off his cell phone. Bringing the bottle up to my lips, I drank way more than

I should have. Wanting to numb my thoughts of Julian and his indifference was the only remedy that seemed worthwhile.

I saw Daniel eyeing me over the rim of his bottle, staring at me with nothing but mischief in his eyes.

I wanted to forget.

And he was the perfect guy I could do that with. He was trouble in the best possible way.

My lips tingled, my face was on fire, and my body was numb.

Good.

It was the first time in forever I'd felt so carefree, throwing my head back and laughing, enjoying the way he made me feel. We exchanged flirty banter, dancing close together to the music. My head was spinning with thoughts of Julian, and I stumbled a little, catching myself in Daniel's arms.

He caressed the side of my cheek, rubbing his thumb over my lips in a back and forth motion. "You're beautiful, Autumn."

Why can't Julian think I'm beautiful?

I pushed off of him, dancing all around while he leaned against a tree.

Were we in the woods? I guess we went for a walk.

Seductively, I worked my hands up the sides of my body, bringing my skirt up with it. Peeking over at him, I moved my hips to the beat of the music, provocatively looking into his eyes as the song continued to blare into the night. I spun around with my back now facing him, closing my eyes. Wanting to get lost in the moment, I lifted my hair off the nook of my neck.

I was sweating.

It was scorching outside.

Texas heat was no joke, and tonight was proving to be one of the hottest nights of the summer.

Slowly, I continued to move my hips in a slow, steady rhythm until I felt a strong arm grab around my waist, tugging me back against his hard chest.

It was super aggressive.

"Daniel?" I was about to spin around when I heard the voice of the man I least expected.

Angrily spewing, "You wanted my attention. Now what are you going to do with it, kid?"

Ten

MY WIDE EYES SNAPPED OPEN, AND I SWEAR MY HEART STOPPED beating.

Was I hallucinating? Was this actually happening? How drunk am I?

Question after question tore through my mind. I couldn't move, I was frozen to the spot. I was standing with Julian's steady arm wrapped around my stomach, holding me firm against his torso. My body aligned perfectly with his like it was made for only him.

I opened my mouth to say something, anything, but Daniel beat me to it.

"Who the fuck are you?" he roared, stepping toward us.

I was shocked when Julian snarled, "I'm the reason she's dressed in that uniform, grinding her ass against your cock. I'm the reason she's drinking and acting out right now. I'm the fucking reason she's even with you. You should be thanking me, you little shit. She's only with you to get my attention."

My mouth dropped open, realizing he knew all along how I felt about him.

Julian didn't stop there, possessively adding, "I'm the man she's trying to make jealous, that's who the fuck I am. You're lucky it was me who found her out here with you drinking, dancing like a slut, and not her brother, or you wouldn't be standing. Now tuck your dick in between your legs and walk the fuck away, or else you're going to have a problem *with me*."

I couldn't form words. The only thing I could do was feel intense ange-

"Daniel, leave."

"You sure?"

"You heard her, run along before I change my mind and show you what happens to little shits like you who try to take advantage of drunk, naive girls who have no fucking business being alone in the woods with you."

"Julian—"

"Don't fucking try me, Autumn. Not. Right. Now. Not with how I'm feeling."

I felt each word beating into my back. He still hadn't let go of me.

"Listen, I don't want any trouble."

"Then go!" I shouted to Daniel.

Finally, he nodded and left.

Julian didn't waste any time, spinning me around to face him. "What the hell do you think you're doing alone out here with that boy? What did you think was going to happen if I didn't show up when I did?"

"We were just hanging out."

"Kid, he was seconds away from lifting your skirt, pulling down your panties, and finger fucking you against the tree. Is that what you want for yourself? A meaningless fuck in the woods? You're better than that."

"You don't even know me anymore."

"Bullshit. I know you're not the girl you mess around with in the woods."

"You would know since you fuck anything that walks."

He jerked back, stunned.

"Well, actually, you fuck anything that walks other than me. Me, you push away. Me, you forget. Me, you don't even acknowledge. Newsflash, I'm not a little girl anymore."

"Really? Then stop acting like one."

"That's your reply?! Are you for real?!"

"What do you want me to say, Autumn? I'm your brother's best friend, and I'm saving your ass. If Christian had seen what I just did, if he knew you had been drinking, trust me, your ass would never be allowed to leave your house again." He eyed me up and down with only craze in his gaze. "And trust me, sweetheart, I'm tempted to tell him, if this is how you're going to be acting. Because of me, nonetheless."

Each word that erupted from his mouth was another knife in my chest.

"And what about you?"

"What about me?"

"You heard me. What did you feel when you saw me? You still want my boyfriend standing?"

"Kid…"

"What? I want an answer! What did you feel? Do you ever feel anything when you're with me? Do you ever think about me? Dream about me?" I knew I sounded like a child, but I couldn't help it. Those questions constantly plagued me. I needed to know his feelings.

Right now.

"I'm not having this conversation with you."

"Why? Because maybe, just maybe, you feel the same things I feel for you?"

"Quit fucking baiting me."

"No!" The liquor coursing through my veins made it easier to ask him all the questions I wanted to know. "Tell me!"

"Autumn, stop! Don't do this to yourself."

"But you said I would always be your number one girl."

"You are. But I can't tell you what you want to hear. I'll never be able to tell you what you need to hear."

"Why? I don't understand! Why do you look at every girl other than me? Why can't you see me? Why can't you look at me? Please, I just want you to look at me! Really fucking look at me! I'm standing right here! Telling you I'm in lov—"

"Don't you fucking dare." He put his finger out in front of him, silencing me. "What do you want me to say, Autumn? You want me to tell you that I wanted to rip him apart the second I saw him pull you into his arms as you made your way over to your brother? You want me to tell you that every time you wear that little uniform, I think about all the ways I could take you in it? Is that what you want to hear? What else do you want me to tell you?"

His expression turned heady, matching my own. Our stares tethered, and for a moment, I saw a certain vulnerability and uncertainty pass through him I could feel deep within my bones. However, just as quickly as it appeared, it was gone. His primal gaze disappeared, shutting off our connection and truths we briefly shared for just a few moments in time.

There he was, balancing on the thin line which had suddenly become us. *Me.*

With a hard edge in his voice, he asked, "What do you think would happen if your brother knew what I just said to you?'

"I don't care."

"Well, I do. Your family has done more for me than anyone in all my life. I won't fuck that up. Not even … for you."

I jerked back, feeling the weight of his statement.

"I'm sorry, kid. I never wanted to hurt you. It's easier like this. Me staying away from you."

"Easier for who?"

"I'm not that guy. I won't fight for you. I won't choose you over them. I can't. Please try to understand and stop trying to force my hand."

I didn't know which was worse—thinking he didn't care about me or knowing he did but wouldn't do anything about it.

"Do you think it's been easy for me to push you away? Do you think it's been easy on me to see you go from a little girl who used to follow me around and look at me like I was the answer to her little fairy tale? Do you think it's been easy on me to know that I'm not? You're not mine, Autumn, and you never will be. Stop trying to make me claim you because I won't."

I didn't want to cry. I wouldn't be able to stop.

It would consume me.

And it did.

I blinked, and tears fell down the sides of my face. I had never felt worse. Only adding to my tears and the hurt of his replies I so wanted to forget.

I wouldn't.

I couldn't.

Getting your heart broken for the first time was like having the wind knocked out of you by the force of a level five hurricane.

I wanted to die.

I felt like I was.

With the back of his fingers, he wiped away my tears. His flesh burned my skin, making me feel like maybe this was hell. The one I'd created for myself.

He held his head up higher, maintaining his strong composure. Every devastated bone in my body wanted to beg him to give me a chance.

To give us a chance.

Knowing it was no use. His loyalty didn't stand with me—it stood with my family, and that was the hardest pill to swallow.

Wasn't I his family too?

"You need to forget about me."

"You say that like it's so easy."

"It should be."

"But all I've ever wanted is you."

"You don't even know what that means, kid."

"That's not fair."

"Life's not fair."

Neither one of us said anything for I don't know how long until he tugged on the end of my hair.

"Let's go get you some food, and then I'll take you home."

"Where's Christian?"

"He left with Kinley. I told him I'd find you and make sure you got home safely."

"Did you know what I was doing?"

"Something like that."

"So now what? We go back to pretending you don't notice me?"

He didn't say anything, but he didn't have to. The expression on his face spoke for itself. It spoke volumes.

"Awesome. Thanks for nothing."

I turned and left him there, ready to go break down in the bathroom at the arena of the rodeo. I didn't realize we'd walked so far out to the woods. My heart hurt so profoundly I was surprised I was still breathing.

Head bowed.

My world tumbling around me.

Tears continued to cascade down my cheeks, and I bet I looked like a mess. Dark black mascara leaving lines on my face.

When it felt as if I couldn't walk any longer, my legs giving out on me, I heard Julian loudly exclaim, "For fuck's sake!"

I stopped and turned around at the same time he gripped onto the nook of my neck and slammed his mouth against mine.

He. Kissed. Me.

Julian kissed me.

I was shocked, confused, and overwhelmed. My eyes shut tightly, my breathing hitched, and my arms fell to my sides in defeat. All the sadness in me was gone. Feeling what I had wanted for so damn long. His lips were rough but smooth against mine. My heart drummed so fast, I swear he could hear it. My knees went weak the longer his lips stayed on mine. It was the most overpowering, mind-blowing, consuming emotion I'd ever felt in my entire life.

There would be no coming back from this. Ruining me for every other boy who might come along.

Reading my mind, he slowly parted his lips and pull me closer. Molding us into one person. I melted against him as I parted my lips, following his lead. Matching the same rhythm he'd set for me.

The second his tongue touched mine, I thought I was going to die. Right then and there, in his arms, with our mouths fused. I pulled back my tongue, and he took it as an open invitation to slide his into my awaiting mouth. Our tongues whirled in their own game of push and pull, turning this kiss into something more than I'd ever expected.

I wasn't the only one losing my mind—Julian was getting lost in me too.

No words could come close to describing what was happening at that moment between us. The feelings he stirred deep within my heart matched my emotions with each stroke of his tongue. Feelings I didn't think were possible to experience. Emotions I didn't even think existed.

I never wanted him to stop kissing me.

When a soft moan escaped my mouth, he pecked my lips one last time before gradually pulling away from me. Leaving me breathless and wanting more.

Wanting him.

Incoherent thoughts ran rapidly in my mind while my eyes fluttered open. Leaning his forehead against mine, he gazed profoundly into my eyes.

"This was your first kiss, wasn't it?"

I swallowed hard.

Eyes wide.

Heart open.

Love pouring out of me.

"Yes."

"*Fuck me.*" I could hear the regret in his tone.

"Please … please don't ruin this for me. Not now. Not after that."

"Let's go," he growled, stepping away from me. "I need to get you home. Now!"

He was mad.

Pissed.

Fuming.

Except for this time, I didn't care…

He loved me.

And with that first kiss, he declared war.

Eleven

I WOKE UP TO MY CELL PHONE RINGING BRIGHT AND EARLY AFTER tossing and turning most of the night. I ended up leaving Julian at the bar with his confessions unsure of how to proceed with it. My mind was spinning, and it didn't stop for the rest of the evening.

For the first time in I don't know how long, I dreamt about the first time he kissed me. The dream played endlessly throughout the night, annoying the hell out of me.

I didn't open my eyes to see who was calling, groaning, "Hello," into the phone.

"Autumn! How could you not tell me you leaked your own story?" Laurel questioned, and I yawned.

"What are you talking about? What story?"

"You didn't tell me you had plans to do this. I mean, don't get me wrong, I think it's brilliant, but why didn't you tell me?"

"Laurel, you're speaking in circles. I don't understand what you're talking about. What story?"

"Your history with Julian. The world loves a second chance romance—they're going to eat this shit right up."

I shot up, sitting in bed. "Second chance romance, what the hell are you talking about?"

She knew Julian's and my history. Of course, I told her. It was why she knew I could handle him, topping it off with the promotion to make part-

"Autumn, it's all over the internet. Charles' interview set the stage on fire."

"Charles' interview?" My heart dropped. "Oh my god." Quickly, I grabbed my laptop off the nightstand, hitting the Safari button.

In less than a second, my whole world and life as I knew it was the headline of every news media outlet. Reading…

High Society Publicist, Autumn Troy, has not only taken Alpha CEO, Julian Locke, on as a client, but she has also claimed his cold, brutal heart. The two go way back—he was her first love. She was his. Can we say second chance romance?

All the blood drained from my face.

"That motherfucker! No, he did not tell Charles we have history! I'm going to fucking murder him! Do you hear me, Laurel? I'm going to jail because I'm going to fucking kill him!"

"Autumn, calm down. Is this not true? Have you guys not rekindled?"

"No! We haven't rekindled shit. The only thing I feel like rekindling is my knee in his balls."

"Oh, honey, this can work to our advantage, though. You need to calm down."

"Laurel, I can't—"

Beep.

I looked at my screen, Mom calling.

Deny.

Dad calling.

Deny.

Christian calling.

"Fuck!"

Definitely deny.

"I gotta go." I hung up, searching Yahoo News and getting smacked in the face with a picture of Julian and me kissing on his bed. It was one of the last pictures he took of us.

"Oh. My. God. He even leaked a personal fucking photo!" Grabbing my phone again, I called Charles.

"Hey, Cherry. You're welcome."

"How could you do this to me? How could you publish an article without my approval? We had an agreement!"

"What are you talking about? I just made your client the most adored man in the world. Did you read the article? Did you see how he spoke about you and your relationship?"

"No! I didn't read the article! I didn't get past the fucking title, Charles! You blindsided me! And we're not in a relationship—other than I'm his publicist, and he's my client!"

"Umm… That's not what he said."

"He was lying! How you, of all people, couldn't tell he was full of shit is beyond me."

"So you guys don't have a history? He wasn't your first love?"

"It's not as black and white as you're laying it out to be."

"Did you or did you not have a relationship?"

I wasn't expecting his interrogation, feeling like I was suddenly on the stand at my own trial.

"If you could call it that."

"So he wasn't your first kiss? Your first sexual experience?"

My eyes bulged out of my head. "He told you that?!"

"I think you need to read the article."

"I think you need to pray that I don't find you and kick your ass!"

"Cherry—"

"Don't you Cherry me! I'm so pissed at you I can barely see straight!"

"I didn't mean to upset you, but he said you guys were back together."

I rubbed my face. "I can't believe you printed a bullshit article. If you would have sent it to me, I would have—"

"He said he wanted to surprise you."

"Oh." I paused, nodding. "He surprised me alright."

"The good news is you're trending across all social media platforms."

"I'm done talking to you now."

"Aut—"

I hung up on him, throwing the sheets off my body. I jumped in the shower and then got dressed, before I ran out of the hotel to meet Julian at his photoshoot with Vanity Fair, but the maid stopped me in the hall.

"Miss Troy."

"Yes."

"I'm so sorry to bother you."

"I'm kind of in a hurry. Could we talk later?"

"This will only take a second. Mr. Locke insisted that I check your bed sheets yesterday morning. He said something about them being wet, and I told him they weren't. They were perfectly dry. Was there a problem I need to know about?"

I scowled, the fury coursing through my veins making my face hot. The son of a bitch had the balls to confirm if I did or didn't have sex.

The nerve of that man!

I bit my tongue. "There's no problem. Thank you." I rushed into the elevator, fuming on my way down.

My blood was boiling, and it didn't simmer down the entire drive to the shoot. I walked into the building ready to spit fire, finding Julian in his dressing room.

Looking up from his phone, he smiled. "Good morning, Miss Troy."

"Good morning my ass!" I slammed the door shut behind me.

"Is there a problem?"

"You bet your ass there's a problem!"

"You need to watch your damn tone when you speak to me. You don't have to yell. I'm sitting right here."

"Julian, you're lucky the only thing I'm doing is yelling at you and not punching you in the face!"

"Oh, so now I'm suddenly Julian again?"

"I'm going to fucking murder you." I threw the article at him. "What the fuck is that?"

"It's *The New York Times* interview I did *for you*," he emphasized the last two words with a conniving grin. "You said you wanted me to be honest with the public. Share my past, my history, show them the man I used to be."

"That is not what I meant, and you know it! You sharing your past has nothing to do with me."

"But you're such a big part of it."

Ignoring his statement, I argued, "We're not a couple, Mr. Locke. Why on earth would you lie about us?"

"Do I need a reason?" He nonchalantly placed his cell phone inside his suit jacket before leaning forward, setting his elbows on his knees. "I thought you wanted people talking? Rumors are the best publicity. Your words, kid."

I glared at him. "Rumors for your announcement, not rumors for our relationship!"

"You didn't specify, Miss Troy. But since you need a reason, how about this one? After your encounters with men yesterday, I decided to take matters into my own hands to prevent any future indiscretions playing out in front of me."

My mouth dropped open. "You lied to the world because you were jealous? What kind of fucked up excuse is that?"

"The only one I have."

"You can't do this!"

"I already did."

"Fine. I'll just deny your allegations."

"Making me look like a liar when I need people to trust me isn't going to sit well with your promotion."

He was right, and I wanted to claw his eyes out. "So what's your plan now, huh? We pretend like we're in love?"

"I'm not pretending."

My stomach dropped, and my heart skipped a beat. Stupid fucking heart. *Did he just tell me he loved me?*

Shaking away the thought, I responded, "I don't love you. In fact, right now it's the complete opposite."

He fell back against the couch, placing one arm over the back. How I could be furious with him, but still find him incredibly sexy and attractive only further incited my rage.

It wasn't until he simply stated, "Well then, fuck me like you hate me, Miss Troy."

That I truly lost my patience with him.

Julian

She grabbed the first thing in her sight and chucked it in my direction. "I wish I'd never met you!"

The vase crashed against the wall, shattering on the floor beside me.

"If you're going to throw shit at me," I snapped, further wanting to piss her off, "then I insist you start with your pussy."

She gasped, and in three strides I was in her face, backing her into the wall. "Are you mad, Autumn? Angry? Seething from the inside out?"

"Yes! Yes! And Yes!"

"Welcome to my fucking life every time I had to push you away."

"Get out of my face!" She shoved me, but I didn't move an inch.

"Be careful what you wish for. For years you wanted my attention—well, now you have it. You're my sole focus, sweetheart. Is it everything you ever wanted?"

"You're ten years too late."

"I gave you my attention back then in my own way."

"Yeah, which usually involved your dick inside of me."

I growled, "Don't degrade what we have."

"What we *had*."

"What we have going on right now is fucking foreplay."

"I didn't know foreplay involved my knee to your balls." She lifted her knee, but I blocked her advance.

"I'm not into that. How about we begin with your mouth instead?"

"Only if you intend on me biting it off."

"The only thing you'll be biting is your lip when I make you come." I narrowed my eyes at her, arching an eyebrow and trying to keep my temper at bay.

"I didn't know you were going to lie to the world."

"That's pretty damn clear."

"You're being unreasonable."

"Which part of me is unreasonable, Autumn? What's unreasonable about me saying something that I should have been saying a long time ago? What's unreasonable about me claiming what has been, and always will be, mine?"

"You can't do this to me. Ten years, Julian! Ten! I waited for you to come back and apologize. What do you want from me? I can't forget about what you did to me. I can't just let it go like you expect me to. It's so fucking easy for you. I didn't leave you. I didn't fuck you over. I did nothing but love you. I'm trying to remain calm and be professional with you, but you're making it really damn hard to not hate you."

"I can't apologize any more than I already have."

"You haven't apologized at all."

I stepped back. "I see you didn't read the article."

"You apologized to me in an article?" She pushed me again. "What the hell kind of apology is that?"

"Autumn, I know I fucked up, and I have to live with the repercussions, but I lost you too. You weren't the only one grieving the loss of our love. I lost everything that ever mattered to me. Including the only family I've ever known. Do you not realize that?"

Bing.

Her cell phone dinged with a text message.

"Oh, don't mind that. It's more than likely another text from my brother. You wanted the whole world to know about our history, and not for one fucking second did you think about the consequences. You're so selfish you didn't think about my brother or my parents and what they would think and say about your interview. We spent years denying and hiding our relationship, or whatever the fuck you want to call it, and you just openly confess it to the entire world without even running it by me first. Now, once again, I have to deal with the fallout. How the hell am I supposed to explain to them when I barely understand it myself?"

"Do you honestly think I'm that much of a heartless bastard? You don't think it killed me to leave you? To leave all of you? Kid, I lost my best friend because of us—the only family I ever knew, ever had."

"As a matter a fact, I do!"

"I've never stopped being yours!"

"You were never mine!"

I needed to catch my bearings and compose my thoughts, having to step away from the situation before it escalated to the point of no return. I couldn't control my temper when it came to her, and it was why she loved to provoke me in the first place. I didn't know what else I could do to make this right.

I was out of answers.

Out of options.

I couldn't fucking think straight when she was glaring at me with so much hatred. I despised not being in control, so I did the only thing I could in this situation.

I unbuckled my belt.

Preparing for more of her bullshit.

Twelve

"WHAT ARE YOU DOING?" I questioned, caught off guard.

He unbuttoned his pants. "I'm getting ready for you."

"Excuse me?" I jerked back. "Have you lost your mind? Do you actually think I'm going to have sex with you right now?"

There was a knock on the door.

"Come in," he called out.

"Mr. Locke," Erin greeted, walking in with a garment bag in her arms. "Here is the suit you requested."

He nodded, unbuttoning his shirt.

I was grateful she'd interrupted us when she did, giving me a chance to calm down and see some sort of reason. What I didn't expect was Julian's tense body catching my attention. From his chiseled physique to every sleek muscle on his chest, arms, and back. His abs contracted, highlighting his six-pack and the V right above his happy trail.

The man was almost thirty-five-years-old and looked better than he did when he was twenty-four. His back muscles flexed as he removed the dress shirt he was wearing to the black one Erin was taking out of the garment bag.

In the matter of a few seconds, I went from wanting to rip him to shreds, to watching him undress like he was my very own private peep show.

Erin just stood there, unmoving, and I couldn't help but feel bothered that she didn't leave the room. Simply waiting for him to take off his suit to hand him the one he was going to wear.

When he started taking off his slacks, my body moved in autopilot, snatching the garment bag from her hands.

"I got it from here, Erin. You can go."

She nodded and left, and as soon as I turned around, Julian was grinning at me like a fucking fool. I never wanted to slap the smirk off his face more than I did at that moment.

"I don't like green on women, but jealousy suits you, kid."

"I'm not jealous."

"No?"

"Not at all."

"Care to elaborate on what that was then?"

"It's unprofessional for you to change in front of her."

"But not unprofessional for me to change in front of you?"

"No. I've already seen you naked." My reply didn't make any sense, but it was the only one I had.

"So has Erin."

My jaw clenched, and he chuckled noticing it.

"Professionally, of course." With that, he grabbed the garment bag out of my hand, beginning to undress again.

Since he was busy, I regarded him with fascination, trying to pretend like I wasn't. Mentally chastising myself that I was falling for his antics. It wasn't until he dropped his pants that my gaze flew to where I had no business looking.

Jesus.

It looked better than I remembered. His briefs perfectly hugged the curves of his cock, and my mind reminisced on what it felt like in my mouth and inside of me. My legs swayed, trembling a little. Thinking about all the times he'd stroked it in front of me while he was going down on me.

Wetness pooled in between my legs.

"Sweetheart, why don't you just bend over since you're staring right at him?"

I. Stopped. Breathing.

My lust-filled gaze shot to his amused expression, immediately washing away all the desire I was feeling for him. However, his dick decided to make an appearance, jutting up and standing at attention. Once again inciting the lust to course through my core at a speed I could no longer control or deny.

"What did you think was going to happen when you're staring at my cock like you want to be fucked?"

I ripped the garment bag from his grasp and presented my back to him. I ignored his question and perfect dick as I walked to the corner of the room where there was a rack of clothing, and discarded his suit on the couch.

"I need to get dressed if I'm going to make your photoshoot. They're waiting on me, and I don't make a habit of being late to anything I commit to."

"Oh. You commit to things? I wasn't aware that you were capable of committing. Anyway..." I continued as if he hadn't said a word. "Your photoshoot isn't in a suit, Mr. Locke. You've been on hundreds of magazine covers wearing a suit. My stylist personally coordinated your outfits. I'm just getting it for you."

After I faced him, he took one look at the Levi's jeans, white t-shirt, black cowboy hat, and boots in my hands and argued, "I'm not wearing that."

"Yes, you are." Making my way back to him, I set his clothes on the couch, ordering, "Now get dressed."

"Autumn, I won't repeat myself."

"Great." I nodded. "Because I don't want to hear your mouth anymore."

There was another knock at the door. "Mr. Locke, are you ready?" a voice asked through the door.

I answered, "He'll be out in five minutes."

We were having a power struggle of who would win.

Me or him?

I should have known better...

He always won everything.

Especially when it concerned me.

Julian

Further drilling her point, she added, "This is what I meant by the world seeing the real you. This is what you used to wear, so this is what you'll wear today." She smiled, playing coy. "Okay?"

I took a deep breath, silently counting to three. "What did I tell you last night, kid? I don't like to be taken by surprise, so the real question is, do I punish you now or later?"

She grabbed another vase, aiming it at me, and I cocked my head to the side, daring her to do it. She thought about it for a second before biting her lip and setting the vase back on the table.

"Good girl."

"Touch me, and I'll scream."

"You already did that." Using the situation to my advantage, I bartered, "If I wear that outfit for you, then you have to be in some of the photos with me."

"Fuck. No."

I walked toward my garment bag.

"Ugh!" She stomped her heel. "Why are you always this much of an asshole? Why can't you just do what you're told? You're worse than a child."

I stared at her, waiting.

"Fine. Alright? I'll take some stupid pictures."

"Great." I got dressed while she called her stylist, telling her she needed a few pieces for the shoot.

I couldn't believe I was doing this for her. I hadn't dressed like this since I'd left Texas. I didn't even own a pair of jeans, let alone a fucking t-shirt. Once I was ready, I stared at the man in the full-length mirror, not recognizing who was staring back at me. It was as if there was a stranger in my reflection, one I hadn't seen in over a decade.

The knock on the door yanked my mind back to the present, and for the next two hours, I shot photo after photo after photo.

Saving the best for last.

Gesturing toward Autumn, I ordered, "Come here."

She'd changed into a soft yellow floor-length dress, reminding me of all the times she'd dressed like that for me. The annoyed expression on her face didn't bother me in the least as I pulled her in between my legs since I was sitting on a stool. Her hair was in a low bun with a clip, and I reached up and freed her long red locks. Grateful she still wore it long, it was one of my favorite features about her appearance.

"I always loved your hair down."

When my thumb began wiping the makeup off her cheek, she jerked back. "What are you doing?"

"Your freckles, I want to see them. Do you remember how much I used to love them?"

"Julian—"

"If you want the world to see me as who I used to be, then I get to show them what my favorite trait about you is."

She narrowed her eyes, taking in what I disclosed. I could see the hesitation in her gaze, knowing I was the reason it was there to begin with. She used to look at me with nothing but love, but now it was somewhere between hate and lust.

"This was always my favorite color on you. Remember all the times you wore yellow for me?"

"No."

If it were even possible, she was more stubborn than she used to be. I didn't expect her to welcome me with open arms, I had my work cut out for me, and I was alright with that. If she thought she could get rid of me that easily, then she was in for one hell of a rude awakening.

I wasn't going anywhere but back into her life where I belonged. At least we were headed in the right direction. The photographer snapped away, and Autumn was so entranced by the way I was looking at her, she didn't notice. She was lost in my truths which were on full display for her.

When she was a child, she could always see right through me. As she got older, I had to hide myself from her, or she would have known how I felt before I was ready to tell her.

The truth was, I was never ready to tell her.

The longer I hid my emotions, the harder it was to push her away. I hated seeing her cry, it was one of the hardest things I had to endure, and I'd been through a lot of bullshit in my life. Her tears were my undoing— they were always my defeat.

With my thumb, I rubbed her lips in a back and forth motion, and her breathing hitched.

I wanted to kiss her.

Claim her.

Though not like this, in a fucking photoshoot of all places. I had to wait—it wasn't the right time.

Would there ever be one?

"You've always been such a beautiful girl, Autumn, but now as a woman, you're truly stunning."

She swallowed hard, hearing the sincerity in my tone. She was captivated by my honest expression and the feel of my hands on her.

"What are you doing to me, Julian?"

"I'm loving you, kid."

My statement broke the spell I had her in, and she shook her head.
Glancing back at the photographer who was still snapping photos, she said,
"You can't use any of those pictures."

"Autumn," I coaxed in a stern voice when all of a sudden, a woman appeared out of nowhere, walking into the shoot.

"Julian, I saw your name on today's itinerary. Of course, I had to come
say hello."

Our attention drifted to the woman in question, realizing all too quickly,
who she was.

And when I used her...

To push Autumn away.

Thirteen

THIS WAS THE FIRST TIME I WAS GOING TO SEE JULIAN SINCE HE'D kissed me two weeks ago. I still felt his mouth on my lips, and sometimes I'd catch myself touching them to feel him all over again. I couldn't wait to see him. I was wearing a yellow maxi dress, anxiously waiting for his arrival.

It was my seventeenth birthday, and my parents were throwing me a huge party. I knew he'd be here. He wouldn't miss it.

"Honey, you look amazing," Mom announced, coming into my bedroom. "Where did my little girl go?"

I smiled. I did look older, and I felt older too.

Would Julian notice?

"Your brother was looking for you."

"What did he want?"

"He said something about Julian's date."

It was as if a pile of bricks fell right on my head. "Julian's date?"

"I know." She chuckled. "Maybe he will actually settle down with this one for a little while. Who knows. I stopped trying to keep track of all his dates when he turned sixteen, but I swear he's been a heartbreaker since he was a little boy."

I wanted to cry.

"Are you okay?"

Our eyes connected. "Yeah."

"Nothing." I turned around, trying to hide my pain.

"Was it something I said? Are you upset with your brother? Is it Julian?"

"It's nothing, Mom."

"Sweetie, it doesn't look like nothing to me. Talk to me. What's going on?"

"I just think Julian hasn't met the right girl yet. That's all. I think you need to give him more credit than his bedhopping ways."

"Autumn," Christian announced, and our stares snapped in his direction. He was leaning against the doorframe of my bedroom. He looked so handsome, wearing a gray button-down and black slacks.

"You clean up nice," I remarked, smiling.

"Don't try to change the subject. Do you really think Julian is ever going to settle down?"

I shrugged. "Maybe."

"Oh, come on!" He laughed. "You can't be serious! Julian Locke? My best friend? The biggest womanizer from here to Dallas? He's going to die an eternal bachelor. Trust me. I live with him, and he brings home different women all the time. Just last weekend, he brought home two."

Last weekend?

I wanted to ask Christian so many things. The pain of hearing Julian had been with not one, but two women since he'd kissed me was an agony I wasn't expecting. And now, he was bringing a date to my birthday party.

My heart clenched, making it almost hard to breathe as I tried not to fall apart in front of my mother and brother.

"Christian!" Mom exclaimed. "I don't want to know that. I just hope he's being safe. With all the diseases and pregnancy, you need to make sure he's wrapping it up."

"Mom, he's been wrapping it up since Dad gave him condoms when he was thirteen after he found a girl in Julian's room."

"A girl here?" I asked, taken back.

"Yeah." He nodded, chuckling. "Just ask Mom how many times they found a girl in his room."

"Too many to count and remember."

It was blow after blow, and I didn't have a clue as to how I was still standing.

"Autumn, why do you look so upset?"

"It's nothing, Christian."

"It's not nothing. Do you have a crush on him or something?"

I knew he wouldn't let this go—his overprotectiveness wouldn't allow it.

"Of course not." *I wish it was only a crush.* "I'm just shocked you're talking about him like this. He's your best friend."

"I'm not saying anything to you I haven't already said to him. Julian is well aware of what I think about him and women. He treats them like shit. You're too good for him, Autumn. Besides, he'd never do that to me. He knows that you're off-limits."

"Now you're telling guys I'm off-limits?"

"No, just him."

Those three littles words made my head spin.

Is that why he abruptly stopped hanging out with me?

"Oh, honey." Mom smiled. "Julian is like another son to us, and she's like his little sister. He would never…" She giggled, eyeing Christian. "You're being ridiculous. Protect your sister from everything, but you don't need to worry yourself over Julian and Autumn. She's family to him."

I couldn't listen to this anymore. "Guests are starting to arrive, Mom."

She stood, kissed my cheek and left, but to my disappointment, my brother didn't follow.

Hoping he'd catch a clue, I remarked, "I need to finish getting ready."

"I'm being serious, Autumn. If you do have a crush on Julian, you need to forget about him. When it comes to women, he couldn't care less about them. The last thing I want is for you to be another notch on his belt. I'll tell you right now, if he broke your heart, I'd fucking kill him."

"Christian!"

"What? Why does that surprise you? It's my job to protect you."

"I know, but you don't have to be so scary about it."

Pushing off the doorframe, he warned, "Don't give me a reason to."

I should have stopped him.

I should have told him.

It could have changed our future, but I didn't. Instead, I watched him leave. My pain overruling our reality. In fact, it won in the end. I did the only thing that made sense to me in a moment purely driven by my chaotic emotions.

I went to look for Julian, finding him downstairs by the bar. A date by his side. I couldn't believe he had the balls to bring someone with him. Of course, she was gorgeous.

Long blonde hair.

Legs for days.

A rack the size of my head.

She was dressed in a tight skirt and bodysuit, emphasizing her perfect figure. I'd never felt more like a child than I did when he reached around her waist and kissed her. The truth of who he was staring me right in the face. With his lips still on her mouth, he locked eyes with me for a minute as though he felt my presence from across the crowded room.

Maybe he felt my pain.

I didn't look at her at all, not for one second. However, I was the first to break our connection. If I didn't, I would have blown up on him in front of everyone.

Our family.

My parents.

Christian.

The party went off without a hitch. Well into the night, there were still hundreds of people dancing, drinking, socializing. I tried to have fun, but my eyes kept wandering toward Julian and his date.

He was caressing her face.

Whispering things in her ear.

Kissing her lips.

Holding her close to him.

He was trying to prove a point, and I couldn't fathom the reason for his actions, so I left. I went out into the woods behind our house, needing air, needing space, needing to break the fuck down.

"What an asshole!" I shouted into the forest, kicking a rock, except it wasn't a rock. It was a stone rooted into the ground. "Ow!" My foot instantly started aching, and I fell to the dirt. "Great, now my dress is ruined too." I took off my heel—the nail of my big toe had sliced in half, and blood was oozing off my skin.

"Shit, kid."

His voice caught in the wind, and my furious glare met his concerned expression. "Get away from me."

He stopped dead in his tracks.

"Go back inside to whatever girl you're sleeping with tonight."

"Do you think if she mattered to me, I'd be out here for you?"

Unable to resist, I sassed, "Two girls at once last week, huh? Must have been quite a night for you."

He gripped onto the back of his neck, bowing his head.

"I can't believe you brought a date to my birthday party after you stole my first kiss! Well, guess what? I want it back!"

"If I could, I would."

Talk about a dagger to my heart.

"I had no business stealing that from you."

His expression quickly turned desolate, and I lashed out, "I thought you said I was your number one girl? If you treat me like this, I can't imagine how you treat all the other women you sleep with."

With a neutral expression, he informed, "I don't cuddle. They never spend the night. I fuck them, Autumn. It's that plain and simple."

I grabbed a rock and chucked it at his head, but he ducked. "You shameless bastard!"

"Keep your voice down."

"Why? No one can hear me! Is the truth too hard for you to hear, Julian?"

He disregarded my outburst, crouching in front of me. "Let me help you. You're bleeding."

I pushed him, and since he wasn't expecting it, he fell back onto the grass. Powerless to control my anger, I lunged at him. "You fucking asshole!" Hitting his chest with all the strength I could muster, I yelled out my frustration, "I hate you! I hate you!" I repeated, wanting it to become part of him as I slammed my fists into his torso.

"You're right! I am a fucking asshole, and you need to stay away from me."

"You're the one who followed me out here! Just like you followed me out into the woods with Daniel! You're the one who kissed me, remember?"

He knocked me senseless, professing, "How could I forget? It was the only kiss that has ever mattered to me."

Fourteen

I hit him harder. "Stop playing games with me!"

All my sadness.

My anguish.

My love for him that wouldn't go away.

My hate for him for pushing me away.

I saw all the girls he'd bring around. All the times he'd ignored me. Every time he didn't look my way. I saw it all. With each blow, I felt a little more of myself die inside.

I went to hit him again, but he caught my wrist, so I tried with my other fist, and he caught that one too.

"Enough!"

"Fuck you!" I flung my body, whipping all around, desperately trying to break free from his strong hold.

On my wrists.

On my heart.

On my soul.

"How could you use me like that? I thought you cared about me! I thought I was different! Why would you kiss me if you were just going to screw me over like you do every girl you sleep with? Why?"

"For fuck's sake!" He immediately flipped me over, getting on top of me, and holding my wrists above my head while the weight of his body held down my legs. "What do you want me to say? You want me to tell you I'm

"No! I don't want your bullshit apologies you'd only be saying for Christian!"

"Did I kiss you for Christian too?"

"Just tell me how many more times you're planning on breaking my heart, you dickwad!"

He jolted back for the first time like I had hit him again, but this time it wasn't by my actions—it was the reality of my words instead.

Julian

Tears slid down the sides of her face, cascading onto the dirt behind her. The guilt was eating me alive.

"I'm no good for you."

"Oh yeah, Christian made that really fucking clear."

"No shit, I heard him."

Her eyes widened.

"And he's right. I'm no fucking good for you. I'm hurting you when I'm with you. I'm hurting you when I'm not. I can't win either way, and I hate seeing you cry over me. I should be the last man you're crying over. Do you understand me?"

"What am I supposed to do, huh? I can't be with you, and I can't be without you. I'm in lov—"

"Don't you fucking dare."

"What? Can't hear the truth? Well too bad! I'm in lov—"

Helpless to hear Autumn say those words, I crashed my mouth against hers. My lips immediately betraying me, I kissed her as if I had a right to, as if she was mine, as if I was hers—as if this kiss would change the course of our lives.

It was uncontrollable.

The urge.

The rage.

The desire to claim not only her lips, but her heart, her soul, her goddamn body were driving me to the brink of insanity. I loved and hated it. The emotions she stirred were ones I'd never experienced before. It was overwhelming, the thrill of her, the thought of her, the feel of her.

My tongue slid into her mouth, and she tasted like everything I ever wanted and didn't think I deserved. Kissing me back like she was trying to prove she was indeed all the things that wreaked havoc in my mind.

She glided her tongue into my eager mouth, moaning, panting, clawing at my senses. My dick throbbed, aching as she writhed beneath me and enticed my cock to rock against her virgin pussy.

The mere thought of knowing she'd never been touched was fucking agonizing to every part of my body. I needed to stop, but I couldn't help myself. The truth was, I did want her.

I wanted her innocence.

Her happiness.

Her love for me.

I didn't deserve it, yet it still felt like it all belonged to me. Where things took a turn in our dynamic was beyond me. It seemed as though it was out of nowhere, hitting me like a fucking freight train. One day she was my best friend's little sister, and the next she was this forbidden fruit I wanted to taste.

It was wrong.

We were all wrong for each other.

I'd spent the last two weeks trying to fuck her out of my mind. From one random girl to the next. It was no use. I couldn't stop thinking about the way her mouth moved with mine. I was well aware of the crush she had on me—it was easy to see. At times it felt like Christian knew it as well. Which was probably why he'd threatened to slice my dick off if I so much as looked her way. I was laying our friendship on the line for his little sister.

What the fuck kind of best friend was I?

Everything with Autumn felt like it was new. It didn't matter how many girls I had been with, no one came close to her. The emotions she incited in me were feelings I'd never expected. Never thought possible.

I didn't believe in love.

But I believed in her.

Our movements became headier and more urgent since we were both searching for something. My hand started roaming, beginning at her hair, then traveled down to her face and breasts. Her nipple hardened against the palm of my hand. She pushed her chest further into my grasp, and I gripped it harder, earning me another moan.

The friction between us was intense, consuming, dry fucking the shit out of one another. Her hips moved faster against my cock, and it was only then that I noticed how frenzied her movements became, how precise her hips rocked, how warm her skin felt.

I opened my eyes.

Her face was flushed.

Her forehead perspiring.

Her hands fisting the grass.

"Fuck!" I stopped and pushed myself off her.

"No!" she shouted, instantly feeling the loss of another thing I refused to steal from her. "I was so close!"

"No shit!" I yelled out, pushing my hair out of my face and holding it back with my hands. Wanting to wring my own fucking neck.

She inhaled deeply and rapidly, trying to steady her aroused body.

"Fuck!" I shouted out again, only pissed at myself. "I shouldn't have done that."

"You did it because you want me as much as I want you."

"Wanting you isn't the problem, kid."

She smiled, sitting up. Her toe was still bleeding, and I needed something else to focus my attention on. Taking off my tie, I wrapped it around her foot before looking up at her through the slits of my eyes.

"What am I going to do with you?"

"I have some ideas."

"I bet you do."

I just couldn't believe...

I'd almost made her come.

Fifteen

Autumn

Day 5 of Press Tour

WE WERE SITTING IN LOCKE'S PRIVATE JET, AND I WAS IN THE seat furthest away from him. Between everything that had happened at the photoshoot three days ago and then ending it with us running into the woman he'd brought to my seventeenth birthday party, I needed some serious space. The last two days were jam-packed with press interviews, and there was no time left over to discuss us.

Thank God.

Today was going to be hard enough. It was probably the hardest day we'd confronted on this tour so far. The timing was shit, seeing as I didn't want to talk about the past, and there we were, going to face it head-on.

Fort Worth, Texas.

Julian Locke was coming home for the first time in over a decade.

A production crew was meeting us there to get footage of him in his old stomping grounds. Beginning with the group home he'd lived at in between his foster placements. I didn't think it would affect me as much as it was, but something inside of me shifted at that damn shoot.

The outfit he was wearing.

The words he was confessing.

The way he was looking at me.

It was all too much to take in at once. Now, we were flying back home, where our tumultuous past existed, and it was breathing fire down my back. By the way Julian was acting in the last forty-eight hours, I imagined he was feeling the weight of our history on his shoulders like I was. Other than when he was answering questions from the press, he was quiet and distant.

We both knew how heavy the load of Texas would be, and the silence was deafening on his private jet. I swear I could hear his thoughts, and every single one included me and my family.

Particularly my brother.

I still hadn't explained anything to them. I'd been dodging their calls and texts, trying to figure out what I would say. The flight was only two hours, and it felt as if an eternity was slowly passing us by. Although the anxiousness I was feeling wasn't only about Texas—we'd be sharing the penthouse floor of the hotel we were staying at while we were in our hometown.

Why did I agree to share a suite with him?

Taking in a deep breath, I counted to three before exhaling on four breath counts. If Locke noticed my unease, he didn't show it. He wasn't talking, and he didn't move from where he was sitting. Aimlessly, he just stared out the window like it had the answers to all the questions that were obviously plaguing him.

I breathed in and out a few more times until I couldn't take his silence anymore and had to ask, "You really haven't been back since you left?"

Without looking at me, he simply stated, "There was nothing there for me anymore."

I winced, narrowing my eyes at him. "You really think that, don't you?"

"I don't think, I know."

"I was there," I reminded, standing my ground on the truth. "So were my parents and my brother. Despite what you said to me the night of his wedding, I was still waiting for you to come back home, Julian. You wanted to cut ties with me, then you didn't need to do that with my entire family. They had nothing to do with us."

"They had everything to do with us."

"Bullshit. That's just an excuse you've convinced yourself of to excuse your shitty behavior. They didn't deserve what you did to them."

"Neither did you."

"I don't want to talk about us."

"Then don't ask questions you don't want answers to."

"I'm talking about my family. They mourned the loss of you as if you died. You didn't even say goodbye to them."

"How many times do I have to tell you it was the only way I could leave you?"

"Oh," I snapped, feeling his response in the pit of my stomach. "So saying goodbye to me made it easy for you to leave?" I nodded. "Good to know."

"I thought you didn't want to talk about us?"

"Ugh! You're the most stubborn man I have ever met! Do you know that?"

"I've been called worse, sweetheart."

"Stop staring out the window and fucking look at me, Julian!"

Reluctantly, he did.

"You could have left town and still had a relationship with them."

"In one way or another, it still would have included you in it."

"Who cares?! We were friends once, and after some time, we could have been friends again."

His expression quickly turned heated. "I've tasted you, kid. From your mouth, to your pussy, to every inch of your body. I stole your first kiss, your first orgasm, your first fuck—there's no coming back from that, Autumn."

"You also stole my heart. Let's not forget that."

"Yes," he agreed. "I stole that too."

"Not only did you steal it, but you also broke it, and don't you ever forget that."

"You have all the answers to your questions built-in, kid."

"Again, that has nothing to do with my family."

"Knowing you were always mine, do you honestly think I would have been able to see you move on from me? Come on, Autumn. You know me better than that."

"If I was able to see you sleep with half of Texas, I'm sure you would have lived, Julian."

"Up until four days ago, my life has been completely private. All it took was seeing you with good ol' fucking Charlie, and I didn't hesitate to tell the world who you belong to." He cocked his head to the side. "How's that for living?"

"You make it sound like moving on from you was easy."

"It would have been worse had I stayed for your parents and your brother."

"I didn't say you had to stay, but you still could have kept in touch with them."

"And the second someone would have told me about a new man in your life, I would have flown back and done something incredibly stupid, landing him in the ICU and me in jail. Is that what you would have wanted?"

"Of course not."

"I couldn't bear to tell your family goodbye. I couldn't explain to them why I was leaving—see the devastation on their faces when I told them. It would have been too hard—too painful. It would've felt like a betrayal." He paused for a moment. "You wanted the truth, kid, and I'm giving you the fucking truth. These are just a few things you need to consider before you start attacking me about what I should and shouldn't have done."

"But lying about our current relationship seems reasonable to you?"

"I didn't lie." He shook his head. "I want you back in my bed."

"The same bed you've probably shared with thousands of women? No thanks, I'll pass."

"No woman has ever been in my bed."

I rolled my eyes. "Is this where you tell me you haven't had sex since me?"

"No. I'm a man, Autumn, I fuck."

Hearing him say those words didn't surprise me, but the next ones he openly shared were staggering, nearly stopping my heart, leaving me awestruck and blindsided when he confessed…

"I've never made love to anyone but you."

Julian

"Has anyone ever told you that you come on a little strong?"

I was prepared for the animosity she'd have toward me, but it still hurt like a son of a bitch that she kept blowing off my sincerity.

Instead of losing my temper yet again, I changed the subject. "How about you tell me how your family is doing?"

She shrugged, not giving me an inch. "Call them and ask them yourself."

"Or you could save them from telling me to go to Hell, and just answer my question."

"Fine." She caved. "My parents are doing great. My dad is still working at his firm, and my mom is impatiently waiting on grandkids from Christian and Kinley."

"Not from you?"

She shook her head. "Not from me."

"What field did your brother end up in?"

"Believe it or not, he's a gynecologist."

Despite feeling out of control, which was never a good thing, I chuckled. "That doesn't surprise me."

"Really?"

"No. Your brother has always loved pussy."

"Ew." She flinched. "Gross. Don't ever say that to me again."

"How are he and Kinley?"

"Good, I guess. I don't see them very often."

"Why is that?"

"I don't live in Texas."

I arched an eyebrow, surprised at her response. "Where are you living?"

"None of your business, Mr. Locke."

"So we're back to that now?"

"We never left."

"You're worse than whiplash, kid. How about you save me the trouble of pulling your records from HR and tell me yourself?"

"That's illegal."

"It would only be illegal if I wasn't your boss."

"How many times do I have to tell you I'm not your employee? I'm not beneath you—I'm your equal."

"But you used to love being beneath me."

"I think that's always been our problem. The love I felt for you."

"Autumn... I've always lov—"

She abruptly stood, cutting me off on purpose. "We landed." She hurried toward the exit, and as soon as she walked past me, I stood and grabbed her arm to urge her to look at me again.

"Mr. Locke."

"I've had enough of your Mr. Locke bullshit, kid. I'm done playing your little games."

"Wow," she rasped. "I played your games for years, and you can barely stand it for six days. How's it feel?"

"Whether you want to face it or not I do lov—"

"No!" She yanked her arm out of my grasp. "I don't want to hear it."

"It doesn't matter if I say it to you now or later, it's going to be said, and the sooner you realize that, the faster we can move forward with it."

"What exactly are we moving forward with?"

"Us."

"There is no us."

"There will always be an us, and you know it."

"Listen." She stepped back, making her way to the exit. "If you want me to forgive you, how about you start with reaching out to my family and we go from there, alright?"

"Will it get you back in my bed?"

"No. But maybe we can be friends."

"We've never just been friends, Autumn."

Before I could stop her, she turned and stepped off my jet.

Bottom line, when push came to shove, she chose to confront our past in Texas rather than dealing with me and my confessions.

Sixteen

Julian

I followed Autumn into the group home I hadn't seen since my eighteenth birthday. The day I became a legal adult I was out of there and never looked back.

She must have sensed my hesitation. "You okay?"

Eyeing the production crew in front of my face, I warned, "You'll be lucky if I don't break that camera by the end of the day."

"Julian," she coaxed. "We need footage for your social media."

"Excuse me?"

"You heard me."

"I never agreed to that."

"I know. I did it for you."

"It's going to cost you, kid."

"I imagined it would." She smiled at the camera. "Can we talk about it later?"

"You mean after I'm done taking you over my knee?"

She glared at me. "I'm not a child, Mr. Locke."

"No, but you're in definite need of some discipline."

"Julian," the director of the facility greeted, bringing our attention over to her. "It's so good to finally see you after all these years."

I nodded, extending my hand, but she smiled, pulling me into her embrace instead.

"I can't tell you how proud we are of you. These kids idolize you. You have no idea how big of a role model you've been to them."

I was never any good at receiving compliments, so I nodded again, pulling away with Autumn hugging her next.

"Good to see you, Miss Jones."

"Please call me Anne." She stepped back, holding Autumn's hands. "Look at you! Oh my God! The last time I saw you, you were what? Ten? Eleven?"

"Twelve."

"Right! Well, you look amazing." She glanced back and forth between us. "I read *The New York Times* article. I can't say I was too shocked over the news of you two falling in love with each other. You've always had such a special friendship, and those always turn into the best relationships. I bet your parents are ecstatic. Do I hear wedding bells in your future?"

Autumn nervously giggled. "I wouldn't go that far."

"I would."

Both their stares snapped toward my direction.

"Julian..." Autumn zeroed in on me, not appreciating my answer.

"What, baby?" I reached around her waist, caging her in with my arms as I held her against my chest to run my nose along the nape of her neck. I inhaled her comforting scent, leaving a trail of longing in my wake. She tensed in my arms, but I didn't give a shit. If she was insistent on taking a trip down memory lane, then I was using it to my advantage as much as I could.

Whispering into her ear, "Smile for the camera, kid."

"Oh, my goodness!" Anne exclaimed. "You two are absolutely perfect! The gorgeous babies you will have!"

"Who knows, Anne." I winked at her while kissing Autumn's neck. "There may already be one in there."

She squealed, and Autumn glanced at the camera. "You can't use that."

"Baby, now's not the time to be shy." For only her to hear, I murmured in her ear, "You want the world to know me, and I'm just showing the best part of me."

Without taking in what I'd addressed, she elbowed my ribs, making me groan and let her go.

"Let's go see the kids." She grabbed Anne's arm, rushing to get away, but before she could take a step, I grabbed her hand.

Determined to remind her who was still in control.

Autumn

For the next few hours I watched in fascination how Julian was interacting with the kids. I had no clue he liked children—we'd never been around any before. This whole time I thought I was going to have to threaten him to play with the kids, but he genuinely seemed happy and not showing off for the cameras who were filming his every move.

Anne wasn't exaggerating—the kids were ecstatic over having him there with them. They adored him, and the feeling was very much mutual. Half the time I couldn't believe what was in front of my eyes. Julian was laughing, joking, bonding with each of them. From playing basketball to soccer, to throwing around a football. At one point, he was carrying around two toddlers in his arms, showering them with affection.

"I'm not surprised," Anne observed, sitting beside me at one of the picnic tables while we watched Julian throw a kid on his shoulders, in order for him to dunk the basketball into the hoop. "Julian has always had a big heart, especially when it came to children."

"Really?" I peered at her.

"Oh yes. He's always known how to calm the little ones down even as a teenager. I think it was because he lived their lives himself. He knew what they needed to hear to feel safe in a new environment. This place can be rough on a child who just lost their parent or parents. Did you know he donates millions of dollars every year?"

I jerked back. "What?"

"Yeah, he not only donates to the group home, but he also helps the kids get into colleges, paying for their books and sometimes their tuition and dorms."

"I had no idea."

"This surprises you?"

"Yeah, it does."

I fed into the gossip from the press. They labeled him as a cold, heartless bastard, and I figured he was like that in every aspect of his life. Especially after being with him the last few days and witnessing it for myself. Never in a million years did I imagine he'd cared about this place, let alone these children living there.

"He's a good man. You're lucky to have him."

My heart fluttered, hearing her say those words to me.

Was I lucky?

The time flew by, and I'd be lying if I'd said I didn't love every second of seeing him with his guard down. His suit jacket was in my lap, his tie was hanging from his neck with the first few buttons undone. He was relaxed, comfortable, and in his element.

My heart wasn't just beating fast, it was hammering against my chest when Julian took off his collared shirt. Sweat glistening off every inch of his muscular, defined chest as he made his way toward us.

I could see it in his eyes—he was coming for me.

"Julian, don't you dar—"

I didn't have a chance to finish my sentence, as he flung his sweaty body on me, wrapping me in his manly scent.

"Julian!"

"What? You used to love it when I made you wet."

"You're all sweaty, and you're ruining my dress!"

"Can't have that now, can we?"

"What's that supp—"

Clutching onto my waist, he sat on the bench, sitting me on his lap. My back to his front, his lips nuzzled my neck.

"Feels damn good to finally hold you in my arms, Autumn."

I smiled. I had to, all eyes were on us. Including the camera.

Julian wasn't deterred, muttering into my ear, "Do you have any idea how much I missed you?"

He was acutely aware of what I was experiencing with his whole body engulfing mine. Completely in tune with my emotions.

We were an illusion.

An act.

A charade.

Nothing about our relationship was real. We were living a lie in front of all these people, and the millions who'd eventually watch this intimate footage the videographer was capturing. Only suffocating me further into the reckless thoughts of what my family and brother would think when they saw us like this.

"Julian, please…"

"You know I love it when you beg."

"You can't do this."

"I already am."

"You need to let me go."

"No, I have waited too long for you."

The space began closing in on me, holding me hostage against my will. Sweat formed at my temples, my hands began to shake, and my heart started beating profusely through my chest.

I couldn't breathe.

All I wanted was to breathe. Just for one second, one moment, one hour in time.

Tick…

"You'll always be my number one girl."

Tick…

"I lov—"

Boom.

I forcefully escaped, ignoring the disappointed expression taking hold of his face.

What did he expect?

"Kid—"

I didn't allow him to finish, quickly walking away. I thought facing our past would be too much to bear, never thinking our future would be harder to endure.

Future? Where did that come from?

He was messing with my head. I took a walk while he showered, and once he was fully dressed in his suit, appearing like the Alpha CEO, it was much easier to be around him. His guard was back up, and I couldn't help but remember that for most of my life, I'd prayed for him to bring it down, and now I wished for the opposite to happen.

We said our goodbyes, and I didn't speak to him the entire drive back to the hotel. Except we didn't go to the suite. When the driver pulled into my favorite restaurant, I was well aware Julian had told him to.

"I'm not going in there with you."

"Autumn, one way or another, you're going to have dinner with me. The choice is yours on how you'd like to enter that facility."

Flinging my door open, I stepped out. Pretty much stomping my feet the entire way in. With one foot in front of the other, I walked inside with Julian behind me at the same exact time my life came tumbling down on me. Right there in front of our faces was our past beating me senseless.

My stare locked with the person I'd least expected, but he was focused on the man behind me.

Both men ready for a battle.

Over me.

Seventeen

Autumn

"CHRISTIAN," I breathed out, overwhelmed by the turn of events.

His eyes flew from Julian to me. "What the fuck is this?"

"It's not what you think."

"Actually, it's exactly what you're thinking."

I glared at Julian. "Stop it."

"Stop what, kid? He knows the truth. There's no need to hide it from him anymore."

"Is this why you texted me to meet you here? For this, Autumn?"

"I didn't text you to meet me here. What are you talking about?"

"It wasn't her," Julian declared in a steady, calm tone. "It was me from her phone."

"Are you fucking kidding me?" I bit. "Why would you do that?" I couldn't believe he'd undermined me again, going behind my back to confront the one person I didn't want to deal with right now. Like dealing with us wasn't already enough for me to handle.

"Because there was no better time than the present. You said you wanted me to reach out, make things right, and that's exactly what I'm doing. I'm done hiding our relationship from him."

"We're not in a relationship!"

My brother chimed in, "So who's lying, Autumn? You or him?"

"Christian, just let me think for a second."

"You haven't answered your phone or replied to one fucking text I sent you in the last three days, and you're telling me to let you have another minute?"

"Jesus! Can you relax? I'm as shocked as you are right now. I wasn't expecting this! He blindsided me too."

In one sudden movement, Julian shifted me aside and stood up to my brother. This was the first time in all our lives I was truly worried about what was going to go down between them. From best friends to enemies in a matter of seconds, at least it was with Christian's perception of the man standing in front of him. I'd never seen him glare at Julian with such disgust and hatred. The tension, thick and palpable swarmed through the restaurant as if bees were suddenly set free, protecting their queen.

Me.

The expression on Kinley's face mirrored my own, her concern evident through her dark brown eyes as she grabbed onto Christian's arm, like she knew he was ready to strike and attack. Taking no prisoners.

"Let's go outside, okay? This is a family establishment, and there's no need to make a scene. I don't want someone calling the cops."

Christian considered his wife's apprehension before his anger quickly turned to rage, and all the color drained from his face as he shoulder checked Julian on his way out of the restaurant. I couldn't take the strain between the two of them. The years of waiting for this to happen was finally here, in a moment I'd least expected.

I hastily followed him out, not knowing what to say or do to make this okay. Once Christian rounded the corner of the building, he snapped back around and got in Julian's face.

Spewing, "Is it fucking true?"

"Christian, please," I begged for I don't know what. I still hadn't read the damn article, but I could only imagine the details Julian revealed just from briefly speaking to Charlie about it.

Julian didn't hesitate, simply stating, "Yes."

Everything happened so fast, yet it still felt like it played out in slow motion.

"Christian, no!" I shouted as his fist slammed into Julian's jaw, causing his body to whoosh back from the impact of Christian's forceful blow.

Julian tried to catch his balance, stumbling around for a second, while I stared with a wide, petrified gaze back and forth between them. Not knowing who to focus on more. Julian caught his bearings, massaging his jaw and moving it around.

Kinley lunged into action, gripping onto her husband's arm. Her attempt at holding him back pitiful. She was no match against my brother's strength. "Babe, come on," she begged. "This isn't the right way. He's your best friend, and that's your sister."

"He was my best friend!" Christian growled, roughly yanking his arm away from her. In one stride he was in Julian's face again, shoving him back with so much force. "Is she the reason you left without so much as a fucking text?!"

I'd never seen my brother so mad before, scaring the absolute shit out of me.

But it wasn't until Julian responded, "Christian, I have loved your sister ever since I can remember."

That I truly almost fell to the ground.

He didn't stop there, speaking with conviction, "I've wasted over ten years being away from her, and I can't do it anymore. I pushed her away so many fucking times—letting our friendship and my gratitude toward your parents get in the way of my decisions and the future I wanted with her. How I left was fucked up, and I'm the first to admit that. I'll apologize as many times as I need to in order to make things right between us, but don't think for one second that I'll ever apologize for loving her. Do you understand me?"

My head wasn't just spiraling, it was tossing and turning, barely keeping up with what was happening and what he was declaring. I desperately wanted to stop Julian, but I couldn't get my lips to move, to speak, to do anything other than watch with an open mouth because of what he was admitting.

I didn't know what to think, let alone how to feel. He was sharing all this information with both of us for the first time, and he didn't stop there...

Professing, "Up until last week, I hadn't seen her since I'd left. Over ten fucking years I stayed away from her for you and your parents and I won't do that again. *I can't.*"

Breaking my heart all over again.

Julian

This was the only way to finally get over our past and move into our future. I was tired of all the games she was playing, so I once again took matters into my own hands. She'd left her purse on the table while she used the bathroom at the group home, and I didn't think twice about it—I found her phone and texted her brother. Telling him to meet us at her favorite restaurant nonetheless.

I was back in control, and it was the only reason I wasn't losing my temper with the man who used to be my best friend. He had every right to be furious, what I did was truly fucked up, but I was there now...

Ready to fight for her.

For us.

No matter what, she was mine. Even if I had to prove it to *her* and her brother. Man to man, we would have it out. Regardless of the outcome.

"Don't fucking try me, Julian! Not right now!" he spit out with a menacing tone, drawing my attention back to the present, where I was willingly putting myself on the line.

For her.

"Or what?" I countered, cocking my head to the side. "You're going to hit me again? Then just fucking do it! Hit me! Hit me as many goddamn times as you want! If that's what it's going to take to make you realize I'm not going away. I'm not leaving her. I'm right fucking here, waiting!"

He shoved me, and since I was expecting it, I didn't waver. Further inciting the fury to course through his veins. "I thought you were my best friend!" He pushed me again. "I thought you were my brother!"

"I know, but it's been over ten years, ten fucking years for us to get to this point. She's not a little girl anymore. She's a grown ass woman, and I fucking love her."

"You think that matters to me? I don't give a shit if you waited for the rest of your life after what you fucking did!"

"Christian, please," Autumn coaxed.

"Kid, stay out of it. This is between me and your brother."

"Actually, this completely involves me! So just shut your mouth and walk away. He's not going to listen to you, and I don't want to either!"

My eyes snapped to her. "Too fucking bad! I'm done playing your little games."

"Julian—"

Christian cut her off, seething, "I had to find out about you guys from a picture of you kissing on your fucking bed, Julian! I had to find out you were her first love, her first kiss, her first fuck in a *New York Times* article I had no intention of reading! I had to find out that not only did you betray my trust, you're also back together—"

"We're not back together," Autumn interrupted. "We were never even together! This is ridiculous. You both need to calm the hell down. Nothing is going to get worked out. I don't want Julian. I haven't in years!"

Just to prove my fucking point, I gripped onto the back of her neck and crashed my lips against hers. Kissing her as if my life depended on it, and in the most significant way, it did. I tugged her closer to me as if she wasn't already close enough, devouring her mouth in the same way I always did her pussy. I softly pecked her lips one last time before I pulled away to look into her eyes.

They were shut tight like she was trying to hide the truth I frantically wanted to see for myself.

"Now," I coaxed, fully aware of the truth behind her closed lids. "Tell me you didn't feel that?"

She didn't reply, not that I'd expected her to.

"You shameless fuck!" Christian roared, shifting my gaze back to him.

"She's my sister, you piece of shit! I loved you, and I fucking trusted you, man! I didn't know you at all, did I? Because the man I thought I knew would've never betrayed me with my own family!"

"Fuck, Christian! What do you want from me? I'm telling you the truth!"

"How am I supposed to get past this?"

"I tried not to love her. I've tried for years… I can't. I never wanted to do this to your family, especially after everything you guys did for me, and you know that."

131

He shook his head, disappointed. "How long were you lying to me? Huh? How long were you fucking my little sister?"

"It wasn't like that, man. She was never just a fuck to me."

"Every woman you ever came across was just another fuck to you, and you expect me to believe that she was any different?"

"She was. She meant ... she means everything to me."

"Is it you?"

I jerked back, confused. "Is it me, what?"

"Christian! Enough! Now!" Autumn pleaded, standing in front of him with her back to me.

"How can you even be with him after what he did to our family?"

"It's not like that," she explained. "Please just calm down and let me explain. I'm just his publicist."

"So what's the difference now? Huh? You don't suck his dick for free anymore? Now he just pays for your pussy instead?"

My fist connected with his jaw, sending him flying back against a car.

Autumn's stare went wide. "Oh my god!"

Kinley darted to her husband's side while Autumn snapped around, getting right in my face. "Are you fucking insane?!"

I sternly pointed to him. "He cannot talk to you like that."

"Why not? You do!"

Unable to control my temper, I roared, "What did he mean by is it me, Autumn?"

"Nothing."

Christian shoved his sister out of the way, standing in front of me again.

"Christian, please!" she pleaded in a desperate tone that shook my body to the core.

"What's going on?" I asked, torn and baffled by what was happening between them.

"How the fuck can you defend him, Autumn?!" His glare flew in my direction. "Is that why you left, Julian?! Huh? Couldn't deal—"

"Christian, stop! Please!"

"It is you, isn't it?! That's why she's defending you! Well, I won't let her take the fall for you again, motherfucker!"

"For fuck's sake! Just out with it, Christian! What the hell are you talking about?"

"It's you!" he raged, knocking me on my ass, and my world as I knew it came plummeting down on my head.

When he added…

"You're the fucking father to her daughter!"

Eighteen

Julian

"D AUGHTER?" I BREATHED OUT, ALL THE AIR FROM MY LUNGS vanishing while I stood there unable to move, but for a much different reason this time. My eyes shot to Autumn. "What is he talking about?"

She stared at me with wide eyes and a terrified expression. The blood had drained from her face, and her chest rose and fell while she was frozen in place.

"Autumn." I stepped toward her. "I won't ask you again."

She placed her hand over her heart like she was trying to hold it together, and in two strides I was in her face.

"Julian, please…"

"Please what, Autumn? I want you to look me in the eyes and tell me what the fuck Christian is talking about." When she didn't respond fast enough, I ordered, "Now!"

She jolted out of her skin, shuddering. "I don't know what you want me to say."

"I want the truth."

"Holy shit." Kinley jumped in, standing in between all of us. "Everyone needs to take a second and calm down, okay? This isn't helping anyone."

I didn't pay her any mind—my focus was still on the liar in front of me. "Either you answer my question, or you'll be answering my lawyer, kid."

"Your lawyer?" she exclaimed, appearing every bit the damsel in distress she was trying to portray. "What do you need to call your lawyer for?"

"For a daughter I didn't know I fucking had!"

"Stop yelling at me!"

"In a second I'm going to be doing a lot more than yelling at you."

Christian shoved me back, placing his sister behind him. "You're going to have to go through me, motherfucker."

I growled from deep within my chest, not backing down. His threat meant shit to me. "I'm only going to say this once, so you better fucking listen. If you think I won't go through you or anyone else who is trying to stand in between me and my child, then you have no idea who you're dealing with."

"You can't take her away from me!" Autumn shouted, shaking her head. "I swear to God, Julian, I'll—"

"You'll what? Keep more secrets? Play more games? Lie to me some more? Tell me, sweatheart, what will you do?"

"You have no right to be angry with me! You left me, remember?"

"Did you know you were pregnant at your brother's wedding?"

She winced.

"Answer me. Did. You. Know?"

Taking a deep breath, she hesitantly nodded.

"I want to hear you say the words."

"Julian," her brother stated. "This isn't helping—"

"Fuck you, Christian!" I pushed him, needing to take out my frustration. "You have the audacity to stand there and come for me, when you knew I had a daughter, and you couldn't bother to pick up the damn phone and tell me?"

He jerked back. "I didn't know she was your daughter—none of us did. She looks nothing like you. She's Autumn to a T. Besides, Autumn told us it was a one-night stand, and no one knew you guys were fucking around up until a few days ago."

"Your parents may have not known, I'll give you that one, but you sure as shit were getting suspicious, so try again."

Autumn stepped aside him to stand in front of me. "I've been telling you this since day one, and I'll say it again. This is between you and me, it has nothing to do with my brother and family."

"Is that right?"

"Yes."

"So you kept the truth from all of us then?"

"What was I supposed to do, Julian? Tell them we were sneaking around and you got me pregnant and then took off like a bat out of Hell?"

"If you would have told me you were pregnant, I never would have left you, and you know it."

"When was I supposed to tell you?" she scoffed out in disgust. "Before or after you told me you screwed someone else at Christian's bachelor party? Or would you have rather I waited until after you told me I was nothing more than a fuck to you? Please tell me when I should have told you I was expecting your baby? Because I just don't know."

"You should have told me the second you found out."

"I was going to tell you the night of the wedding. It's why I went outside by myself. I knew you'd follow me. But you didn't give me a chance before breaking my heart and then stomping all over it."

"How long did you know?"

"I really don't want to talk about this in front of my brother and his wife. Can you at least give me that?"

"I don't have to give you shit."

"I know, okay? I'm asking for mercy."

Before I went off again, I abruptly walked away.

"Can you guys go please? I need to handle him alone."

"Fuck no," I heard Christian retort. "I'm not leaving you alone—"

"We're a phone call away," Kinley interrupted him. "Okay?"

My glare shot to Christian when he warned, "We're not done here, Julian. It's far from over." He turned and left with his wife following close behind him.

Once they were gone, I got right down to the point. "Where's my daughter?"

"None of your business."

"Oh, trust me, kid. It's going to be my business when I'm serving you with custody papers."

"Are you insane? She doesn't even know you!"

"Whose fucking fault is that?"

"Yours! You left me, asshole! What did you expect me to do? Grovel and beg you to stay for me and a baby you didn't want?"

"I wanted you, Autumn. I've always wanted you."

"Well, you had a shitty way of showing it. I've been trying to tell you—"

"You haven't been trying shit. You want to know how I know? Because I still don't know the fucking truth!"

"Oh my God! Will you ever stop?!"

"Do I look like I want to be yelled at?! Do I seem like I want to be fucked with?! Now tell me where my daughter is before I lose the last bit of patience I have with you."

She pushed me. "Get out of my face! You have no right to make these demands! You told me you'd never love me!"

I stood closer to her. "How could you keep this from me? Christ, kid. After everything, how could you not tell me we made a baby?"

"I thought you would come back, alright? I waited for you. I didn't think you wouldn't come back for me and after time went on, I realized you weren't ever coming home again. By that time it didn't matter anymore."

"Oh, it mattered, Autumn. How the fuck could you keep this from me? Were you ever going to tell me?"

"Yes. I was trying to figure out the right time."

"You expect me to believe your bullshit lies?"

"I'm not lying."

"Well, I don't trust you."

"Great. Don't trust me. If you want to stand there and pretend like I'm the villain, then go right ahead. I'll be the bad guy, if that's what it's going to take for you to not involve your lawyers in this. Please, Julian…"

I shook my head, eyeing her up and down as I backed away. I had to remove myself from this conversation before I said something she could use against me if we needed to settle this in court.

Unable to hold back, I threatened, "This whole time you've been saying I'm an asshole. Well, sweetheart, you haven't seen anything yet."

Fear replaced the anger in her expression, and for some reason, my mind kicked to another place and time.

Where looking at her didn't make me hate her.

Nineteen

Julian

Then

I SAT IN MY CAR WITH A BOTTLE OF TX STRAIGHT BOURBON WHISKEY in my grasp, staring at a house that held one big, happy family. For the last three hours, my car was parked behind a huge oak tree. No one could see me, not that anyone was looking. I chugged my bottle, drinking away the uncertainty of what I was going through. I didn't think I had it in me, but there I was…

Sitting.

Waiting.

Fucking numb.

I'd only just searched for her in the last month, never imagining I'd actually find her.

Them.

Their toys were scattered all through the yard, there was even a fucking basketball hoop in the driveway. A white picket fence circled their home with a bright red door. This house was straight out of a *Home and Gardens* magazine. The grass was perfectly cut, flowers and plants accentuated the property flawlessly. There was a white swing on the porch with pillows and a blanket. This house was everything you would want to raise a family in.

When an Audi SUV pulled into the driveway, the next thing I knew, I was getting out of my car, watching as they exited their vehicle too. The woman stepped out last, heading straight toward the back-passenger seats where she opened the door to reveal a car seat. She unstrapped a baby and pulled it into her arms as two other kids flew out and hauled ass toward their father, who was walking out the front door.

A boy.

Two girls.

Three children.

Happy.

Laughing.

Loved.

I was powerless, unable to stop myself from witnessing the reality of a family I wasn't good enough for. I couldn't help but notice that the man was an older version of me. He was sporting a beard with gray hair intermixed, and it was also around the temples of his head. Though, it was his piercing blue eyes that caught my attention the most—they mirrored my own. It was almost like I was looking into a mirror of what my appearance would be in thirty years.

I didn't expect to see him or meet him. I was only prepared for her. After all these years, I always assumed she was the one who gave me up. Now to learn that it was both of them triggered feelings I didn't know I felt until that very moment.

Sadness.

Confusion.

Abandonment.

The emotions were endless, piling up one right after the other.

Taking a deep, reassuring breath, I inhaled through my nose and exhaled out of my mouth, trying to shake off the bullshit they evoked. From then on everything sort of played out in slow motion.

The man greeted, "Hey, honey," kissing her on the lips.

She responded, "Hey," smiling lovingly at him. "Can you help me with this little guy?"

He smiled and grabbed their son from her arms, throwing him up in the air, making the baby squeal in delight. I felt as if my body was giving out on me—the emotions were ruthlessly taking ahold of me.

Why didn't they want me? What was wrong with me? Why was I so easy to give up? Why not them?

Maybe they were too young and thought I'd ruin their future. We might have looked the same, but I would never abandon my kid to the fucking system of all places.

One thought led to the next, making me sick to my stomach. I never considered them still being together and having a family. I wanted to give them the benefit of the doubt. But the longer I stood there, the further my resentment and anger grew.

It wasn't until the woman's gaze found mine through the yard that I truly wanted to scream, *"Why didn't you want me?"*

She didn't move.

She didn't speak.

She didn't show me anything.

Nothing of what I'd hoped I'd see.

Seconds, minutes, hours could have flown by, and not once did I look away, openly showing her my agony and dismay. She knew who I was, that much I could see. Except, she didn't give a flying fuck. She was the woman who'd brought me into this world, and at that moment, it was obvious that it was all she'd ever be. I wasn't her son. I was just an accident and mistake she gotten rid of. She must have read my mind, because she simply turned and left. Everyone followed her into their home, and I continued to stand there and consider my options. I could knock on their door, make a big, ugly scene. Confront them, ask them everything, but in the end it wouldn't matter.

It wouldn't change one damn thing.

Instead of getting answers, I locked up my emotions like they never existed to begin with. Getting in my car, I left. Wanting to get lost and not be found. My mind was a jumbled mess of what the fucks. My head was pounding so hard I could barely see straight. It felt like a hammer was beating in my skull.

I drove around aimlessly, drinking away my sorrows before I snapped out of whatever stupor I was in. The last thing I needed was to get a DUI. By the time I'd made it back to my house, it was well into the night. Past midnight. The whiskey was long gone, and all I had left was my misery.

Christian wasn't home, which meant he was at his girlfriend's, or should I say fiancée now. Seeing as he'd asked her to marry him a couple months ago, spending more time at her place ever since. I was glad he'd found someone to spend the rest of his life with. That future wasn't in the cards for me, not when I couldn't be with the one I wanted the most.

"Get your shit together," I uttered to myself, wanting to wash away the day and the booze. I walked into my bathroom to take a quick shower, and after I pulled my shirt off, I remembered I'd left my toiletries in Christian's bathroom. The drain in my shower was clogged, and I'd forgot to pick up Drano to fix it.

Grabbing a beer out of the fridge first, I made my way into his bedroom and stopped dead in my tracks when I saw her.

Sleeping.

Peaceful.

Fucking beautiful.

Christian gave her a key to our place in case we lost ours, and I was beyond grateful for it. Especially then. Her head was on a pillow, wrapped in a throw blanket she'd bought me for my twenty-fourth birthday last month. She must have gone into my bedroom and grabbed it before she'd fallen asleep in her brother's bed.

Over the last year, since she'd turned seventeen, I'd kept her at arm's length. Pushing her away was the only way I knew how to live. She wasn't mine and never would be, yet I couldn't stop myself from picking her up and carrying her into my bed with me. Softly, I laid her on my pillow, watching her for a minute.

Fuck, she was gorgeous.

There was no resisting the urge to feel her beneath my body. Careful not to wake her, I laid on top of her and caged her in with my arms around her face. She fit seamlessly against my chest.

"Kid," I whispered, faintly rubbing my lips on her mouth.

"Mmm…" she groaned, stirring awake.

"Wake up, Sleeping Beauty."

Her eyes fluttered, but sleep won out.

"Autumn, if you wake up, I'll give you anything you want."

"Mmm-hmm," she hummed as I kissed my way down her neck.

Once I reached the top of her breasts, I lightly bit her hard nipple through her dress. Her breathing hitched, and her eyes snapped open, big and wide. Coming face-to-face with the last person she expected to see hovering above her.

The world seemed to stop spinning, stop moving, and time just sort of stood still for us. In the last year there were times I couldn't help myself and gave into the temptation that was her mouth.

We'd kissed.

Made out.

Nothing went further than dry fucking. Anytime we got close, my reaction was to push her further away the next time I saw her. She hated me for it but loved me way more. I was toxic for her—she was poison for me. With the way I was feeling that night, I needed her in a way I'd never needed anyone in all my life.

Her warmth.

Her comfort.

Her love.

Home.

Despite the dim lighting in my room, I could still see her bright green eyes grasping the compromising position we were currently in.

"How did I get in here?"

"I carried you."

"Oh." Her eyebrows pinched together. My demons might have been silenced by her presence, but Autumn's was lying right on top of her. "Why?"

"Because I wanted you in my bed."

She searched for something in my gaze, narrowing her eyes. "I must have fallen asleep."

"Why were you waiting for Christian?"

"I wasn't. I was waiting for you."

"For me?"

"Yeah."

"Why?"

"I don't know. I was heading home from a study group, and out of nowhere it felt like you needed me. By the expression on your face, Julian, I was right. Are you okay?"

"I am now."

"What's wrong?"

"I don't want to talk about it."

"You never want to talk about anything." She placed her hand over my heart. "Please don't push me away. Just let me in."

"Kid, I've let you in so much I don't know how to kick you out."

"I'm not a little girl anymore."

"I can see that."

"I'm eighteen now."

"I know how old you are, Autumn."

Almost immediately my mind battled my heart, raging a war I never had a chance to survive. It was her innocence and vulnerability that were eating me alive, swallowing me whole. There was no denying our connection, and for the first time in our relationship, I sought refuge within her.

"Will you tell me later?"

"There's nothing to tell."

"Julian…"

"Don't whine, kid. I don't like it."

"I'm not whining. I'm just trying to be here for you."

"You are. You're lying beneath me. It's all I need right now."

"Have you been drinking? You smell like whiskey."

I smiled, rubbing my lips against her mouth.

"Have you eaten?"

"No." I grinned. "Are you offering?"

She giggled. "You're drunk."

"And you're breathtaking. Do you know that? Do you have any idea how fucking beautiful you are?"

She blushed, making her freckles much more enticing.

"Those freckles of yours are going to be the end of me."

She rolled her eyes. "I hate them. I can't wait to get them lasered off."

"Your long red hair and the scattered freckles on your nose and cheeks are two of my favorite traits about you. Don't ever change, Autumn. You're perfect just the way you are."

She blushed again, biting her bottom lip.

"Your pouty mouth is another one of my favorites."

"Oh, yeah? What else?"

"Your green eyes. They show me everything I need to know."

"So you love my face the most?"

"No. Your perky tits, your slender waist, your luscious ass, I like those too."

She chuckled, stirring my cock to twitch.

"But it's your laugh, your smile, your heart, the way you can see through my bullshit—it's what really takes ahold of me."

She mischievously smirked. "See through it or put up with it?"

"Either or."

I knew one thing for sure, tonight I wouldn't be pushing her away. Giving into temptation, I claimed her lips.

With no intention … of just stopping there.

Twenty

Julian

I KISSED HER UNTIL NOTHING ELSE MATTERED, KNOWING DEEP DOWN in the pit of my stomach this wouldn't change anything between us. She was chasing away my demons while I was merely becoming one of hers.

Our mouths were starving for affection.

Aching for relief.

I desperately wanted to lose myself inside of her.

"You want me, Autumn?"

"Always."

It was all I needed to hear before I reached for the hem of her dress and slid it off her body, leaving her in nothing but her panties. With a predatory regard, I devoured every inch of her bare skin. From her rose-colored nipples to her perky, supple tits, down to her narrow, slender waist, and her luscious ass and thighs.

"Fuck," I groaned, slipping off her panties, I crawled my way up her body, kissing, licking, caressing.

The addictive sounds she was making.

The way her body kept shuddering beneath mine.

The smell of her fucking arousal.

It all had me losing my goddamn mind.

"Autumn," I rasped. "I want to fuck you with my tongue."

She swallowed hard, her chest rising and falling, waiting, eager, ready...

This was definitely a bad idea, but I was going to make her feel so fucking good, and it was the only thing that mattered at that moment.

She moaned in response and there was no hesitation on my part when I took in her pink flesh for the first time.

"Autumn." I blew on her clit. "You have the prettiest pussy. All this under your yellow dress."

She moaned again, and her thighs clenched.

Grinning, I nudged my nose along her folds, faintly blowing against her heated flesh. Lightly running the tip of my tongue over her clit, her breathing instantly became heavy and intoxicating. I knew her heart was beating rapidly out of her chest, making it difficult to catch her next breath. With each stroke of my tongue, I showed her how fucking weak I was when it came to her.

"Tell me, kid. Have you ever touched yourself?"

She thought about it for a second, blushing profusely. "No."

"Are you being shy? There's no need for it—my face is already buried in between your legs."

"Julian…"

"You are being shy." I smiled, peering up at her through the slits of my eyes. "Sweetheart, you have nothing to be shy about. You have the prettiest pussy I've ever seen. It's the perfect shade of pink."

She covered her face, and I licked from her opening to her clit.

"Are you going to be a good girl for me, Autumn?"

"Please," she begged in a breathless tone.

"Please what? All I keep thinking about is how good you're going to taste when I make you come in my mouth."

Her eyes widened.

"How fast do you think I can make you come?"

"Oh, so you're being cocky now?"

"Not cocky when I'm about to make you sit on my face."

"Wha—"

I flipped us over, placing her pussy where I wanted it. Our eyes locked, and all I could see was lust.

"Tonight, you're mine, and you're going to give me what I want. Fuck my face, Autumn."

She purred.

"You like that, do you? The wetter you are, the harder I'm going to tongue fuck you."

And the little minx replied, "Prove it, Julian."

I didn't have to be told twice. I sucked her clit into my mouth, and she loudly moaned, melting against my lips. There was no stopping there—I was just getting started.

Savoring the taste of her.

The feel of her.

Her hips rocked against my face as I pushed my tongue into her cunt before sucking her clit into my mouth. Up and down, side to side, I took what I wanted. What she was giving. Knowing I was the first man to have her this way did something primitive to me. I turned into a fucking caveman.

She was so wet.

Tasted so good.

Her pussy throbbed.

Her body shook.

It didn't take long to have her come undone.

"Julian," she panted, climaxing in my mouth. "Julian, please…" she begged for mercy, but still—I didn't stop. I couldn't.

She consumed me.

From my mind to my soul, to my goddamn cock.

A heady growl vibrated from deep within my chest, conscious of the fact that she was trying to save me from myself while I was destroying her in the process. Ruining her for every other man. The mere thought pissed me off, and I took my frustration out on her cunt.

"Julian!" she exclaimed, coming down my neck. Her body fell forward, and she held herself up on the headboard.

"Are you a squirter, baby? We're about to find out. Give me what I want, Autumn."

She did, proving that she was indeed a dirty little girl. Squirting down my face and chest, but it wasn't enough for me. I was a man possessed, licking her fucking clean, from her opening to her clit. I wanted every last drop of her come. Not allowing her any time to recover, I flipped us over and crawled my way up to her mouth, kissing her and making her taste herself.

She moaned, sucking on my tongue.

"So fucking good." I sat up on my knees, never once breaking our heated stares as I unbuckled my jeans to kick them off with my boxer briefs.

Through dark, dilated, hooded eyes, she took in the size of my hard cock for the first time. I fisted my shaft, jerking myself off in front of her. She watched with an expression full of desire and nothing else. I smiled, appreciating the look in her eyes.

I was a fucking goner. There wasn't a chance in hell I wouldn't have stolen her virginity.

It was mine.

It belonged to me.

I'd stolen everything else, and this would be mine as well.

Still fucking my hand, I made my way back up her body. "I can go as slow as you need."

It was her turn to smile as she sat up, kissing me. Silently demanding I keep going. When I didn't move fast enough, she reached for my dick and wrapped her hand around my shaft, causing my breath to hitch against her lips and my dick to jerk in her grasp.

"Yeah, baby, just like that," I scoffed out, biting her bottom lip. "Stroke my cock. Harder. Faster."

She was a very good listener. Driving me to the brink of insanity. I'd never been with a virgin before. It was too personal, and I was the fuck 'em and leave 'em kind of man.

With Autumn, it was different, and there was no denying that.

"After I'm done with you, I'm going to fuck you again. Just so you remember, only I belong inside of you."

She slid her tongue into my mouth, and I let her take the lead.

"Julian, I want you." She positioned my dick at her entrance.

I groaned, "I want you more than I've ever wanted anything. Are you ready for me?"

"Yes, I've always been ready for you."

"Once I thrust my cock inside of you, there's no going back, kid. You know that, right?"

She beamed. "Promise?"

"I don't deserve you. Not your heart or your pussy, but I'm a selfish bastard, and I want both regardless."

"I'm yours forever."

"Don't say things you don't understand."

"I love—"

"Don't say things I don't understand."

"Julian—"

I kissed her, mostly to shut her up. I didn't want her to have expectations after this, and I was beginning to realize she would. And still, I couldn't stop myself.

Slowly, inch by inch, little by little, I thrust inside of her. She felt incredible, like nothing I'd ever felt before. The sensation of her walls tightening around me was indescribable.

My balls ached.

Her barrier pushed against the head of my cock. "I'm right there, baby. About to steal another part of you."

"I know. Just do it already."

I chuckled, and in one deep thrust I tore through her virginity. She gasped, clinging onto my back.

"I know it hurts, but I'll make it better." Reaching below, I rubbed her clit, trying to make this better for her.

"Yes…"

"Yeah? You okay?"

"Yes, I like that. Keep going."

"I'm going to start fucking you now."

She moaned, fisting the sheets as her head fell back against the bed. Preparing for the pain and pleasure my cock would bring.

Thrusting in and out, I played with her nub. Her pussy constricted every single time I massaged her clit up and down. The faster my fingers moved, the harder and deeper my thrusts became. It wasn't just her blood on my dick that made her soaking wet and drip down my balls.

Her cunt loved my cock.

Spasming.

Squirming.

Falling apart.

"Your pussy was made for me. How are you this fucking delicious?"

"*I* was made for you."

Hearing her affirm what I'd spent years disregarding was another emotion I wasn't expecting. Unable to confront the truth, I hid my face in the crook of her neck. Aware it wouldn't matter in the end—she owned my heart and soul.

Always had.

Always would.

Our mouths parted, both of us panting profusely, helpless against our bodies coming together as one. She gasped the second she felt my cock hit her g-spot, and I picked up the pace of my assault.

"Julian … right there…"

"Here, baby? You want my cock, here?" My dick throbbed to come balls deep inside of her now.

"Oh, God … yes … right there…" Her moans got louder and louder, squeezing the hell out of my cock.

"Yeah, baby, just like that. Come hard for me."

"Yes… Don't stop … please don't stop."

"I won't. I can't. You own me."

She pulsated, and her sweet pussy sucked my cock dry. I came so hard, my vision blurred, and my body trembled right along with hers. Both of us going over the edge together, where I could barely see straight. We stayed like that for I don't know how long, in our safe haven that would eventually turn into our hell. It felt as if an eternity had passed between us, and it still wasn't enough time with her.

It was never enough time with her.

Kissing all over her face again, I slowly, unwillingly, pulled out of her, causing her to wince from the sting of my dick.

"I'll be right back." I kissed the tip of her nose and got up, going straight into the bathroom. Needing a minute to myself for what I wasn't prepared to face. "Fuck." I looked in the mirror. "We didn't use a condom."

My emotions held me hostage while I cleaned myself up. Taking a solid breath, I dampened a washcloth and made my way back into my bedroom.

"Autumn—"

"Don't say it. Please don't ruin this for me." She was staring up at the ceiling. Lost in her own thoughts with my white sheet wrapped around her naked body.

"What exactly do you think I'm going to say?"

"That you regret it."

"Kid, look at me."

She did, her eyes already welling up with tears.

"Awe, baby." I went to her and kissed her lips.

"Every time something intimate happens between us, you always push me away after. Please, just give me this. I can't hear you say that you regr—"

"I don't."

"Really?"

I shook my head.

She sighed, fresh tears falling down the sides of her face.

"Don't cry for me, Autumn."

"They're happy tears."

I didn't want to ruin the moment, but I had to ask, "Are you on the pill?"

"Ummm . . . no."

"Fuck!" I sat up, and she went with me, grimacing when the bed hit her core. "You're going to be sore."

"It's fine. Don't freak out, okay? I'll get on the pill."

"A little late, kid."

"I mean for next time."

I arched an eyebrow. "Next time?"

"Yeah, there's going to be a next time, right?"

I opened my mouth to reply, but nothing came out.

"Julian, this isn't a one-time thing, right?"

"I need to clean you up."

The next thing I knew she was kissing all over my face, wrapping her arms and legs around me, seeking the comfort she needed in my embrace. I kissed her, softly pecking her lips, taking my time with each stroke of my tongue as it tangled with hers.

I tasted her tears.

Her hope.

Her love.

When I opened my eyes, I saw every sentiment I felt through her gaze. We locked eyes.

I surrendered.

To her.

To us.

Because for the first time, I didn't stop when she wholeheartedly expressed, "I love you," all in one breath.

Twenty-One

Autumn

Day Six of Press tour

H E COULDN'T EVEN GIVE ME A DAY TO FIGURE SHIT OUT.

Not. One. Fucking. Day.

We were supposed to be getting footage of him at the old junkyard he used to work at, not sitting at a rectangular mahogany table in the building he owned in Texas which was another extension of his office in Miami.

Of course, Julian Locke was sitting at the head of the table, and I was parallel to him with our lawyers by our sides. They were both personally flown in on Julian's private jet—God forbid he give me any time to think things over. I didn't want to involve lawyers. We could have worked this out on our own, but now I had no choice in the matter.

Like with everything, he'd stolen that away from me too.

For the last twenty minutes, all we did was fight back and forth over his ridiculous demands. He wanted joint custody, one week off, one week on, when we didn't live in the same state. Along with exchanging of holidays, switching each year on who would get Thanksgiving and Christmas. The last demand he had was a real kicker—Julian wanted our daughter to carry his last name.

I'm sorry, what?!

The desire to punch him and his stuffy lawyer, Anderson, in the face was palpable.

Especially when Anderson stated, "May I remind you, Miss Troy, that Mr. Locke has been more than flexible with the terms of his agreement."

"Flexible?" I choked out. "You call this flexible? He just found out about our daughter yesterday, and he hasn't even given me any time to explain anything to her. This is the complete opposite of flexible! This is entirely selfish on your part and utter bullshit, Julian! She doesn't even know who you are!"

"Whose fault is that, Autumn? It sure as hell isn't mine."

I glared at my lawyer. "He doesn't even know her name! Greg, do something!"

He nodded, looking over at them. "Miss Troy has been the sole parent for the last nine years—"

"I don't need to hear your bedtime story. She either agrees, or I'll take her to court for sole custody."

"Julian! Do you hear yourself? What the fuck? You can't do this to her!"

"I'm doing it *for* her. Big difference, kid."

"I'm trying to keep my calm, alright? Do you know how hard that is for me right now? Please." I paused to let my words sink in. "Just think about it for a second. She doesn't know you, and I know deep down you understand how hard it will be to uproot her from everything she's known for the last nine years. I promise I won't keep her from you. I want her to get to know you, but we can't do it the way you want."

"You've left me no choice."

"We don't even live in the same states. How is joint custody going to work?"

"I have three private planes, Autumn. Pick one."

"So you're just going to completely turn her life upside down? What about school? And her friends?"

"I can get her a private teacher, and she's a kid—she will make friends in no time."

"Do you hear how insane you sound? You! The man who grew up from foster home to foster home. Why would you want her to go through that?"

"She's not being tossed away like I was. I'm her father, and I have just as many rights to her as you do, sweetheart."

"You're being unfair."

"I don't give a shit what you think I'm being. I stand by my demands. If you don't like it, I'll see you in court."

I wanted to bash his face in. "I've raised her for the last nine years, and no judge in their right mind would give you sole custody of a child who doesn't even know you."

"It's a risk I'm willing to take, but as you know, I never lose, kid."

"What is that?" I jerked back. "Is that a threat? You have judges in your back pocket, Julian?"

"What you're doing is called entrapment, Autumn. And I'm not stupid enough to fall for your desperate antics."

"I'm not trying to trap you. I'm just trying to make you see reason."

"What do you suggest we do?" He leaned back against his leather chair. "What's reasonable for you?"

I sighed in relief, feeling like I was starting to get somewhere with him. "I don't think joint custody is the right answer, and I'm not saying it's not something we can't discuss later, but for right now, it's too much for her. She needs to get to know you first."

"And what exactly does she know? Have you told her anything about me?"

"For the last year or so," I reluctantly gave in, but he'd left me no choice. "She's been asking who her father is."

"And?"

"And since she's so incredibly stubborn like you, I had to tell her, but I didn't give her your name. The last thing I wanted was for her to Google you and find out that you're Alpha CEO."

He narrowed his eyes at me, unaware of what I meant by that.

"You're an asshole. That's no surprise to you. The last thing I wanted was for her to find out the man you've become." I took a deep breath, already dreading the fact that I was going to admit this. "To say I was shocked when Claire called me to help you would be an understatement. It was like fate or something. I guess, I mean … I know. It's one of the reasons I agreed to take you on as a client. I thought … I hoped … I could change you back. Okay? I wanted to help you become the man I used to know, not for me, but for Capri."

"You named her Capri?"

"Yeah. I wanted her to have a part of you, and you always liked the name. I know it's silly, but it was something I could use without my family getting suspicious of who her father was. I couldn't give her your last name, Julian, so I worked with what I had."

"After knowing I was raised without a father, how could you do that to me? How could you betray me like this?"

"What was I supposed to do? You left me."

"I would have taken the first flight back if you'd told me, Autumn."

"And then what? Huh? What would have happened next?"

"It's really quite simple, kid."

Never did I expect him to declare, "I would have asked you to marry me, and we could have been a family."

Julian

"You don't mean that."

"I never say anything I don't mean."

"Other than when you're lying to me."

"If you're going to bring up our past every time you don't get your way, we're in for a rough road ahead."

"We're in one nonetheless." She abruptly stood. "You can't say shit like you would have asked me to marry you!"

"Whether you want to hear it or not, it's the truth."

"It's so easy for you to say that now, in retrospect, but back then … it wasn't like this. *You* weren't like this. You spent years pushing me away. Years, Julian!"

"I know, and you don't have to remind me every chance you get. I was there, Autumn."

"You're so fucking arrogant. How can you sit there and make all these demands when the only reason we're in this situation is because of you and your choices in the first place? You're the reason things went down this way."

I slammed my fist on the table, making her jump. "Don't you think I know that? I'm trying to make it right. I've been trying to make it right all week."

"It's going to take longer than a week to make things right between us, and now you're throwing our daughter in the mix, and it's not fair!"

"You want to know what's not fair? I'll tell you what's not fucking fair! First and foremost, missing out on your pregnancy, watching your stomach grow with our baby. Feeling her kick, seeing you pregnant with my child, glowing, radiant, and fucking breathtaking. The first ultrasound, finding out we're having a baby girl, and then preparing for it. Her birth, cutting the cord, seeing you hold her for the first time, me holding her for the first time, taking her home from the hospital, her first bath, her first steps, her first word, her first birthday! All the firsts I missed! Every. Single. One. Now that's not fucking fair! You took everything away from me, and you're damn lucky I'm not demanding to knock you up, so I don't miss out on those first again!"

She didn't just fall back—she stumbled from the truth of my words. With wide eyes, she replied, "Knock me up again? Are you hearing yourself? We're not together, Julian!"

"Again, not by my choice, sweetheart. If I thought for a second there was a possibility of you saying yes, I'd get down on one knee and ask you to marry me, right here and now."

"I'm not eighteen anymore. You don't need to marry me because you got me pregnant."

"That's not the only reason I'd ask you to marry me, kid."

"I don't want to talk about this anymore."

"Great. Sign the papers then."

"Julian, please… I don't want to keep her from you. She deserves to know who you are and to have a father. I promise I'll do whatever I can to make this easy on all of us."

"If I agree to wait this out, what do I get out of this new arrangement?"

"You'll get to know your daughter."

"I'll get that regardless."

"I don't know. What do you want?"

I folded my arms over my chest. "I want a month."

"What?"

"You heard me."

"What does that mean? A month of what?"

"A month of getting to know our daughter."

"Julian, I don't understand—"

"For the next month, I want you and Capri to move in with me."

She jerked back. "Move in with you?"

"Take it or leave it."

"I can't move to Miami for a month."

"Not Miami. Here. In Texas."

"You want us to move into a penthouse suite?"

"No. I own a ranch about an hour out of Fort Worth. We can live there. It's close enough to your parents where we can see them, and I can try to fix what I broke with your parents and your brother."

"I have to work."

"No, you don't."

"Yes, I do."

"I'll handle Laurel."

"Laurel? What, you're on a first-name basis with my boss now?"

"She's going to make you partner, and that means you're in control. You can start your new position next month."

"I can't work, but you can?"

"I haven't taken a day off since I started Locke Enterprises. I'm more than due."

"What about the rest of your tour? Your announcement is in four days."

"My tour is over tomorrow, and I can make my announcement any-where. Including the ranch."

"People are going to think we're a couple."

"They already do."

"Ugh! You have an answer for everything!"

"It's what makes me Alpha CEO."

She shook her head. "You're delusional if you think I'm going to agree to this."

"From where I'm sitting, you don't have much of a choice. Either you agree to my new terms, or you deal with settling this in court, where I go after full custody of Capri."

"Wow. Now you're bribing me?"

"Again, you've left me no choice."

Her stare shifted to her attorney. "Greg."

"Autumn, I think this is the best it's going to get. If he does take this to court, there's a huge chance he will win."

"How? He doesn't even know her."

"I know, but you're leaving it up to the judge and they could rule in his favor. He has money, and you lied to him about having a daughter—that'll hold up in court. I've seen it happen before."

Anderson added, "Mr. Locke is being more than fair, Miss Troy."

"Unbelievable. Now it's three against one?"

"Believe it, kid. This is your best option. You'll be there, and you can help me get to know our daughter and her to get to know me."

"I don't even know you."

"Then we can all get to know each other. After we finish the tour tomorrow in LA, we can fly straight from there to pick up Capri. You guys can pack, or I can buy you all new things. We can head back to Texas in the morning."

"Oh my God, Julian. This is too fast."

"On the contrary I'm being very lenient with you."

"You're being an asshole is what you are!"

"At this point, it's your term of endearment for me."

"I hope you can get our daughter to like you, because I sure as hell don't."

"I'll take that as a yes."

She threw the contract across the table. "I want my own room. Furthest away from yours."

I grinned, looking at Anderson. "Write it up."

For the next month, she would be mine. They both were.

And I was going to make damn sure it stayed that way.

Twenty-Two

Autumn

ONCE AGAIN, WE WERE SITTING IN JULIAN'S PRIVATE JET. EXCEPT this time, we were flying from LA to San Diego, where I lived with our daughter. I couldn't believe this was happening. One minute we were fighting about his demand's, and the next he was hitting me with a whole new one, which might as well have been worse than his first ones.

I was stuck by his side for the next month, as if the last week wasn't hard enough. Now, we were also involving Capri, and I was sick to my stomach. I told her I was coming home, but I didn't tell her with who. I honestly didn't know what to say or where to start, and I knew Julian wasn't going to allow me to go by myself to get her. This was my only choice. He was going to meet her for the first time, and my nerves were on edge.

I swear I could strangle him for putting us through this. I never imagined he'd take it this far, and that was my first mistake.

Julian always got what he wanted. Especially when it came to me.

I anxiously waited in my seat, trying to play it off like I wasn't losing my shit.

"You need to relax."

"You need to go to Hell."

He chuckled. "You're going to have to reel in that feisty attitude once we're around Capri. You don't want her to think her mommy hates her daddy, do you?"

I glared at him. "I swear you're enjoying this."

"I'd be lying if I said I wasn't."

"You actually think this is going to go over well, don't you?"

"I'm going to try like hell to make sure it does. There's nothing I can't give her. *Either* of you."

"That's your answer to everything. Money can't buy love, Julian."

"You're right, but you loved me when I had nothing. Now I can offer you the world if you want it."

"I don't need the world."

"Then what do you need, Autumn?"

"I don't need anything. Especially from you."

"At some point you're going to have to forgive me, kid."

"I was starting to, but you fucked it all up again by making us move in with you. But it's what you do best. You always fuck things up in my life."

"I don't regret getting you pregnant, and if you'd let me, I'd do it again."

"Stop! Stop saying shit like that to me. If you say stuff like that in front of Capri she's going to—"

"Get the happy family I'm sure she's dreamed about with two parents who love each other and want the best for her?"

"I don't love you, Julian. How many more times do I have to say it for you to believe me?"

"I'm not the one who needs to believe it."

"Oh, that's rich."

"You might hate me, kid, but you also still love me. It's a very thin line, you and I."

"If you break Capri's heart like you broke mine, I'll take you for everything you're worth."

"You don't have to worry about me breaking anyone's heart, Autumn. It's you who holds that power now."

"You know what?"

"What, baby?"

"I fucking hate you."

"Great." He deviously smiled. "Now say it again until you believe it."

"We're done talking now." With that, I stood and walked into the back. Trying to find the bathroom, instead I found a bedroom. "Awesome, I wonder how many times he's joined the mile-high club?"

"I haven't."

He was standing behind me, and I could feel his heat searing into my body.

"Want to make me a member?"

I couldn't take it anymore—it was all too much to take. I felt as if I was that eighteen-year-old girl all over again, completely at his mercy. I snapped. Spinning around, I went for him. Hitting him on his chest. "I can't believe you're doing this to me! I hate you! Do you hear me, Julian? I fucking hate you!"

"That's enough!"

"Fuck you!"

He gripped onto my wrist, and in three strides I was on my back with him hovering above me on the bed.

"Get off of me!"

"Not until you calm the fuck down!"

"How do you expect me to when you're forcing your hand on everything?!" I thrashed my body around, trying to get free, but it was pointless. He was much stronger than me.

With one hand he held my wrists above my head, hooking them, while the other began skimming the inside of my thigh and I froze, locking eyes with him.

I cleared my throat, trying to steady my voice. "You're obviously ignoring what's in front of your face."

He looked me up and down. "Sweetheart, you're the only one that's in my face." Slowly, he slid his fingers higher. "What do you want to do about that?"

I had nowhere to go.

I could barely move.

"Because I can think of plenty of things to do with that sweet little mouth of yours that loves to push all of my buttons."

"I—"

"Did I say you could talk?"

My eyes widened, and mouth dropped. "Who the hell do you think you are? This is not how it's going to go, Mr. Locke."

"So, I'm Mr. Locke when my hand is near your pussy?" His eyes dilated, dark and daunting. "Or what, kid? What are you going to do? I'm not the one under you, now am I?"

I jerked my body around, trying to break out of his hold, but the second I felt his fingers get closer to my core I froze again.

"Miss Troy, you're not going anywhere unless I want you to."

"You can't keep doing this to me."

"And what's that? Making you wet?"

"Julian—"

"Oh, now I'm Julian again?"

I changed the subject. "I'm over your cockiness. It doesn't work on me."

He arrogantly smiled, calling my bluff and my body's response to him. Back and forth, he caressed the soft skin of my bare thighs. My breathing elevated, proving to him I was lying.

"I am doing what's in the best interest of our daughter, Autumn. You can think I'm asshole for it, but I honestly don't give a fuck. I've lost nine years of her life and I plan to make up for it. With or without your consent."

"You could still do that, and we don't have to move in with you for the next month. What the hell are you doing with a ranch in Texas anyway? You don't even live there anymore."

"If I tell you, what do I get?"

"What do you want?"

"You."

My thighs clenched, hearing his response. Seconds later, his fingers glided closer to my core, and I resisted the urge to moan.

"What's wrong, sweetheart? Where's your smartass mouth? My tough girls gone? I guess she's not so tough when I'm lying on top of her."

I sucked in air, alarmed by his reply. He continued his gentle torture, loving the feel of my skin against his calloused fingers. As if reading my mind, he tilted his head to the side, enticing me with whatever he wanted to do. I could see, feel his internal struggle. Julian was fighting something deeper than what I imagined.

"You can't have me," I found myself saying, though I was torn. I may hate him, but my body seemed to love him.

"Fine," he stated. "I'll take your pussy in the meantime."

"You know what?" I challenged, my pussy challenging him for me. "I should just let you to make you back off."

"Kid, if you think that than you're surely mistaken."

"I'm serious."

"As am I."

"No, not about that… I mean about the ranch. Why do you own one?"

"If you must know, I've owned it for a while."

"Wait, what?"

"You heard me."

"I don't understand."

"You don't seem to these days. I'll make it very simple, I bought it for you. It even comes with farm animals like you've always wanted."

The memory of the day I told him my dream of owning a ranch and a farm played out in front of me like I was saying it to him right then and there.

"You gotta be kidding me?" You bought a ranch for me? Julian, we're not even together, that makes no sense."

"I have no intention of letting you leave."

"I don't care what your intensions are. I'm leaving when our contract is up."

"We'll see." He grinned. "Not that I need a reason for purchasing your fairytale, but Capri needs a steady home and she'll get that in Texas. We're near you family and that's important to me."

"What about Miami?"

"What about it?"

"You live there."

"I may live there, kid, but it's never been my home. Texas is where my heart is." The tips of his fingers lightly touched the edge of my panties. With a wicked expression, he taunted, "Should I keep going?"

"What does it matter what I say? You're going to do what you want anyway."

He grinned again, and instead of pushing my panties aside, he simply grazed my folds through the silk fabric. "I know you want me to touch you, and all you have to do is say the magic word."

I cunningly smiled. "Fuck off."

"I'd much rather fuck you."

When his finger slid over my clit, I released a heady moan, my body once again betraying my mind.

Causing me to counter the same words he bribed me with at my hotel suite, "I'll make you an offer you can't refuse."

Twenty-Three

H E ARCHED AN EYEBROW. "WE'RE MAKING SEX DEALS NOW?"
"Why not? You've been making them for everything else. My offer is I'll have sex with you right now."

"If?"

"If you'll let me tell Capri about you alone."

He opened his mouth to reply.

"No," I sternly interrupted. "Hear me out. I want to tell her who you are and that you're with me, by myself. I don't care where you are, you can wait in the car if you want. But please… let me talk to her first. I need to try to explain things to her before she meets you. I haven't seen my girl since I've been with you and I'd like to tell her what's going on, on my own. Can you give me this? Please, Julian."

His gaze zeroed in on me, thinking about it for a second. There was so much emotion behind his stare, and I knew it mirrored mine. There was no need for words. Our eyes spoke for themselves as his fingers began to really caress me. My mouth parted, and he laid his forehead on top of mine, his lips inches away from my mouth.

I could feel his erection.

Inhale his musky scent.

I felt him everywhere and all he was doing was rubbing my clit. His fingers were soft yet demanding, controlling yet eager, and fucking intense as all hell. I couldn't remember the last time I had a man's hands on me in this way, between being a full-time mom and having a full-time job, both of them occupied most of my time.

On top of that, I never found another man who caught my attention quite like Julian. Through the years, I often wondered if I'd ever find someone and be able to move on from him. He may have broken my heart, but a huge part of me felt like it didn't matter—he owned my soul. I had no interest in dating or to give my heart to someone else.

Maybe you were only allowed a love like ours once in a lifetime and I guess I'd become complacent with that.

Peering into his eyes, I erratically breathed out, "Julian." Trying to catch my next breath, I added, "Do we have a deal?"

My thoughts.

My words.

They all seemed to be intertwined with one another.

Especially when he slipped my panties to the side, touching my pussy for the first time in over a decade. I shuddered against him, melting into his caress, wanting to kiss him.

Why wasn't he kissing me? I refused to demand it.

His rough fingers moved to my opening, soaking up my wetness before he glided them back and forth on my clit. "Fuck, you're so wet," he growled. "Your pussy has always been so responsive to me, it's one of the many things I love about you."

Did he just say he loved me? I refused to ask that too.

He slid his fingers into my core, ordering, "Fuck my hand, Autumn." Curving his fingers toward my g-spot, he rhythmically stimulated it in a come-hither motion. I began to rock against him as he increased his speed, harder and faster he manipulated me. No one knew my body quite like Julian, he was the first and last man to give me an orgasm.

"Please," I shamelessly begged. "Make me come…"

He released another growl from deep within his chest, vibrating against my breasts. I opened my eyes needing to look at him. He was staring at my face through a hooded gaze, completely taking me in. Showing everything I always wanted to see.

His love.

His devotion.

His regret.

It poured out of him, and I had to close my eyes again.

Don't fall for his trap. You're just doing this for Capri. It's a deal. Nothing more. You don't love him anymore.

Softly, he rubbed his lips against my mouth. "When's the last time someone touched your pussy, kid?"

"Really?" I panted. "You want to talk about this right now?"

"I can't think of a better time than now." He fucked me faster with his fingers, and I rode him harder.

"I don't know… it's been… a while."

I didn't have to open my eyes to know that he was smiling wide.

"How many men have you been with since me?"

"I'm… not…" He worked me over fervently. "Jesus… that feels amazing…"

"I'm waiting, kid."

"What?" I shook my head, overwhelmed by his touch and questions.

"Men, Autumn. How many?"

"Oh… god…" My eyes rolled to the back of my head. "None of… oh fuck… business…" I bit my bottom lip, feeling my legs quiver and my pussy pulsate. "Don't ask questions… you don't want… answers to."

"Is that right?" he asked in a devilish tone, breathing into the side of my neck, making shivers crawl up my skin and throughout my entire body. "You're not being a good girl." Before I could retort, he slapped my pussy, catching me off guard and my body jolted forward. "You want me to finish you off?"

"If you don't, I'll kill you."

He smiled with nothing but mischief in his eyes. "Then answer my question."

"Ugh!" I fell back against the bed. "Four."

His eyes glazed over with a predatory regard that made my stomach flutter.

"Including me," he stated as a question.

"Yes."

He leaned forward, close to my mouth. "Was one of them good ol' fucking Charlie, Cherry?"

"I'm not answering that."

"Oh, you'll answer it."

"I don't want you to get him fired."

"You just did."

"Julian! You better leave him alone."

His fingers slid back inside me, causing my back to arch. "Did any of them make you come?"

Giving him what he sought, I admitted, "No."

"I'll tell you why," he adamantly affirmed. "It's because I'm the only man who knows where and how to touch you, I know how to lick you and how hard to fuck you." His voice was laced with possession. "You're mine, Autumn. I'm yours. Always and forever, kid."

I whimpered into his mouth, but he quickly repositioned his face in between my legs and I just about came undone when I felt his tongue on my clit—licking, sucking, tasting. Devouring me as if he had something to prove.

"Say it," he insisted, eating and finger fucking me still. "Who do you belong to?"

"Not a chance."

Deeply, he growled, for a much different reason that time. "You don't have to say it. Your squirting pussy will do it for you."

"Julian…" I let go, coming all over his face and fingers.

After I was done riding the high that was Julian Locke, he looked profoundly into my eyes as he got up off the bed. Slipping his fingers into his mouth, he licked them clean.

Simply stating, "Your pussy doesn't hate me, Autumn. You still taste as sweet as ever."

Twenty-Four

Autumn

WE DIDN'T TALK FOR THE REST OF THE FLIGHT. *WHAT COULD we say after that?* It was a clusterfuck. Now we were sitting in the backseat of an SUV, Julian was on the phone yelling at someone while I looked out the window, lost in my own thoughts as the driver drove us to my home. I was a wrecking ball of emotions, good and bad. I couldn't believe I allowed him to touch me. I didn't think it through. All I did was evoke more feelings I thought were long gone.

They weren't.

They were staring me in the face, like a fucking beacon of bright lights. Blinding my sight with nothing but conflicting emotions about him, us, our family.

Shit. Did I just say our family? You're not a family, Autumn. He's the father of your child. You're moving in with him for Capri to get to know him with you being there to make the transition easier for her. This is for your daughter.

Not. For. You.

Not. For. Him.

I repeated the words, desperately trying to believe them. I should have never let him touch me. It just added more fire to our already blazing inferno.

"Robert," Julian bit. "You either make it happen or I'll find someone who will." With that, he abruptly hung up his call.

"Wow, you're just peachy keen to everyone today."

Smirking, he placed his cellphone back into his suit jacket. "You of all people should know my patience wears thin."

"You are aware our daughter is going to test all your limits, right?"

"She's different."

"How? Patience is not your virtue. You just admitted it yourself."

"I have over nine years to make up for, Autumn. My patience is going to be endless when it comes to her."

"We'll see." I looked at the driver. "You can pull up to my window and I'll punch in my code into the security box."

"Or you could just give it to him."

My gaze shifted to Julian's statement. "I don't want you to have access to my neighborhood."

"We're back to this?"

I ignored him, dialing the code.

"Let me guess, it's either your birthday or Capri's?"

"Nope."

"Would you tell me if it was?"

"Nope." I looked at the driver. "It's the house at the end of the road, 2473."

He nodded through the mirror and moments later we were pulling into my driveway. My home was beautiful, it was three stories, coastal living kind of vibes since we were on the water. It was perfect for Capri, Emily, and me. Emily was our nanny, she'd been with us since Capri was three. I actually met her through one of my mom's friends, she was around her age, and had moved with us through a couple of cities and states. She was the best and we were lucky to have her.

"You did good for yourself, kid. Your home is beautiful. I'm sure Capri has fond memories here."

The satisfaction I felt by hearing him say those words was a feeling I didn't think I'd have.

"Thanks."

"When you're ready for me to come inside, you know where to find me."

I nodded, instantly feeling relieved he was following through on our deal. Although, I knew he meant his statement as a double innuendo. "Okay." I opened the door, but at the last second, I turned around. "Oh, and umm… thank you for allowing me to talk to Capri alone. I appreciate it and I know she will too."

"I would have allowed it regardless of you coming in my mouth."

My gaze snapped to the driver. "I'm sorry you had to hear that."

He chuckled. "I've driven for Mr. Locke for a long time. There's nothing I haven't heard."

I shot Julian a questionable expression, wondering how many women he might have entertained in the back of his car.

"I have an extended office in San Diego as well."

"Great, is there any state you don't have an office in?"

"I own the world."

"I see that."

"And now I have a family to enjoy it with."

"Julian, I'm not your family."

"You've always been my home."

I knew I wouldn't win this argument with him, so I shut the door and made my way toward the entrance of my house. My heart was beating out of my chest, I had no idea what I was going to say or how I was going to say it to her. I figured it would be easier and smoother if I spoke from my heart and not a speech I had prepared.

Capri could always see through me, she had the same power as her dad. It was one of the reasons I moved from Texas to begin with. The older she got, the more she started to possess a lot of his traits or maybe it was obvious to me since I knew the truth.

His stubbornness.

His perceptiveness.

Having no filter.

She was wicked smart like him too. She even had some of his mannerisms, holding her fork in the same way he did, she was left-handed like him. Loved old classic cars like Julian.

It was surreal.

Capri had my appearance, but she was her father's daughter in every other way. Pushing away those thoughts, I inhaled a solid breath as I unlocked the door and walked inside.

"Capri?" I called out, laying my purse on the entryway table.

"I'm in the kitchen with Emily, Momma!"

Quickly, I rushed into the kitchen. Excited to see my girl.

"Momma!" She jumped into my arms. "I missed you so much! I'm so happy you're home early! I thought you weren't coming back until tomorrow?"

I tightly squeezed her against my chest. My girl was getting so big. She'd be ten in a couple of months.

"I missed you, baby." I kissed the top of her head.

"Momma, are you okay?" See, perceptive as all hell.

I nodded, glancing at Emily. "Thank you for everything."

"Of course. I'll let you two get reacquainted. I'm going to get the groceries for the week."

"Oh, yeah... umm... you can just buy groceries for yourself. Capri and I won't need anything."

"We won't?" Capri asked, looking up at me. "Are we going somewhere?"

I nervously laughed. "Something like that."

"Sounds great," Emily replied. "You can tell me all about when I get back."

I smiled, and she left.

Giving my girl another big hug, I coaxed, "Baby, we need to talk." Julian was waiting in the SUV, I didn't have a lot of time to tell her what was going on, needing to get right to the point sooner rather than later.

"Am I in trouble?"

"No, you're not in trouble, but what we need to talk about is serious, so let's go in the living room and sit down."

"Okay."

Once we were sitting on the couch, I grabbed her hands in my lap.

"Momma, you look really pale. Are you sure you're alright?"

"Mmm-hmm... I'm just having a little trouble finding the right words to say."

The concern was evident on her beautiful face. "What's this about?"

"You know how I told you that I was taking on a client that I used to know?"

"Yeah, you spent the last week with him, right?"

"Yes, I did."

"Is this about him?"

"Yes, baby, it is."

"What is it? Do you like him or something? Because it wouldn't bother me, Momma. I'd love to have a daddy. All my friends have daddies."

"Honey." I paused, needing a second. It absolutely killed me she missed out on having a father and was starting to feel his absence so profoundly. I tried my best, always playing both roles, but in the end… she longed for her dad. Making me feel intensely guilty I waited this long to tell him.

Maybe I was wrong?

Resisting the urge to cry, I pushed through. "On the topic of that, do you remember when you asked me about your dad?"

"Yeah. Why? Is this about him?"

"Yes, baby, it is."

Her eyes lit up like a Christmas tree. "Momma! Tell me! Please!"

"I'm getting there. There's just no easy way to say this to you."

"Just say it, Momma. I'm a big girl, I can handle it."

"You are a big girl, but you'll always be my baby."

She smiled. "I know. Now tell me! What is it?"

"Okay, here goes nothing. So, the client I've been with this last week, well… he's… I mean… it's your dad."

She jerked back. "I don't get it. Your client is my daddy?"

"Mmm-hmm. It's one of the reasons I took him on as a client."

"You've been with my daddy this whole last week?"

"I have."

"Why didn't you tell me?"

My heart dropped, the last thing I wanted was for her to be upset with me. I couldn't take it. Not after everything Julian has put me through.

"I hadn't seen him in a very long time, sweetie."

"How long?"

"Since before you were born."

"Why?"

"He moved away."

"Oh…" She considered it for a minute. "Did he know about me?"

I shook my head. "No, baby, he didn't."

"Why didn't you tell him?"

"Listen, it's a long story, and it really doesn't matter."

"But does he know about me now?"

"Yes." I nodded. "And he's very excited to meet you and get to know you too."

She beamed. "Really? My daddy wants to be my daddy?"

My heart was breaking into a million pieces. "Yes, honey, he would love that."

"Really, Momma? You swear? You promise?"

"Cross my heart."

"Then when can I get to meet him? Today? Tomorrow? Oh, please, Momma! Please! Can I meet him soon? I'll be a good girl! I'll be the best girl!"

Talk about a kick to my stomach. "You're always my best girl."

"Yay! When can I meet him? Please say soon!"

"Well, babe, you can actually meet him right now."

She jumped up off the couch. "What?! He's here? Where?"

"He's outside in the SU—"

She took off.

"Capri! Wait!"

She didn't listen, not that I expected her to. This wasn't going how I imagined. If I thought my heart was beating fast when I walked through the front door, there was no comparison to how it was pounding now. I hurried behind her, trying to catch up with her pace, but she was too fast. Too excited. Too eager. Nothing was going to hold her back, not even me.

The door swung open and I knew my whole life would never be the same. It wasn't just Capri and me anymore. Now our lives were about to…

Forever intertwined with Julian's.

Julian

When the front door opened, I never expected to see our daughter hauling ass out of it. From that point forward, I moved in autopilot. Swinging open the door, I stepped out of the SUV and rounded the back. Coming face to face with a mini Autumn. I gasped at the sight of her. She was breathtakingly beautiful, exactly like her mother. She had freckles on her nose and cheeks, green eyes and bright red hair.

She halted in front of me, smiling wide. "Hi, I'm Capri."

I tugged on the end of her hair. "I know who you are, sweetheart."

She giggled, sounding so much like her mother at that age. "Momma says she's been with you all week! She said you wanted to meet me, and I've always wanted to meet you too. But Momma says you didn't know about me, and I don't know why she didn't tell you, but she says it doesn't matter.

Will you tell me? You don't have to tell me now! I'm so happy to finally meet you! My name is Capri Marie Troy and I'm a super cool girl. I have a lot of friends at school and I'm really smart. All my classes are advanced. My best subject is math! I love numbers. Did you know that?"

I shook my head, trying to keep up with everything she was sharing. Hearing and seeing her for the first time was almost just crippling as not knowing anything about her.

"I'm sorry. I talk really fast when I'm excited and I'm just so excited to meet you! But I can tell you everything and all about me! Is that okay? Do you want to know?"

Choked up from all the emotions, I expressed, "I'd love that more than anything."

"Okay, good! I love to talk. It's one of my favorite things. Momma says I can talk her ear off and my teachers nicknamed Chatty Capri, but you can call me anything you want. Momma usually calls me baby even though I'm a big girl. I'll be ten in five months! Momma says I still can't have a cellphone." She rolled her eyes. "Maybe when I'm eleven."

I swear I was thrown back to another place and time, sitting in Christian's truck with Autumn in the backseat, asking for my cellphone.

"Do you live here? Are you close? Can I come to your house?"

"Your mom didn't tell you?"

Autumn walked up to us, mirroring the expression on my face. "She didn't give me a chance."

"Tell me what?" Capri enthusiastically asked.

"You're going to move in with me."

She gasped. "We are?"

"Yes, but only for a—"

I cut Autumn off, "You're moving into my ranch in Texas."

"Texas?!" she squealed. "Oh my God! I love it there! Are we close to Grammy and Grampy? I miss them so much."

"Yes," I replied. "You can see them as much as you want."

Before I could get another word in, she threw her arms around my waist, hugging me as hard as she could. "I'm so happy! Thank you! Thank you!"

I blinked away my tears and cleared my throat. "I'm happy too." I closed my eyes and held her as tight as I could against me too, trying my best to keep it together.

Capri was the first to pull away, and I resisted the urge to pull her back toward me and never let her go. I locked stares with Autumn when I opened my eyes. She was hugging herself in a comforting gesture, with tears in her eyes.

"Momma!" Capri hugged her next, looking back at me.

Although, my stare never wavered from her mothers.

"Daddy," Capri said for the first time, instantly tearing my attention to her. "When do we leave?" She must have misinterpreted the expression on my face. "Oh, I mean… is that okay? Can I call you my daddy?" Looking up at me, she waited for an answer with nothing but love in her eyes.

Her mom used to look at me in the same way. I'd give anything for her mom to look at me like that again.

"Capri, baby girl, I'd…" I couldn't form words. Never did I imagine I'd be a father. I didn't date or do relationships, my life consisted of work and casual sex. Right then, in that moment, I'd give my soul to the devil to have the last nine years with my daughter. From the second Autumn told me she was pregnant. "I would be honored if you called me daddy."

"Yay!" she exclaimed, jumping into my arms again. "We're going to finally be a family!"

"Capri," Autumn cautioned, and I recognized that tone.

There was no hesitation on my part, I tugged her into the side of my body. Holding my entire world in my arms in what seemed like a lifetime.

I gazed down at our daughter, simply stating the truth, "Yes, baby girl. We're going to be a family."

Twenty-Five

Autumn

PACKING WAS TAKING LONGER THAN EXPECTED AND WE DECIDED to leave tomorrow morning instead. Julian invited himself to spend in the night in my house. He was going to sleep in the guest bedroom. Yesterday didn't turn out as planned, and although we did share his penthouse suite, we steered clear of each other, both of us lost in our own thoughts.

The anxiety I felt having him in my home wasn't as emotion I'd expected. This was my safe haven, the place I'd go to escape the stressors of life. He was invading my personal space in a way I wasn't prepared for or anticipated. It didn't help that he was bonding with Capri right off the bat. He was in her room, helping her pack while I cooked dinner.

It felt like we were playing house, and it was too close for comfort.

Capri walked into the kitchen alone.

"Where's your dad?"

"He's taking a shower and asked me to tell you he needed a towel."

Julian clean.

Wet.

Naked.

It sounded like a bad idea to me, but I couldn't exactly say that to Capri. I nodded, grabbing a few from the linen closet before walking across the house toward the guest bedroom.

I knocked on the door. "Julian?"

He didn't answer, so I opened the door to find the bedroom and bathroom empty. I realized all too quickly the son of a bitch probably had the balls to use my shower. Stomping one foot in front of the other, I marched into my bedroom, and the first thing I heard was the sound of the shower in my sanctuary.

I shook my head, the audacity of that man. As soon as I opened the door, I shrieked and instantly placed my hand over my heart while my other hand was firmly placed on the doorknob. There was Julian, in all his naked glory, water glistening off his chiseled physique. He was freshly showered and stepping out onto the tile.

My gaze shifted from his face, to his chest, to the place I had no business looking.

His cock.

Jesus.

I. Stopped. Breathing.

Licking my lips, I actually envisioned myself licking from the V in between his hips and tracing my tongue down to his dick. The memories of us showering together and having sex under the showerhead immediately assaulted my mind.

When my lustful glare finally met his, I noticed the cockiest fucking grin plastered on his handsome face, and it instantly washed away all the desire I was feeling for him. It didn't matter he was fully aware of the effect he still had on me which was more than likely the reason he decided to use my shower instead of the one in the guest bedroom. Knowing I'd walk in here with a towel in my hands to drool over his perfect dick.

"What are you doing in here?" I asked, throwing the towel at him, and he caught it mid-air.

"What does it look like I'm doing, kid? I'm showering," he simply stated, drying off and not bothering to cover his cock.

"No shit, smart ass. But why are you showering in my room?"

"I wasn't aware you assigned showers for your guests."

I rolled my eyes. "Don't play that game with me. You know exactly what you're doing. Down to telling Capri to ask me to bring you a towel."

"I don't know what you're implying. All I wanted was to shower. It isn't my fault you don't know how to control yourself, and you're still staring at my cock."

"Oh my God! Then fucking cover it!"

He laughed, wrapping the towel around his waist. "Seeing as I have no clothes, I might have to wear just this towel for the rest of the night."

"I'm sure I can find something of Christian's for you. He's always leaving his clothes behind when he comes to visit."

"Or I can use the clothes you've stolen from me over the years."

"Like I still have them."

"I saw my black hoodie in your closet, kid."

My mouth dropped open. "You snooped through my things?"

"No, but it got you to admit you still have my shit."

I glared at him.

"You shouldn't poke the bear."

"Oh, so you're the bear now? Here I thought you were the asshole."

He winked. "Sweetheart, I can be both."

"You're just a shameless bastard at this point."

"At least I'm not asking you to call me daddy."

"Ewww ... don't ever say that again."

He chuckled, tugging on the ends of my hair. "Have I told you how beautiful you look today?"

I smirked. "Just today?"

"You know you're drop-dead gorgeous, kid."

"What's with the flattery? What do you want?"

"For you to tuck me in."

"It's too early for your bedtime, Mr. Locke."

"We're back to Mr. Locke, are we?"

Backing away from the bathroom, I informed, "Dinner's almost ready. I don't think your hoodie is going to fit you anymore. You're bigger than you were back then."

He arched an eyebrow. "How about my cock? Is that bigger too?"

"No." I shrugged. "It wasn't ever that big to begin with."

He growled as he reached for me, but I was quicker and jumped out of his grasp.

"I'll get you some of Christian's clothes. Don't come out of my room. I don't want to scar our daughter with her thinking men are all this small."

This time I wasn't fast enough, and he threw me over his shoulder and smacked my ass so fucking hard.

"Julian!"

"I'll show you fucking small, kid."

"Put me down!"

"Keep your voice down, or our daughter is going to think I'm torturing you."

"Umm … you're spanking me! Same difference!"

"If you'd be a good girl, you wouldn't need any discipline."

"Julian, put me down!"

He did, tossing my ass on my bed. Except, he hovered over my body and caged me in with his arms around my face. My heart beat rapidly against his chest, feeling his dick against my core.

To prove his point, he thrust against my pussy. "How's that for small?"

I smiled. "Didn't feel a thing."

With that, he flipped me over and pinned my hands above my head, locking my wrists together.

Rasping, "I used to love you in this position."

I inadvertently moaned.

"There's my good girl."

When his hand slipped in between my legs, Capri called out, "Momma, Daddy? Where did you guys go?"

"I guess it's true what they say about kids being little cock blockers." He let me go, and I got up, slapping him on the chest.

"Don't look so disappointed," he teased. "You could always play with your pussy later with the arsenal of toys you have in your drawer."

My face paled. "You *did* snoop through my thi—"

Capri walked in. "There you are." She peered back and forth between us, smiling. "What are you guys doing?"

"I was just about to get your dad some clothes. Do you know where Uncle Christian left his sweats and sweater the last time he was here?"

"I think they're in the laundry room cabinet. I'll get it for you, Daddy." She excitingly ran out of the room.

"Payback's a bitch," I threatened in a lighthearted tone. "Just wait until I snoop through your things."

"What's mine is yours—you can look through anything."

I tried to hide the smile on my face as I walked out the room to go finish dinner, playing it off like his words didn't affect me.

Julian

Autumn cooked my favorite dish, and we ate together as a family. It was crazy how effortless this was. How natural it felt being here in her home, watching as she finished up dinner while Capri set the table. I enjoyed watching their routine, thankful to be a part of it. How Autumn was able to balance being a successful publicist, and a loving and attentive mother was not lost on me.

It was sexy as fuck.

She was amazing with our daughter, and I could tell that she and Capri were very close. Seeing their special relationship warmed my heart. Making me realize how much I'd truly missed out on.

After Autumn introduced Emily to me, she told her to stay and eat with us, but Emily didn't want to intrude, saying she wanted us to eat together alone.

During dinner, Capri asked, "Daddy, what was your high and low today?"

I cocked my head to the side. "High and low?"

"Yes. My high was meeting you, my low was eating this broccoli."

I chuckled.

"It's just this thing we do during dinner."

Capri nodded. "Momma, what was yours?"

"Well, my high was coming home to you. My low was… I don't think I had a low today."

"That was your high, kid?"

Her eyes burned, understanding my subtle reference to what had happened on my plane earlier today."

"Kid?" Capri noted. "Why do you call Momma kid? She's not a kid. She's big."

"She wasn't always."

"You knew Momma when she was a kid?"

"I've known her since she was born."

She beamed. "Really?"

I nodded.

"What was she like? When she was my age?"

"A lot like you."

"That's what everyone says."

"She was always up to no good."

"Not true," Autumn disagreed. "I was always a good girl."

"And look how much that's changed."

"How did you know Momma?"

"Well, I was her b—"

"I think that's enough questions for tonight."

"Oh, come on, Momma…"

I grinned, loving the fact I had another teammate now. Two against one were always the best odds. After Autumn finished clearing the table, she told Capri to go get ready for bed while loading the dishwasher.

I grabbed the glass out of her hand. "You cooked—I got this."

"You're going to clean up?"

"I do know how to load a dishwasher."

She smiled. "You're Alpha CEO now. I assumed you had maids who do everything for you."

"I do, but you're not my maid, kid."

Taking the glass out of my grasp, she suggested, "Why don't you go tuck Capri in. I'm sure she'd love that. She picks out a book, and I read it to her, but she's usually passed out before I get to the third page."

I didn't want to intrude on their time. "Are you sure?"

"I've read her a bedtime story for the last nine years. I think I can give you one night."

"You know I'm going to want a lot more than one night."

"I know, but let's begin with one."

"Fair. I'd like for Capri's life to stay as normal as possible, and also for Emily to live at the ranch with us."

"I'd love that."

"Great. Let her know I'll be responsible for her salary now."

She shook her head. "You don't need to pay her. I've been pay—"

"You have me now."

"You're not going to let me win this, are you?"

"I don't lose, kid."

"Fine."

I left before she could change her mind, walking up the stairs to Capri's room. She was already laying in her bed with a book in her hands. Her bright green eyes lit up when she realized I'd be tucking her in.

I didn't have to look up to know Autumn was watching us from the doorway, listening to every word I was reading. I could feel her presence anywhere, and for years I felt it from states away. Although, Capri fell asleep in the crook of my arm, I continued until I was done with the story. I didn't want to let her go. I was going to capture every moment for as long as I could. Once I was done, I kissed her forehead.

"Hmm... I love you, Daddy."

I froze hearing her say those words to me for the first time. Letting my lips linger, I replied, "I love you too, baby."

By the time I actually left Capri's room, it was well into midnight. On my way to the guest bedroom, I walked by Autumn's door. It was closed, and I resisted the urge to open it and demand to sleep in her bed. I'd been demanding everything else, and this shouldn't be any different.

When my hand was on the doorknob, I heard her exclaim, "That son of a bitch!"

I smiled, I couldn't help it. Deciding I didn't need to sleep in her bed for her to know I was near. She was about to play with herself, thinking about me.

Too bad for her...
I stole all her toys.

Twenty-Six

Julian

"Wow," Capri breathed out, looking all around. We'd just taken off. "You have your own plane?"

"I have three."

"My daddy has three planes! That's so cool! Momma, did you hear?"

"I heard." Autumn was sitting the furthest away from me, staring out the window.

She was quiet which was never a good thing. It usually meant she was overthinking. It didn't matter that she was no longer the eighteen-year-old girl I'd left, her personality hadn't changed. I could still read her like the back of my hand. She might have thought she wasn't the same young girl, but in reality, she absolutely was.

"Daddy, what do you do that you have so much money?"

I chuckled, and Autumn scolded, "Capri! You can't ask—"

"I'm an entrepreneur, and you can ask me anything."

Autumn groaned, snapping her attention out the window.

"What does entrepreneur mean?"

"It means I made something from nothing."

"Oh, that's so cool. How do I do that? I want to make a lot of money too."

"Capri!"

I laughed. She had no filter, exactly like me. "I'll tell you what, baby girl. You can take over my empire one day."

"Really?" Her gaze went wide. "I can be an entrepreneur too! Momma, did you hear? I'm going to be just like Daddy!"

Autumn pinched the bridge of her nose. "Julian, do you have any pain meds? I have a pounding headache."

I pressed the button by my chair.

"Yes, Mr. Locke," Katie, the stewardess, announced through the speakers.

"I'd like some ibuprofen."

"Yes, sir. I'll be right out."

"Daddy, do you always order people around?"

I grinned.

"Momma says I'm bossy." She shrugged, giggling. "I guess I get it from you."

"You're too smart for your own good." In my eyes, she was perfect.

"Daddy, do you think we can get a puppy?"

"Capri," Autumn chimed in. "I already told you. I don't have time to take care of a puppy."

"I know, Momma, but it'd be *my* puppy, so I would take care of it."

"I can barely get you to clean your room."

"Why do I have to clean my room when we have a cleaning lady?"

I nodded. "Valid point."

Autumn rolled her eyes. "Why do you think we have a cleaning lady?"

"But, Momma, a puppy would give me responsibilities. Don't you want me to be a responsible child?"

This kid.

"No puppy, Capri."

"I didn't ask you—I asked my daddy."

"Sweetheart, don't speak to your mother like that." I winked at her. "Even though you have a solid argument."

She smirked, reminding me so much of her mother. Christian was right—I swear, Capri could be Autumn's twin.

"Daddy, can I tell you about all my favorite things?"

"I'd love that."

She unbuckled her seatbelt and walked across the aisle to sit next to me. For the next hour, she did all the talking. Catching me up on her favorite colors, shows, books, clothes, numbers, food, ice cream, and everything else in between. I loved every single second of it.

When she grabbed my hand, laying her head on my arm, I was a fucking goner. She had me wrapped around her little finger, and I'd only met her a few hours ago. Kissing the top of her head, I allowed my lips to linger for a moment before I leaned my chair back and laid against the headrest. I never slept much, but having my baby girl holding me close made it easy to pass out.

I woke up to the airplane landing, and Capri was now in my arms, her head on my chest with half her body over mine. There was a blanket covering us, and I didn't have to wonder who did that, knowing it was Autumn. Our stares connected. Her eyes were red, and her face was flushed. She'd been crying.

I cocked my head to the side, silently asking.

She replied, "I just have a migraine."

I opened my mouth to respond, but the pilot announced through the speakers we were home. Unaware of how true his words were, Capri grabbed my hand, holding the stuffed animal I'd bought for her, not wanting to meet her for the first time emptyhanded.

My driver was waiting for us on the tarmac. I opened the door for Capri and Autumn. After they were inside the SUV, I sat down, and Capri slid closer to my side again. I could sense Autumn was getting jealous of the attention she was giving me. She was used to having her all to herself. Instead of allowing it to become an issue, I moved a seat over from her, leaving the empty one in the middle for Capri.

Autumn hid back a smile when she realized I'd done that for her.

Autumn

In less than an hour, we were driving past the gold security gates of Julian's estate. To say this ranch was massive would be a definite understatement. I'd seen some huge properties with my clients, but this one might take the cake. We drove down a long, circular driveway which was surrounded by beautiful landscaping and a fence that looked like it was made out of high-end wood. No one could see onto the land unless they had access to enter though the security box.

A ranch-style home was in the center of the open field, surrounded by stone pathways in between the tall columns that split up the different wings of the house. There was a big garage port on the side of the main home, where I imagined several of Julian's vehicles were housed. The smell of the farmhouse from the back of the estate made me smile wide.

"Wow, Daddy." Capri took the words right out of my mouth. "Is this where we're going to live?"

He simply nodded as if this place wasn't incredible. His driver parked in front of the courtyard doors, revealing four older women dressed in maid uniforms. They greeted us as we exited the SUV. Of course, Julian instantly dismissed them with a wave of his hand.

"You don't have to be an asshole to everyone, you know?" I whispered in his ear.

"But it's one of my best qualities, kid."

I rolled my eyes, walking into the house where angled grand stairs were the first thing you see. It opened to a wide foyer with shiny marble floors. Walls as far as I could see. I let go of Capri's hand, knowing she wanted to look around and wander.

"Daddy! Can I go see my room?"

He gestured to one of the maids, who quickly took over and led her up the stairs, away from us.

My jaw dropped as I turned in a full circle, taking in my surroundings. I only stopped to look at him. He nodded again with a small smile playing on his lips, giving me the okay to go explore. I made my way into the stunning main sitting area. The sun was shining bright through every window in the wide-open space, illuminating the furniture and décor.

I heard his footsteps coming in my direction, abruptly stopping when they were close. I turned around, peering at him as he leaned against the archway, his strong arms crossed over his chest.

"This house is exactly what I described to you, Julian."

"I'm fully aware."

"How did you find this?"

"I had it built like this for you."

"What?" My voice echoed through the mansion.

His intense gaze never left mine. "I bought the land and had it built several years ago. It was initially supposed to be an investment property that I would eventually sell off, but I could never bring myself to actually do it. Up until yesterday, I had every intention of following through, but when the terms of our agreement changed, I figured the time had finally come to put your ranch to good use."

"Julian . . . several years? We only just saw each other a week ago. Why did you build my dream home when we weren't in each other's lives?"

"It's really quite simple, kid. I was going to come back for you."

My eyes widened. "What? When?"

"After I bought the land."

"Then why didn't you?"

"Because old habits die hard. I broke your heart and didn't know where to begin to piece it back together. Each year, I told myself this would be the year I'd come for you. Then the following would come around, and history repeated itself. I just didn't know where to start with you anymore."

"Oh my God."

He stepped toward me, and I stepped back, holding my hand up to stop him. He raised his hands in a surrendering gesture, meaning me no harm. However, it wasn't his caress I was afraid of this time. His words were affecting me far more than his touch.

"All I want is to make a life with you here, Autumn."

"Julian, my mind is spinning."

"For the first time in my life, mine isn't. I'm standing in front of you, hoping that you'll stand with me."

"Jesus," I breathed out. "And I thought you were coming on strong before."

"I go after what I want. It's who I am, it's how I'm made. I don't ask for anything, kid. Yet, here I am, asking you to be with me. Truly be with me. Out in the open—no secrets, no hiding. Where we're together and nothing else matters. I know you still love me, and I'm not asking for this to happen overnight. But I have a month, and I need you to seriously consider what I'm saying. You can't push me away forever. You have to give me a chance. Not just for us, but for our daughter too. She deserves to have what you had growing up, Autumn. Two loving parents under the same roof, a family." He grinned. "And several siblings."

"Siblings?"

"Yes, I plan to knock you up. A lot."

"Do you hear yourself right now?"

"I'm not the one who needs to hear me, kid, it's you."

"I don't know what to say. I barely know what to think when it comes to you."

"I'm coming for you. And it's going to make this last week look like child's play compared to what I have planned for us this month."

My heart beat rapidly against my chest, waiting for I don't know what. At this point, I wouldn't be surprised if he got down on one knee and professed his undying love. The irony was not lost one me. For years I waited for this exact moment, even after he'd left. Now, here it was, and I didn't know how to handle it.

Without wavering, he finally uttered the three little words I'd been waiting for all my life...

"I love you," he expressed all in one breath. "I've always fucking loved you, Autumn."

Although my mind was a jumbled mess, I knew without a shadow of a doubt that this was the first time he'd ever professed those words to anyone before.

And the fact that it was me resonated deeply.

Twenty-Seven

Autumn

Then

I T HAD BEEN OVER TWO MONTHS SINCE I'D LOST MY VIRGINITY, AND Julian and I were spending a lot of time together behind everyone's backs. We were lucky that Christian was engaged to Kinley, spending most of his time at her place, letting their apartment become our little oasis.

We spent a great deal of time at their place, pretty much christening every surface we could. From his bedroom, to the couch, to the kitchen counter, against the wall, in the shower, in the tub, on the floor, on his dining table, and even on his bedroom furniture. There wasn't an inch of my body he hadn't explored. Even down to my back door.

Yeah … he'd stolen that from me too.

"What are you thinking about over there, kid?"

I smiled. We'd just eaten dinner. He'd cooked me spaghetti and meatballs.

"Of all the spots we've had sex here."

He grinned. "I think we've covered every crevice by now."

I was on the pill, and Julian definitely took advantage of that. Saying I was the first girl he'd ever gone bareback with.

"What would you do if Christian came home right now?"

He lifted his phone in the air, showing me the text from him, confirming he was indeed staying the night at Kinley's.

"What do you think about them getting married in a few months?"

He shrugged. "I don't think anything. It isn't my life."

"I know, but he's still your best friend. Are you scared you're going to lose him to married life?"

"That isn't what I'm scared of losing him to." With that, he got off the couch and walked into the kitchen. I knew what he meant by his not so subtle response.

"Is that the end of our conversation?"

Opening the fridge, he grabbed a beer. "I wasn't aware we began one."

"You can't fool me. I know everything about you. Especially when you're blowing me off."

He twisted the cap from the bottle and threw it in the trash before making his way over to me. "It's why I fuck you so much. I need you to keep me around despite my shitty personality."

"Your personality is not shitty, Julian. I'd say you were more of an alpha asshole than shitty."

His hand went under the blanket, tickling my inner thigh. I laughed, thrashing around.

"You need to go put some clothes on."

"I thought you preferred me naked."

"I do, but I want to take you somewhere."

"Where?"

He smiled, big and bold. "For a joyride."

I arched an eyebrow, confused where he was going with this.

"You better hurry before I change my mind and eat you out instead."

"Well…" I giggled. "That isn't going to get me to move any quicker. If anything, I think I'll lay here and make you follow through with your threat."

He laughed, pulling off his hoodie to throw it over my body. Grabbing my panties off the floor next, he stated, "You won't be needing these anytime soon."

For a moment, I took in his chest and arms. Making my mouth water. Julian was a work of art. Chiseled muscles, broad shoulders and back, a six-pack showcasing a V—he was completely breathtaking.

"If you keep looking at me like that, we're not going to be leaving this couch, and I really want to take you for a ride."

"All the more reason to keep looking at you then."

Grabbing my hand, he pulled me up and put his hoodie on me instead. "I like seeing you in my clothes, kid."

"Good, because I love wearing them."

Holding my hand, he dragged me off the couch and led the way into his garage. When he opened the door, I gasped. There in front of my eyes, was a bright green Audi R8.

My eyes shifted to him. "Did you rob a car dealership today?"

He chuckled. "No, not today."

Julian always had different cars every month. They were usually classic cars he'd fix up. This was new.

"Who's is this?"

He winked. "If I told you, I'd have to kill you."

I laughed. "You're wicked."

Rounding the front of the car, he opened the driver's side door. "Want to go for a ride?"

"You're serious?"

"I mean, I'd much rather you ride my cock, but it'll happen soon enough. Especially if you go for a ride with me right now."

"I can't think of a better way to end my day."

He stepped inside the car, and I followed suit, sitting on the passenger side. He started the car, and the engine purred to life, vibrating my entire body.

Particularly my pussy.

"You feel that, kid?"

"I do."

"Good. I'm only getting started."

It all happened in a flash, although it felt like it played out in slow motion. The adrenaline pumping wildly through my veins was a feeling I'd never forget. I felt every roar of the car as his foot eased down on the clutch. Popping the shifter into reverse, he backed out of the garage.

"Holy shit!" I exclaimed. "This is amazing!"

Quickly shifting into second, then third, he tore down the street. Fifty, sixty, seventy miles per hour, he gunned it onto the highway. I watched in astonishment as he downshifted to first, fishtailing out onto an old, abandoned road. The only sounds that could be heard were the squealing tires while he did a burnout.

It was such a thrill.

I was hot, burning up. Part of it was from the engine, and the other was from Julian. The rush surging through his veins controlled his actions, and I was damn lucky it did.

The next thing I knew, he ordered, "Spread your legs for me, Autumn."

"What?"

When I didn't move fast enough, he did it for me. Reaching over, his hand slid in between my thighs. "I'm going to do two of my favorite things at once, driving this sports car and making you come."

Halting all the air in my lungs, I sucked in a breath as soon as he started rubbing my clit. He downshifted into second, jerking the wheel to make a sharp right turn. The car slid, and my head fell back from his skilled fingers working me over.

The engine revved as he shifted into fourth gear, sliding his finger inside me at the same exact time. The adrenaline coursing through me was releasing endorphins I didn't know I had, sky-rocketing my entire body and bringing me to a new high. It took over all my senses, my entire being. My chest heaved, trying to catch my breath.

"Oh God…" I panted, as he hit my g-spot over and over again.

Shifting from gear to gear, he floored it down the street, the speedometer indicating we were hitting ninety.

"Let's see what this baby can do."

"Julian…"

Going faster and faster, he ripped through the secluded back alley. Harder and harder he fucked me with his hand. Waves of ecstasy barricaded my mind as wetness rolled out of my core. Our heated emotions were running wild, fueling my need to come.

One hundred miles an hour.

One fifteen.

One twenty-five.

I was a ticking time bomb, counting down until I exploded.

The engine was loud, rumbling, coming to life the faster he drove. Taking everything along with it, like a tornado spinning around in circles. It elicited feelings I never thought possible.

I felt every loss of breath.

Every curve of his finger.

It cluttered my mind, and I couldn't keep up with his skilled assault.

"Come for me, Autumn."

That was all it took for me to fucking ignite. I shattered, coming apart at the seams. I came so hard that my vision blurred, and my body shook uncontrollably. Julian didn't miss a beat, slamming his foot on the brake, and causing the car to do a complete three-sixty. Around in a circle we went. My body flew to the side from the impact until we came to a stop.

Before I could say a word, he threw his seat back and gripped onto my waist and carried me onto his lap. His cock was out and inside me before I even blinked.

"Ride my cock, baby."

I didn't have to be told twice, I did as I was told—riding his dick as if I was in a rodeo. He gripped onto my hips and moved me harder against him. It was something I'd learned about him early on—Julian liked it rough.

"Come on my cock, Autumn, like you just came down my hand."

Once again, I exploded. Seeing fucking stars.

Galaxies.

A lunar eclipse.

I didn't hold back, repeating, "I love you, I love you, I love you."

Which was also new between us, I told him I loved him all the time. Every chance I could get. And since the first time I expressed those three words the night he stole my virginity...

He never stopped me anymore.

However, he never said it back either.

Twenty-Eight

Julian

Day of Locke Enterprises Announcement

MSNBC, FOX BUSINESS, AND YAHOO FINANCE WERE ALL SETTING up their camera equipment in my office on the ranch. Autumn wanted the world to know the man behind the expensive suits, and this was the perfect place for them to learn who I was.

Over the last three days, Autumn had kept her distance, and after what I shared, I knew that she would. I'd spent most of my time with Capri—my daughter was the light of my life. She was catching me up on the last nine years of hers, from all her favorite memories to her interests. I was surprised when I learned of her love for classic cars, considering I owned several. I had them imported from Miami, and now they were stored in the garage at our home.

We'd spent most of our time hanging out in the garage, her helping me fix up a few car projects that had kept my mind occupied when I needed to think of something other than work. Capri could barely hold in her excitement the day they'd arrived.

"Daddy!" She walked around the front of my 1967 Chevy Truck. "Are these all your cars?"

"Mmm-hmm."

"How do you have all these classic cars?"

"I've collected them over the years."

"That's so cool!"

"I'm glad you think so. Your mom wasn't much of a fan of your old man's

"Oh my God!" Autumn chimed in, walking up behind me. "That is not true—don't believe your father. I used to love all his cars. If you think these are something, he had an arsenal of them back in the day too."

"Really?" Capri exclaimed. "How many cars do you think you've owned in all your life?"

I thought about it for a moment. "At least fifty, sixty maybe."

Her eyes went wide. "Daddy, that's a lot."

"All those cars helped me figure out how to make an eco-friendly sports car."

Capri nodded. "That makes sense. Can I help you in the garage with these that still need to be finished?"

"I'd love your help." I gazed at Autumn. "Maybe your mom can help too?"

"Yesssss, Momma!"

"I think you guys can handle it on your own."

She walked inside, and I turned my attention to our baby girl, trying to play it off like I wasn't disappointed that Autumn didn't want to help us.

The best part of my day was when I'd walk in the house, wearing jeans and a shirt covered in grease and motor oil, my hands covered in it too, and I swear the look in Autumn's eyes had the power to bring me to my knees.

With a grin, I called her out, "Like what you see, kid?"

She instantly looked away, and I wasn't going to let this one go. I came up behind her, wrapping my arms around her waist.

"Julian! You're all messy."

"You used to love me all messy."

She turned around, placing her hands on my chest. "That was when I wasn't wearing a thousand-dollar dress."

I smiled. "I'll buy you a new one."

"I don't need you to buy me anything."

"I know you don't, but it doesn't mean I won't."

"You need to take a shower."

I grinned again. "You should join me. You know, to make sure I get everything off."

"I have a feeling that isn't the only thing you'd be getting off."

I laughed and backed away, leaving her with the residual effect of my touch.

My appearance brought me back to another place and time when she undeniably loved me, immediately making me regret the choices I'd made when it came to us. I tried not to let my mind wander to any of that. She knew where I stood, and all I could do was wait for her to come to me. After today, I hoped it'd lead her in the right direction.

Into my arms.

My life.

Our future as a family.

Capri walked into my office, where I'd be making the announcement of Locke Enterprises going public.

"Daddy, what does going public mean?"

I smiled. My daughter's thirst for knowledge resembled mine. "It means my company is going from a private entity to a public one where people can buy shares to make money."

"Oh…" She scratched her head. "I don't understand."

"It's a bit confusing. You'd have to learn about the stock market."

"Daddy, will you teach me?"

"Of course, baby."

"Good." She nodded. "Because I want to be just like you."

I beamed, hearing her say that made my heart soar every time.

"So you're going to tell the cameras, and then what?"

"They're going to ask questions."

"What kinds of questions?"

"Number, stats, reports—boring stuff like that."

"Are they going to ask you about us?"

"More than likely."

She cocked her head to the side. "What are you going to tell them?"

"What would you like me to tell them?"

"Hmm…" She thought about it for a second. "I think you should tell them all about us."

"I think you're right."

"Daddy." She sat on my lap, playing with my tie. "Can I be in the announcement with you?"

"If you'd like." At least one of my girls wanted to be seen with me.

Her eyes lit up. "Really?"

"Of course."

"Yay! I'm going to go change into my pretty yellow dress!" She jumped off my lap and ran out of my office, almost running into Autumn on her way out.

"Why is she in such a hurry?"

"She's—"

"Mr. Locke," the reporter interrupted. "We'll be ready to go soon."

I nodded.

"You clean up nice," Autumn coaxed, bringing my attention to her. "I've gotten used to you looking like you used to."

"Do you still like me all messy, kid?"

She blushed, bowing her head. "Should we go over what you need to say?"

"No," I replied, disappointed by her changing the subject yet again. "I can handle it."

"Okay. I'm going to go answer a couple of emails. I'll be back toward the end of the interview."

"Or you could stay, be in the announcement with me."

"I don't think that's a good idea."

"You're right—it's a great idea."

"Julian…"

"What more of a family man can I portray with you sitting beside me? It's what we're aiming for, right?"

"Yes, but this is your business, and I don't need to be involved in that."

"I'd love to have you involved in everything. Including my company. All I have is for us."

"Okay, Casanova, I'm going to get some work in. I'll be back in a bit to check on how things are proceeding."

Reluctantly, I let her go. What other choice did I have in the matter? At least our daughter would be present on one of the biggest days for my business. Capri hurried into my office, wearing a yellow sundress. Her hair was in pigtails, and she was holding the stuffed animal I'd bought her.

"I'm ready, Daddy." She posed for me. "How do I look?"

"Beautiful, exactly like you're mother."

She smiled, sitting on my lap. "Okay, let's do this."

I chuckled, I couldn't help myself. She was fucking adorable.

Lights.

Camera.

Action.

The reporters sat in their chairs while we were behind my desk. For the next ten minutes, I made my announcement with Capri never moving from my lap. She was smiling the entire time, nodding when she thought I'd said something important, really trying to understand what I was informing the world of.

She was a CEO in the making.

"Mr. Locke, how about we address the elephant in the room?" the MSNBC reporter stated. "Who is this gorgeous little girl who has taken over your announcement?"

They didn't know how to mind their own business on a normal day, let alone on an occasion like today. Question after question about my personal life was about to be thrown in my face. This was what Autumn wanted, and it was the least I could do after what I'd been putting her through.

"This is my baby girl, Capri," I hugged her close to my chest.

"Hi. I'm Capri, and I'm ten years old, but one day, when I'm bigger, I'm going to be just like my daddy."

I grinned, honored I'd become her hero.

"Your baby girl?" the Yahoo journalist chimed in. "Oh wow, so not only are we learning about Locke Enterprises officially going public, but you're also telling us you're a father?"

I nodded. "No better time than the present."

"And who is the mother of this lovely girl?" the same journalist questioned. "Although, I don't think you need to tell us. She looks identical to Miss Troy."

"Then I don't need to tell you."

"Tell us anyway," he added.

"Yes," Capri replied, handling them like a pro. She must get it from her mother. "My Momma is Autumn Troy, and she's the best publicist in all the world. My daddy is her client, and now we're a family."

Bringing her little hand up to my mouth, I kissed it. "I worship the ground her Momma walks on. Have for as long as I can remember."

"That's right!" another *Fox* interviewer exclaimed. "We all read *The New York Times* article—you two have known each other all your lives. Your relationship started when she was young, correct?"

"Something like that."

"We know you're a very private man, Mr. Locke, but I think we can all say we're loving this new you. Can you tell us about your first kiss?"

"Not with my daughter present."

Everyone laughed.

Even the loud eruption of chatter in the room didn't steal the memory of the first time I stole her mouth.

"To follow up on that question," *Yahoo* added. "In the article you said you've always loved Miss Troy. When did you know it was true love and she was the one?"

"I gravitated toward her without even realizing it was happening. She consumed me, I've always been held captive by the beauty that is Autumn Troy."

Autumn

I watched from the television in the other room with tears falling out of my eyes.

"As you read in the article, I was a foster kid. Her family is all I've ever known. If it weren't for them, especially her brother who used to be my best friend, she'd already be carrying my last name. I was a different man back then. If could I go back and make things right, I would."

My heart skipped a beat the second he went on with, "She's always been my whole world."

"Mr. Locke," *Fox Business* addressed. "Can we expect to see more children in your guys' future?"

"If it was my choice, she'd already be pregnant."

I can't believe he's sharing this. I wiped away the tears.

"How do you feel about that, Capri?"

"I'm not sure." She shrugged. "As long as I can still have my own pony."

Julian scoffed out a chuckle.

After all these years, all the bullshit we'd been through together, the ups and the downs. This moment seemed surreal.

Our spark.

Connection.

Love.

It was all wrapped into one.

The interview continued, and I prepared for the aftermath that was

Julian Locke. Once everyone left, I walked into his office. Capri was in the farmhouse, feeding the baby chickens.

"I can't believe you blindsided me. You couldn't have told me that our daughter was going to be in the announcement with you?"

"She requested it. And as you know, I can't say no to her."

"I've spent years making sure the press didn't find out I had a daughter, Julian. And you just throw her to the wolves without even discussing it with me first."

"We both know why you didn't want the press to know about Capri, and it has nothing to do with you protecting her from the world. You were hiding her from me."

"It doesn't matter. I still have the right to know what you're planning on doing when it concerns her."

"What do you want from me, sweetheart? You wanted the world to know the man behind the expensive suits, and I gave you exactly what you asked for. Now, you're giving me shit for it? You need to learn how to pick and choose your battles. This is a war in which you fucking started."

"Julian—"

"I'm not going to sit here and have you come for my balls. I did nothing wrong. You got what you asked for—end of story."

"Listen, you stubborn asshole—"

He slammed his fist on his desk before he was in my face, backing me up against the wall. Caging me in with his arms on either side of my face, he leaned forward close to my lips. "Why can't you just admit the real reason you're giving me shit, kid?"

His scent was making me dizzy, the smell of his cologne driving me insane.

"What's worse, Autumn? The fact that I told the world how much you own every last part of me, or the fact that you want me to kiss you right now?"

My eyes followed the movement of his mouth, and I swallowed hard, unable to wait any longer. In less than a second, I kissed him for the first time in what felt like a lifetime. He didn't hesitate, gripping onto my ass and wrapping my legs around his waist. Pinning my back against the wall, he devoured my mouth.

Our battle was far from over. We'd fight again, but for a moment, his words had me surrendering.

To him.

To us.

To our family.

Our kiss took on a life of its own. Something neither one of us could understand or deny. Something neither one of us could control. It seemed like all we had to do was look at each other and sparks flew from here to kingdom come. My lips parted as he slipped his tongue into my mouth, demanding a response that only he stirred within me.

He kissed me deeper.

Harder.

Slower.

My breathing picked up, engulfing him in nothing but my need to keep going and have him claim my body the way he used to.

But…

This time it wasn't me who stopped.

It was him.

He pulled away, dropping me on the ground to my feet. I lost my footing, trying to catch my balance. My legs were unsteady, wobbling from his embrace.

"Fuck," he rasped, backing away. "I won't play this game of cat and mouse with you anymore."

"Julian—"

"There's more at stake now, Autumn. You either want me, or you don't. I won't mess with Capri's emotions because you can't make up your mind."

I bowed my head. "I just… I don't want you to hurt me again. I won't survive it."

He tugged on the ends of my hair. "I love you, Autumn. I loved you then, I love you now, I'll love you always."

"Do you have any idea how long I waited for you to say that to me?"

"I know. I couldn't say it back then, but I can say it now. And I'll say it to you every single day for the rest of my life to make up for the years I didn't."

"Momma!" Capri ran into his office, breaking our intense conversation. "Did you see? I did the announcement with Daddy!"

"I did, baby. You were perfect."

She ran into her father's arms. "Thank you, Daddy. I'm so happy to have you in our lives. Promise me you won't leave this time?"

The pained expression on Julian's face rendered me speechless as he crouched to the floor, getting eye level with her.

Capri caressed his face. "I'm sorry. I didn't want to make you sad. I just don't want you to leave Momma again. Cause then you're leaving me too this time."

He kissed her hand. "You're stuck with me, baby girl. I love you more than anything."

She smiled while tears rimmed my eyes. "I love you too, Daddy." Throwing her arms around his neck, she hugged him tight.

He embraced her, except his gaze was locked with mine when he mouthed…

"I love you," to me.

Twenty-Nine

Autumn

Then

"A RE WE ALMOST THERE?" I QUESTIONED. MY ASS WAS NUMB from sitting in his car for the last three hours.

"How many times are you going to ask that question?"

"Depends on how much longer we have to drive to get there."

He glanced at me. "We're almost there, Miss Impatient."

"This better be the best classic car show ever."

"Would I lie to you?"

"So I would join you on this long-ass journey, maybe."

"One day I'll own every car we're about to see today, and then you're going to thank me for taking you to this."

"Cars are your thing, not mine."

"What's your thing, kid?"

"Mmm… I'm not telling, or you'll make fun of me."

"Do I ever tease you?"

"Every chance you get."

He grinned. "Tell me anyway."

"Nah."

"Come on, kid. Tell me your dreams. I want to hear them."

"Fine, but you can't make fun of me."

He did a cross over his heart.

"I want to own a ranch."

"A ranch?"

"Yes, with a farmhouse and animals."

"I can't see you shoveling shit, Autumn."

"I won't. I'll have a crew who will do that for me. My job is to feed them and give them all the love."

"And what kinds of animals live in your farmhouse?"

"Goats, chickens, pigs, horses, maybe a pony, cows—you know, the usual."

"I see. That's quite an interesting fairy tale."

"My house will be the best part, Julian."

Now that piqued his attention. "Your house?"

"Mmm-hmm…"

"You've thought about your house?"

"Of course. I'm a girl—I think about everything."

"Fair." He nodded. "Tell me about this house?"

"Well, it will have a huge iron gate that no one can get through unless they have the code. The estate will be private, surrounded by tall trees and beautiful landscaping. My house will be in the middle of the property, and it will be breathtaking. There will be marble floors, huge bay windows where the sun can come through in every square inch of the place. I want a grand angled staircase right when you walk in. A massive foyer. It will have the works."

"That's quite a floor plan. You've given this a lot of thought. Where did this dream come from?"

"We live in Texas. I think that answers for itself."

He laughed. "I like your dream."

"I didn't get to the best part yet?"

"You'll have a sex room?"

"Only if you want one." I giggled. "But I was talking about a massive carport where you store all your classic cars."

"Oh, I'm in your dream too?"

"Of course."

The expression on his face turned serious, and I quickly played it off like it wasn't a big deal when it was. I didn't want to scare him off, and Julian scared easily with anything that involved me.

"It's just a silly dream, Julian. You don't have to read that much into it."

He didn't say anything for what felt like forever, until he finally revealed,

"I think we should just stay in the here and now and not think too far ahead, Autumn. Especially when it comes to me in your future."

I flinched, quickly looking out the window. It was pointless to hide my emotions from him because he could sense my disappointment.

"Yeah, whatever you want."

"You know what I want?"

"Hmm…"

He gripped onto my inner thigh. "To hear that contagious laugh."

"Don't you dare—"

He squeezed, sending me reeling into a fit of laughter. Almost making me pee my pants.

"Please!"

"Begging me isn't going to help your disposition, kid. You know how much I love it when you beg me."

"Oh my God! Stop!"

He squeezed harder.

"You're going to crash the car!"

"If I can finger fuck you while I'm driving a sports car, I can certainly tickle you."

"Julian!"

"I love it when you scream my name." Finally, he stopped and pulled his hand away. "Now, be a good girl and tell me more about your dreams."

"I thought you didn't want to hear about my future?"

"I never said I didn't want to hear about it. I just don't want you to include me in them."

"You're my brother's best friend, and my parents consider you a second son—you're going to be in my future whether you want to or not."

"Is that all I am?"

I shrugged again, and neither one of us spoke for the rest of the drive. Once we parked in the open field, I opened the door, but he grabbed my hand and held me in place, and I looked over at him.

"I don't like it when you get quiet on me, kid."

"You weren't talking either."

I could see it in his eyes, he wanted to say something, and I eagerly waited for his response. Julian never gave me hope for the future. He knew I was head over heels in love with him. However, he never expressed his feelings for me, through actions or words. He never gave me an inch, and I stupidly waited for a centimeter.

Gripping onto the back of my neck, he kissed my lips. "I know your dreams will come true."

"Really?"

He nodded.

"How?"

Silence.

He simply pecked my mouth and exited the car. I was shocked as shit when he reached for my hand as we were walking toward the entrance of the car show. Julian never gave me any public affection, and I didn't know if he'd noticed that he was. Instead of making a big deal out of it, I internally squealed.

Maybe it was because we were hours away from home, and no one would know us here, but either way, it didn't matter. I cherished this moment and lived in the present with him.

Silently praying, my future consisted of only him.

Julian

Hearing her say she envisioned me in her dreams wasn't a surprise. It was the fact that I wanted what she was saying more than anything, but I refused to give her false hope. All we had were these stolen moments where no one could see us, and I didn't fear losing the only family I'd ever known.

Being thrown around like I was nothing more than garbage for all my adolescence made it hard to live in anything other than the present. Despite being on my own and that life far behind me, it was difficult to think of a future other than financial stability. Coming from nothing gave you another perspective on life. I valued each day for what it was, and not knowing what tomorrow would bring was the only way I'd survived for so long.

Autumn was the light in my life.

Her smile.

Her laugh.

Her love.

It was everything I'd ever wanted and didn't think I was worthy of.

Without her being aware of it, for the next few hours I showed her my world. I was determined to make something of myself and never again be that little boy always looking in at someone else's life. I wouldn't allow my mind to wander to a future that included Autumn.

All we had was the now, and I took full advantage of that.

"Which is your favorite car?"

I led her toward the black Lincoln Continental with the suicide doors, nodding to it.

"This is one sick ride, Julian."

"She is a beauty." And I wasn't referring to the car.

"Too bad we can't christen this one, huh?"

I pulled her into my side. "Never say never, Autumn."

If I had one life goal, it was to make love to her in that vehicle. At the end of the day, I couldn't tell her I loved her, even though…

I did.

By the time we got back to my apartment it was dinner time, and I ordered us a pizza and chicken wings. We were sitting on my bed when we heard the front door open. Our eyes went wide.

"Fuck," I breathed out.

Her car was in the driveway, there was no hiding she was there with me.

"Autumn?" Christian called out, and her eyes went wide.

Neither one of us moved, but the second we heard his footsteps coming toward my room we both stood up. Once he stopped in front of my door, his stare shifted back and forth between us until he focused on me.

"What is my little sister doing in your room?"

"Christian, I was looking for you," she replied, bringing his gaze to her.

"In Julian's room?"

"No." She smiled. "He was just showing me his new TV."

His eyebrows pinched together. "Mom says you've been hanging out here a lot, and I haven't been here much, so explain that one to me?"

"Christian, just ask what you want to know," I snapped, unable to bite my tongue.

"I just did. What's my little sister doing here all the time if I'm not here, Julian?"

"Stop calling me your little sister, I'm not a child."

"That doesn't answer my question, Autumn. What are you doing with Julian?"

"We're just hanging out. He's my friend too."

"Since when?"

"What are you insinuating?" Autumn asked, not backing down. "I've known him all of my life, Christian. It's no different than coming here to hang out with you."

"I'm your brother."

"Most of the time I'm looking for you."

"You can text me, and I can tell you if I'm here or at Kinley's."

"I will next time."

That response seemed to appease him, and I could see it in his eyes—he definitely suspected what was going on.

"Anyway, it's getting late. I'm going to head home." Autumn glanced back at me as she was leaving. "Good choice on the new TV. It's awesome." She hugged her brother. "I'll see you at dinner tomorrow."

Once we heard the front door close, Christian didn't waver. Not that I expected him to. "What the fuck was that?"

"I don't know what—"

"Don't give me that shit. You know exactly what I'm talking about. Why are you hanging out with my little sister?"

"You don't have to keep calling her that. I know what she is to you."

"Doesn't look like that to me."

"You need to relax. I was just showing her my new TV."

"What about all the other times she's been here? What were you doing then?"

"What are you insinuating, Christian?"

"You fuck anything that walks, Julian. I don't need to remind you Autumn's off limits, do I?"

I shook my head. There was no need for the reminder. I thought about it every time we were together, and when I was inside of her.

He nodded, slowly backing away, never taking his intense stare off of me. I knew what he wanted to ask…

Are you fucking my little sister?

He just couldn't bring himself to say it, and to be completely honest,

I wasn't sure if I'd be able to look him in the face and lie to him. He was my best friend, my brother, and I was fucking it all up by betraying his trust.

"Great, keep it that way." He turned and left.

For the rest of the night, I thought about what I was putting on the line for Autumn. His bachelor party was coming up, and I was going to have to prove to him one way or another that there was nothing going on behind his back.

My phone dinged with a text message, and I didn't have to wonder who it was. Grabbing my phone from the nightstand, I read it.

Please don't push me away again.

I didn't reply. I couldn't. Unable to lie to her.

Although, her text didn't matter. I knew deep down in every fiber of my being…

This was the beginning of the end for Autumn and me.

Thirty

J ULIAN WASN'T WORKING, AND NEITHER WAS I. AFTER THE AFTER-noon in his office last week, things had taken a turn for us. We started doing things as a family. Eating all our meals together, taking Capri to all of Julian's favorite places, and showing her a bit of our history. My favorite day was today—we took her to her first rodeo.

"Capri, your momma had a first here too."

"Julian…"

He leaned into her ear. "You want to know what it was?"

"Yesssss!"

Julian didn't heed my warning, simply stating, "She got her first kiss here."

I groaned, leaning against my seat.

"What?! Momma, who was your first kiss?"

"You're looking at him," he casually replied.

"Oh my God! Daddy was your first kiss? That's so romantic."

"Romantic isn't the word I'd use for it."

"Kid, I almost beat up your date for you. I think that classifies as romantic."

"You did?" Capri asked, completely enthralled and amazed that her father was suddenly Prince Charming.

"Your mom tried to make me jealous with a boy who was half my size."

"He was not half your size."

"The boy was a wimp. I would have swept the floor with him. It's the only reason I didn't. He would have wound up in the hospital, and everyone would have learned about us."

"What do you mean 'learn about you,' Daddy?"

"Your mom and I were secretly seeing each other without your grandparents and uncle knowing."

"Julian!" I scolded. "You did not just tell her that!"

"You want me to lie to our daughter?"

"Yeah, Momma, you want him to lie to your daughter?"

I laughed, it had become two against one.

"Tell me more, Daddy. Why did you have to hide?"

"Well, your uncle was very protective of your mom."

"Oh yeah," Capri agreed, nodding. "He's like that with me too."

Julian smiled. It was obvious he appreciated Christian looking out for our baby girl."

"So what happened?"

"It's a long story," I stated, not wanting to talk about this anymore.

"It's okay. We're in the intermission. Tell me, Daddy. I want to know."

Of course, he gave her what she wanted. "Your uncle used to be my best friend."

"Oh," Capri breathed out. "I didn't know that. He's never talked about you before. Is that why you left, Momma?"

"Something like that."

She scratched her head. "Do Grammy and Grampy know who you are?"

"They do. Your grandparents did a lot for me back then. I didn't have a family."

"What do you mean you didn't have a family?"

"My parents gave me up when I was born, and I was raised in foster homes."

Her mouth parted. "They gave you up? Daddy, I'm so sorry."

"There's nothing to be sorry about. I'm a better man for it."

She grabbed his hand and then mine, linking ours together. "It's okay. Because now you have us. We're your family. Right, Momma?"

Julian and I locked eyes.

"Yeah." I nodded. "Now you have us."

He beamed, not trying to hide it.

"Can you tell me more?"

"I'll tell you everything you want to know."

And he wasn't lying. Capri didn't stop until she knew everything about us. She'd spent most of the rodeo asking Julian our history versus watching the bull riders. As much as I loved watching the show, I couldn't help but pay attention to his every word.

Later that night, when we got back to the house, I went up to my bedroom and grabbed the photo albums I'd brought with me before I went back downstairs to find them on the couch, watching a movie. Capri was tucked into the crook of his arm, and I sat down beside her.

"Momma!" She recognized her baby album. "I didn't know you brought these."

"I did," I replied to her, only looking at her father. "I brought them for you too, Julian."

Julian

Capri grabbed her baby book, placing it on her lap. "Daddy, do you want to see?"

Unable to find the words of what I was feeling, I simply nodded. Her little hands opened the photo album, and right there in front of my eyes was a picture of her birth.

"She was six pounds, five ounces, and I was in labor for thirty-six hours."

It was like I was there, but I wasn't. It was the first time in I don't know how long that I felt so unbelievably helpless. I thrived on being in control, and in that moment, I had none. The more photos Capri showed me, the further my heart fucking broke. I'd never felt pain like this before. Not even when I'd left Autumn.

To see the last nine years of her life playing out before my eyes was a kick to my fucking stomach.

Autumn continued narrating all the pictures. From the first time she'd crawled, walked, ate solid food, to her first birthday, her first bike, her first everything. I'd missed it all. The longer I sat there hearing Autumn's voice and seeing all those memories I'd missed because she didn't tell me we had a daughter, the further the pain inside of me grew, and it quickly turned into anger.

Fury blazed through me like a fucking tornado, taking down everything in its path.

"Daddy, are you okay?"

I abruptly stood, needing a second to compose myself before I lost my shit on Autumn in front of Capri.

"Capri," Autumn coaxed, taking the album off her lap. "Honey, I think this is a lot for your daddy to take in. Let's show him the rest later, alright?"

"Yeah, okay. Daddy, can you tuck me into bed?"

I nodded again. I was so pissed I could barely see straight, but I kept it together for Capri. Holding her hand, I led her out of the living room and into her bedroom. She went to her bookshelf and grabbed a story. I couldn't tell you what it was. I moved in autopilot, reading it to her. She passed out cold before I finished, and I kissed the top of her head. Capri was a solid sleeper, and nothing could wake her up.

"I'm so sorry," I found myself whispering to her, needing to get it out. I had to say it to her. Although she couldn't hear me, it felt like I owed it to our daughter. "I missed so much of your life, and I'm trying so hard to let it go. But… I can't get those years back. With you or your mother. I feel like I failed both of you, and I'd give everything I have to get back that time with you." A tear slid down my face, and my chest heaved.

I was a grown-ass man. However, in that moment, I felt like nothing more than a father who'd wished he could have been there to watch his baby girl grow up. I missed out on so much, and I didn't have anyone but myself to blame. I wanted to take my anger out on Autumn, and a part of me felt some resentment brewing.

She could have told me.

I would have been there.

God, I would have fucking been there.

"My life hasn't been easy. My parents didn't want me, and I always promised myself I would never be like them. I would never abandon my children, and yet here I am, hoping that one day you won't hate me for missing so much of your little life. The things I've seen, the stuff I've endured, I wouldn't wish that on anyone. I can't help thinking that maybe I'm being punished for something because why would your mother not tell me about you? Why would she do this to me? Knowing how I grew up?"

More tears slid down the sides of my face, and I felt as if I was breaking down, shattering in my baby girl's bed with her in my arms and her mother in my heart.

"Seeing those pictures of you tonight… I don't think I've ever felt pain quite like this before. I thought I could get past it. I thought I could push through. But seeing you, so little, so innocent, looking so much like your mother, it's just… I'm finding it hard to breathe. I can't tell you how profoundly sorry I am for not being your daddy. When all I've ever wanted was to have one of my own. I swear to you. I promise you I will be there for you for the rest of your life. I won't miss another milestone, another moment, another birthday. It's me and you, Capri."

The sound of a shudder brought my attention to the door. Autumn was standing there. Fucking wrecked. Her face was flushed with tears streaming down her face.

"I'm so sorry, Julian. Please… I'm just so fucking sorry. I never meant to hurt you. I never met for Capri to not have a father. I was young and stupid, and if I could go back, I swear I'd change everything. I would have told you. I would have begged you to stay for us, but you broke my heart. You killed me inside, and for years it felt as if I was only surviving for our daughter. I thought about you every day. There were so many times I wanted to call you and tell you, but I couldn't find the words to say that I'd fucked up. When I finally did find the nerve to call you, your number was disconnected, so was your email. I couldn't reach you. What else was I supposed to do? I hate myself for hurting you. I hate myself for hurting her. I just… Fuck…" She sucked in a breath, her body shaking, her heart breaking. "I never stopped loving you. Not for a second, a minute, an hour. I've loved you all my life. All I ever wanted was you, and I know the only reason I was able to go on was because you'd left me with a huge part of you."

"Autumn." I sighed, getting off the bed, careful not to wake Capri. "I don't want to resent you, but I'm not going to lie to you. I'm trying to forgive you for keeping her from me for nine years when you know without a shadow of a doubt I would have been there. By your side, through it all."

"You said it yourself, Julian. Old habits die hard, and it was the same for me. I didn't know where to reach you, and when you became this big shot and were all over the news and tabloids, it was hard to see you for the man you once were. You know what everyone said about you, and I couldn't bring myself to tell you about Capri because I was terrified you were that man everyone said you were. And I wasn't going to let you break her heart too."

"I became that man because I'd left my heart and soul with you."

Her hands flew to her face as she openly began to bawl. "I don't know how to fix this. Maybe we're just too broken beyond repair. We've both hurt each other so much, and I can't keep doing this. It hurts too fucking much."

"Kid—"

"I love you, okay? I fucking love you."

She turned to leave, and I chased her down the hall. Grabbing her arm, I turned her to face me, but I couldn't get a word in. She started hitting my chest, her fists pounding into my pecs.

"Why?! Why did you have to lie to me? Why couldn't you just have faced them with me? We could have told them! They would have accepted it! My parents loved you, and so did Christian! Why did you have to break us?"

I let her hit me.

Over and over again.

I wanted her agony. I deserved it.

"I'm sorry, kid. I'm so fucking sorry."

"You ruined us! We could have been a family!"

"Don't you think I know that? Don't you think I fucking hate myself for it? I can't change the past, and looking at that photo album proved it. I want so desperately to make things right with you. I can't live without you anymore. Not after being with you these last few weeks. My life belongs to you, Autumn. Always has, and it always will."

She sobbed, falling to the floor, and I went with her. I held her in my arms.

Until there were no more tears.

No more hurt.

No more mistakes.

Until there was nothing but the future for ours to take.

I carried her into my bedroom and stripped off all our clothes.

Leaving us bare where only our skin touched. I didn't kiss her, I didn't make love to her, I didn't do any of the things I truly longed for.

Instead, I held her close to my heart. Where she could feel it only beating for her. She cried most of the night, and I kissed away every last tear. Breaking down with her.

Knowing we both needed this ... to heal.

Thirty-One

THE DAY HAD FINALLY COME, AND MY FAMILY, INCLUDING MY brother and Kinley, were coming over for the day. Julian had invited everyone. This was the first time I was going to see my brother since our altercation over two weeks ago. We'd been living here for seventeen days, and the truth was—it was starting to feel like home. Capri was loving every second of it, and I'd be lying if I said I wasn't also.

I was beyond nervous of what today would bring. Fully aware of Julian's intentions, they were pure. He wanted my family in his life. I knew he'd missed them, probably in the same way I'd missed him. Christian didn't want to attend our gathering at first, but our mom was able to change his mind.

Julian spared no expense, having it fully catered with some of my family's favorite food. The liquor bar was stocked, our home was ready, and the atmosphere was perfect. The minute my parents' SUV pulled up, Capri hauled ass outside to greet them. We hadn't seen my parents in a couple of months, the same with Christian other than the day at the restaurant.

"Grampy!" Capri jumped into my dad's arms.

"Sweet pea, look how big you've gotten!"

"I know! Momma says I've grown an inch since you last saw me. What do you think, Grammy? Do I look bigger?"

My mom hugged her tight. "You sure do. You have to stop growing, or who's going to be my baby girl?"

"I'd love to give you another grandchild, several actually."

He hasn't seen my parents in over a decade, and that's the first thing he says to them?

"Julian," Mom announced, looking at him with so much affection in her stare. "You always did speak your mind. It was one of the things I loved the most about you."

He smiled, and she didn't hesitate, opening her arms to give him a hug. They embraced, and my father hugged him too, all of them peering at each other with warmth and love.

"Look how handsome you are." Mom beamed. "I always knew you'd accomplish big things. We can't tell you how proud we are of you."

"Thank you," he replied. "You have no idea how much that means to me, and I just want to start off by saying I'm so sorry about—"

She waved him off. "It's in the past. You're here now, and that's all that matters."

"The way I left after everything you guys did for me. It's inexcusable, and I'll spend the rest of my life trying to make things right with the both of you."

"We just want you to be happy. It's all we've ever wanted."

"I know." He looked over at me. "Autumn has always been the woman to do that for me."

I hadn't spoken to my parents about anything pertaining to Julian since *The New York Times* article hit the stands. I didn't know what to say, and I figured it was better to discuss it in person than over the phone or through text. The expression on Mom's face was enough—she had questions. Lots of them.

We showed them around the estate, and I could tell my parents were enamored with the property. It was as if no time had passed between Julian and my parents. Despite them being hurt by his actions, I always knew they wouldn't hold a grudge. Now, my brother was a much different story. Christian and Julian had been best friends, and Christian had missed Julian like I did when he'd left. At least I got a goodbye—not a very good one but one, nonetheless.

Julian went out to the farmhouse with my dad and Capri, while my mom and I stayed behind in the kitchen.

Which was made for a queen.

Me.

"Okay, spill, Autumn. I can't hold it in anymore. You've been ignoring my calls and texts."

"I wasn't ignoring you."

"Then how do you explain every miscall and text?"

"I just didn't know what to say. When I first learned about the article, I was so mad at Julian."

"First learned? You didn't know about it either?"

"Absolutely not! I would never want any of you to find out that way, but Julian … he's Julian Locke, Alpha CEO, and he does what he wants."

"He's always done what he's wanted, Autumn. You were too young to realize that before."

"I've always known. I just ignored it back then."

"And now?"

"He drives me absolutely insane."

"What's going on between you two? Is it true? Are you guys together because of the way that man looks at you, I can't imagine this is just a publicity stunt."

"I don't know what we are, and that's the honest truth."

"Alright… And the article? What happened back then?"

I deeply sighed. "We lied to everyone."

"So he was your first love? You were his?"

"Yeah, well, I mean he was mine, but I didn't know I was his until the article hit the stands."

"Oh wow." She shook her head, dumbfounded. "How did we not see any of this?"

"We were really good at hiding."

"I guess I don't understand why you guys were hiding in the first place."

"We didn't think you guys would approve, and we knew Christian definitely didn't."

"Oh, honey … all we've ever wanted is for you to be happy. Both of you. And if you found that with one another, who are we to say anything about it? Your brother has always been so overprotective of you, but he would have eventually come around. His little sister, his best friend, he couldn't ask for a better outcome."

"You would think, but you should have seen him a few weeks ago when Julian told him to meet us at a restaurant."

"I saw your brother's busted lip. I can imagine what happened."

"Did he tell you?"

"He told us he saw you guys, and Julian and he exchanged words. Christian is hurt, but he'll come around."

"I can't believe you guys are so forgiving. I know how sad you were with the way he left."

She lovingly smiled. "Honey, it was a long time ago. Julian has always been a very complex man, even as a child. At first, of course, his abrupt departure was painful, but I know he didn't mean to hurt us. Now, finding out about you guys, I understand why he thought leaving the way he did was the best idea."

"Really? Because I barely understand it."

"You were raised in a loving home. Julian may have stayed at our house a lot, but he's always been thrown away like he was nothing more than yesterday's garbage. Kids that are abandoned like he was and thrown into the system usually tend to mess everything up before someone they love can do it for them. It's sad, and I'm not making excuses for him. I know he believed he was doing what was in everyone's best interest."

I nodded. "I know. I'm glad you guys are so forgiving. You mean a lot to him. He loves you, both of you."

"And we love him. He's always been a special boy, and we knew he'd amount to great things. I had a suspicion it would be something to do with cars. He's always had a passion for them. How are he and Capri? From the looks of it, they've already taken to each other."

"They're two peas in a pod. I'm the odd man out these days."

"Give it time. It will all work itself out."

"I'm trying."

She pulled me into a firm embrace, murmuring, "All the pieces will fall together."

"I love you, Mom."

"I love you more."

The front door opened, and Christian called out, "Autumn?"

I pulled away and swallowed hard, making my way toward the front door to greet him. "Hey."

He smiled, pulling me into a tight hug, and I was relieved. My brother was very important to me, and I didn't want us to have any issues. Especially when it came to Julian and me.

"Hey, Kinley." I hugged her next, whispering into her ear, "Thank you for making him come."

"Believe it or not," she replied. "He came willingly."

Which surprised me more than anything.

Julian

"Daddy! Do you see? Look! I'm riding Buttercup all by myself!"

"I see, Capri!"

She was riding her pony with one of the ranch employees, while Autumn's father and I were talking.

"I want to thank you for coming today."

He put his hand on my shoulder, reminding me of all the times he did. "You look good, Julian. Happy, content, relaxed. Fatherhood suits you, son."

I nodded, feeling his encouragement in the same way I did as a boy. With just a couple of words, he always had the ability to make me feel like I was wanted, cared for, loved...

"I don't think I've ever felt this happy about anything in all my life."

"Not even when you grossed your first million?"

"Money has never made me happy. I don't think I've ever taken a moment to realize how far I've come. I'm always contemplating what's next, what happens now. It was so hard for me to be present until Autumn came back into my life. All I was doing was moving from one day to the next, but for the first time in over a decade, I'm actually standing still and enjoying every second of life. I haven't worked since I made Locke Enterprises announcement, and it's been some of the best days of my life."

"Glad to hear it. You deserve it."

I looked into his eyes. "I've always admired the man that you are. Always strived to be like you. I can't tell you how relieved I am to know you don't hold any grudges. What I did was truly fucked up."

He chuckled. "It was very fucked up."

I chuckled back.

"We spent a lot of years wondering if we did something wrong."

I rubbed the back of my neck. The weight of his words was unsettling.

"My intention isn't to make you feel bad, Julian. It's to make you aware."

"Either way it's hard to hear."

"You've always been like another son to us. When we read the article the other day, it all made sense, and we understood why you handled things the way you did."

"I never meant to betray your trust with Autumn. I spent years pushing her away, but you know your daughter—she's hard to resist."

"The apple doesn't fall far from the tree. Her mother is the same. If you would have told us back then what was going on between the two of you, we would have understood. You grew up together, so it was only natural if things took a turn in your relationship."

"I know that now, but I didn't back then. I was so grateful for everything you guys did for me, and I couldn't bring myself to disappoint either of you. I didn't want to make problems in a home where there weren't any. Toward the end, Christian was getting suspicious, and I didn't know what else to do. I knew if I'd stayed in Texas, I wouldn't have been able to stay away from her. I loved her, I still do. She's the only woman I've ever loved, and all I can do is make amends with everyone."

"We don't have to forgive you, Julian, we already do. It's you who has to forgive yourself."

"You may not have to excuse my behavior and betrayal, but I know I have my work cut out for me with Christian. He's far more stubborn than your daughter."

"You bet your ass I am."

Our stares shifted toward Christian, who was walking up behind us.

I nodded. "Glad to see you could make it."

"I came to see my niece and sister."

"Christian—"

I stepped out in front their old man, interrupting him. This wasn't his argument to fight—it was mine.

"I fucked up."

He got in my face. "I fucking loved you, man. How could you betray me like that?"

"Don't you think I know that? I missed nine years of my daughter's life because I fucked up so bad. I'm the reason she's spent all her life without a father." I pointed to myself. "Me. The man who grew up in foster care, going from piece of shit parent to piece of shit parent, and you think I wanted this for her? You don't think I've been punished enough for my poor choices?"

"I knew." He sternly nodded. "I fucking knew you were messing around with Autumn. That's what hurts the most! You blatantly looked me straight in the face, making me feel like I was crazy for even implying you two were hooking up behind closed doors."

"You're the last person I would ever want to betray, Christian, and you know that. It's why I left the way I did."

"You're nothing but a coward."

"I know, and I have to live with that. I lost everything that ever mattered to me. You were the only family I ever had. I fucking loved you too. It's why I had to leave. I couldn't tell you that I was in love with your sister, but I can now. And it's the truth. I've loved her for as long as I can remember. I can't lose her again—I won't. I'll spend the rest of my life trying to be the man she deserves and the father Capri needs." I paused to let my words sink in. "I'll prove to you how much I've always loved Autumn, but I need you to forgive me. I'm sorry, Christian. I'll apologize to you until I'm blue in the face. Anytime I think about how I handled things it makes me sick to my stomach. You're one of the most important men in her life, and she wants your approval. It would help me tremendously if you gave it to us."

"I don't know if I can do that. At least not right now. I just… I'm here for my sister and my niece. It's all I can offer you, Julian." With that, he turned around and left.

And my mind was thrown into the past.

Thirty-Two

I KNEW HE WAS GOING TO DO THIS SHIT TO ME AGAIN. I WAS EXPECT-ing it. For the last two weeks, Julian had been blowing me off and push-ing me away. How he could go from one extreme to the next was not lost on me. I couldn't believe he had the audacity to think I'd sit back and take his cruelty. I thought we were past the back and forth mess, but then Christian had to unexpectedly show up and ruin everything we were building.

He was beginning to let his guard down, and it was such a beautiful sight to witness, and knowing I was the reason made everything he'd put me through worth it. I wanted to go off on him. I was a ticking time bomb, and he wasn't going to be able to manipulate his way out of this one.

I wasn't a little girl anymore. He couldn't treat me like I was his every-thing one day, and then the next I was suddenly just his best friend's little sister he needed to stay away from. Christian was not responsible for the decisions I made in my life. He was just my older brother, and they both needed to understand I could make my own choices.

My happiness was mine, and they were ripping it away from me as if they had a right to.

Grabbing my phone from my back pocket, I texted Julian.

Answer your door. I'm outside.

Seconds later, the door flung open, and there was Julian dressed to the nines. The smell of his cologne immediately assaulted my senses. Tonight, was Christian's bachelor party, and Julian looked like he was made exclusively for sex. He was wearing a light blue collared button-down shirt with black slacks. His bright blue eyes were mesmerizing, and I found myself enraptured in his gaze before he ruined it.

Angrily spewing, "What the hell are you doing here? Christian was just here, Autumn."

"I know." I nodded. "I saw him leave."

He shook his head. "You shouldn't be here."

"That's all you have to say for yourself? This is bullshit, Julian! We've gotten so close these last few months, and now you're back to treating me like I'm just some girl you were fucking! I thought I meant more to you than that?"

"Keep your voice down. Our neighbors—"

"I don't give a fuck about your neighbors!"

He grabbed my arm, dragging me inside his apartment before shutting the door behind me. "You will when they're telling Christian his little sister was standing outside screaming at me."

"What the hell do you expect? I haven't seen you since Christian caught us in your room, and you haven't answered any of my calls or texts! You've completely dropped off the face of the earth, and it's complete and utter bullshit!"

"Kid, I'm not going to stand here and have you yell at me like I'm a fucking child."

"Well, you're acting like one!"

He inhaled a deep breath. "What the fuck do you want me to do?"

"I want you to treat me like I'm more than just a random fuck to you!"

"Autumn," he calmly stated, placing his hands out in front of him. "I'm trying to do the right thing."

"The right thing? Isn't it a little late for that? You already stuck your dick in my ass, Julian!"

He didn't hesitate, viciously countering, "It was a mistake! From the very start it's all we've been! One big fucking mistake!"

"Which part?" I stumbled back from the harshness of his response. "Taking my virginity or leading me on?"

"All of it. I had no right to steal any of that from you. I'm a selfish bastard, and for that I'm very sorry, kid. You don't deserve a man like me."

"That's not your choice to make! It's mine!"

"This never should have started between us."

It was blow after blow, after blow. It felt like he didn't care about how much his brutal honesty was affecting me, how much it was destroying me inside. Julian had the ability to shift from hot too cold at the drop of a dime. Showing me this Jekyll and Hyde side to him too many times to keep track of.

Words failed me, and all I could do was fight for us. He was worth the hurt and devastation along with my tears and sorrow, my love, my devotion, the uncertainty of a future that felt destined from day one.

Trying to hold my heart together, I placed my hand over my chest. Arguing, "You don't mean that."

"You have no idea how much I do."

Tears welled up in my eyes. "You can't do this to me again."

Sweeping the hair away from my face, he tucked it behind my ear. "I don't have a choice, kid."

"Yes, you do. Choose *me*, Julian. I love you. I'm in love with you."

He didn't answer, barely demonstrating any emotion. I did the only thing I could. I bared my heart and soul to him, only to have him crush it into a million tiny pieces.

"What do you want from me, Autumn?"

"I want you to fight for me! Who cares about my parents and Christian? This is our lives, and if we want to spend it together, then it's no one's business but our own."

"I don't see it that way."

I started to sob, feeling like a little girl when I should have been stronger. Harder.

However, I always wore my emotions on my sleeve. It was who I was—it was how I was made. I didn't want to shatter in front of him, breaking like a cheap piece of glass.

At this point, I'd come this far, and I couldn't hold back. Openly bawling, I asked, "Why don't you want me? Why don't you love me like I love you?"

"Oh, kid…" He tugged me into his arms, holding me close to his heart while I broke down. Proving to him I was just a child, begging the man I was hopelessly in love with to love me back.

I cried in a way I never had, sobbing until I felt as though I had no more tears to shed.

Words to say.

Pain to feel.

It was all a clusterfuck of emotions and memories. Good times that were some of the best days of my entire life. Where nothing else mattered but being with him.

In his presence.

His bed.

His heart.

Home.

He was always my home, and for the life of me I didn't understand why I couldn't be his.

"Autumn, I'm barely hanging on by a thread here. Please don't cry over me."

"Then stop making me."

"Baby…" He picked me up and carried me to his bed. Laying me down, he hovered above my body, and I desperately wanted to remember the feel of him on top of me.

Using this position to my advantage, I expressed, "Why am I not good enough for you?"

"It's the other way around."

"Why won't you be brave like me?"

"It has nothing to do with being brave, Autumn, and I wish you could understand that. I'm so deeply sorry for fucking with your heart, but I can't lose your family. They mean everything to me."

"But you're willing to lose me? Do I mean that little to you?"

"Kid, I can't answer that. I'm sorry."

I lost my shit, heaving, hyperventilating, wailing. I was a blubbering mess, and there would be nothing left of me after this. He was stealing it all. Every last part of me now belonged to him.

"Is this what dying feels like? Because you're killing me, Julian."

He kissed away my tears, and what once gave me peace, now gave me war. It created havoc in my body, not refuge anymore.

I was desperate.

Aching inside.

Instead of leaving with a bit of my pride, I did the only thing I could in a moment where I felt lost.

I kissed him.

Praying I could use my body to change his mind.

Julian

I could physically feel her agonizing emotions radiating off her in waves as she kissed me like her life depended on it. I wish I could tell you I didn't expect what happened next, but I'd be lying.

I should have stopped her.

I should have told her no.

I should have done something, anything…

Except allow her to slide her dress off her body, leaving her in nothing but panties. When my stare didn't leave her face, it wasn't long until I lost this sudden power struggle we were in. Her delicate hands moved down my chest in a gradual, struggling motion, causing my breath to hitch. Her touch was different.

It was afflicting.

Torturous.

And so damn loving.

When her hands started moving lower toward my belt, I roughly shoved them away. It didn't stop her assault—if anything it only provoked her.

But then…

She bit her lip, fucking baiting me.

"What do you think is going to go down here, kid?" My hands craved to grip onto her waist and show her who was in control which was exactly what she sought. My fingers pleaded with me to touch her, feel her, aching for something I shouldn't, completely aware it would only lead to more trouble.

Chaos.

Conflict.

"Please," she interrupted my thoughts with the sincerest expression I'd ever seen. "Don't push me away." Grabbing my hand, she placed it over her racing heart.

Revealing, "Feel my heart—it's breaking for you."

Thirty-Three

Julian

I GROANED. "WHAT DO YOU WANT FROM ME, AUTUMN?"

I could see all the buildup in her eyes, days of anticipation, long-ing, and desire in her gaze as she hesitantly leaned forward, placing her hands on my chest. Slowly, she brought her lips to meet mine. It started off with just a peck until she opened her mouth, seeking out my tongue.

This was all her now, showing me everything *I'd* taught her. I let it go on. Carelessly letting my walls and reserve come crumbling down. I'd spent the last two weeks feeling like a dick, but I couldn't continue with her. Not after Christian warned me she was off limits again. I remembered the first time he'd threatened me. She had just turned fifteen. Even back then he'd suspected something might eventually occur between Autumn and me.

Her kiss had me on the verge of fucking losing myself, getting lost in the moment. Becoming lost in her. A man could only take so much, and I was at my breaking point.

I wanted her.

In every way possible.

And more…

I never stopped kissing her, hovering above her heady frame, causing her breathing to escalate when she realized she was getting to me.

"For fuck's sake, what are you doing to me, Autumn?" I rested my fore-head on hers, looking down at her swollen lips.

She was so beautiful.

So loving.

So fucking mine.

The way she was looking at me as if I was everything she'd ever wanted simply encouraged me to keep going. I couldn't help myself. I never could with her. I kissed her more aggressively than before, crashing our lips together. Chastising myself mentally the entire time as I continued to consume her mouth.

Her hands went to the back of my neck, pulling me closer, but not nearly close enough. The kiss turned urgent and demanding, as she met each and every pull I was delivering. It was full of emotion, mixed with pure lust and something else I'd never felt before.

My hands continued to roam over her body. Knowing I was the only man to have ever touched her this way was doing all sorts of things to my cock, like it always did. She tilted her head back, giving my lips more access to her flushed skin. My mouth moved, kissing from her neck down to her collarbone, stopping just above her breasts that were rising and falling with every movement of my lips.

I ran my tongue along her nipple, leaving goose bumps in its wake. Looking up at her through hooded eyes, I lightly blew her aroused flesh, watching her come undone in the way she always did. My mouth kissed down her stomach, savoring the elevated heat of her body pressed against mine, getting hotter with each caress of my lips, touching her skin as I made my way to where I wanted to kiss her the most.

A moan escaped her lips.

And that was my undoing. Like a fucking atomic bomb dropping on my head, my mind took the control back from my cock, realizing what I was just about to do. Having sex with her wasn't going to do anything other than lead us back to square one.

I jumped off the bed, leaving her there panting and exposed. Breathless and stirred. I tried to shake off all the emotions she'd triggered inside of me. Holding my head between my hands, I paced around the room. Knowing I'd just royally fucked up.

AGAIN.

I took a deep breath while grabbing my hoodie off the chair and tossed it at her. "Put some clothes on," I snapped, mostly pissed at myself for letting it go this far.

The last thing I wanted to do was to lead her on more than I already had, and it was all I had done since day one. I walked out onto our patio, leaving the slider open behind me. Leaning over the railing, I needed to calm down. She stepped out shortly after, closing the slider behind her.

"Hey…" She grabbed my arm, turning me to face her. "What happened back there?"

"I can't do this with you anymore. This is my fault. I never should have kissed you, or crossed the line with you. But throwing yourself at me isn't the right answer either. I stole all your firsts—it's why you think you're in love with me. It's an illusion. You're young, and I should have known better. I'm the adult here, and I took advantage of you. I fuck, Autumn. I'm not your boyfriend—you're just my best friend's little sister." I regretted the words as soon as they came out of my mouth, and she jerked back like I had slapped her in the face, and I guess in a way I had.

"Kid…" I reached for her, but she stepped back.

"Just your best friend's little sister?" she repeated, hurt and dismayed. She stood taller, eyeing me up and down. "You're not fooling anyone but yourself, Julian. You're a coward, a fucking pussy, who's pushing me away because I'm getting too close to you. You're in love with me too! You can pretend and deny it all you want, but I know you. I feel you. You can fight it all you want, but we're connected in a way that even you can't destroy. We're soulmates whether you want to be or not." She stepped toward me, getting right up in my face. "If you didn't love me, then you wouldn't have chased away Daniel—you wouldn't have been jealous! You wouldn't have dry fucked me on my birthday. You claimed me. Making sure your lips, your hands, your fingers, your tongue and cock were all my firsts. You made damn sure it was only your touch, your scent, your body that I'd remember."

"Autumn—"

"You want me to be yours, and that fucking scares you more than anything, because you've never wanted that from anyone else. Not any of the women you've slept with. My brother will understand, and if he doesn't, then I don't fucking care! This is my life, and I want you in it in every possible way."

I arched an eyebrow and cocked my head to the side. "You think you got me all figured out? Well, here's the truth, sweetheart. I don't love you. I'm not in love with you. You're not my girlfriend and I don't want you to be. I'm sorry I risked my friendship for you, but you're not worth the sacrifice."

She shook her head, her eyes immediately watering with tears.

I spoke with conviction, even though it killed me inside. "The truth hurts, Autumn. You deserve better than me. Now take your ass back inside and leave my house. You don't belong to me."

Tears streamed down her beautiful face. I watched them pour out for a minute, unable to witness it any longer. "If you won't leave, then I'll do it for us." I sidestepped her and left her there.

Her heart broken on my floor.

It wasn't the last time I'd walk away from her, but it was the first time I wanted to stay. That realization alone sent me spiraling down a bottle of fucking whiskey. Losing the only family I ever had wasn't an option, but staying in Autumn's life wasn't one either.

There was no one I could vent to, so I had to go through this alone. Which shouldn't have been a shock to me, I had been abandoned from the moment I was born.

Before I knew it, I was sitting on a black leather couch, in a house we ended up at for Christian's bachelor party. I was exhausted from the day and the never-ending plaguing emotions torturing me day in and out.

Christian had been watching me like a fucking hawk for most of the night. I had to prove to him I wasn't fucking around with his little sister behind his back. There was no way out of it, and I needed to do what I had to.

End of story.

"What's your name?" the luscious brunette enticed with her red, pouty dick-sucking lips. Wearing nothing but a tiny G-string and a bra that barely covered her tits.

"Don't worry about it."

The stripper laughed, swinging her long hair over her shoulder. I didn't have to look over to know that Christian was staring at us. Waiting to see how I'd react and what I'd do. She took it upon herself to straddle my lap, grinding her pussy on my cock to the beat of the music.

"I want you," she breathed out, leaning in to kiss me, but I turned, and she got the corner of my mouth.

From where Christian was sitting, it appeared like we were making out. I gripped onto her hair at the crook of her neck, tugging her head back, hard and making her whimper. Getting pussy had never been an issue for me, and she wasn't any different.

I let go of her hair and slowly moved my hands from her neck to her ample tits, down to her narrow waist. She licked her lips, sucking in another breath when I suddenly gripped onto her hips. I placed her on the table in front of me so Christian could get the show of a lifetime, feeling sick to my fucking stomach the entire time.

Autumn and I weren't together. I wasn't cheating on her, yet it still felt like I was betraying her in every way that mattered.

I stood, spreading her legs to stand in between them. Getting close to her face, I rasped, "If you go into the bedroom with me, I'll pay you whatever you want to say I fucked you."

She inhaled, holding her breath as my hand continued its descent, running along her smooth, heated skin and down to the seam of her panties.

"Say that you did?"

"Yes, I don't need you to ride my dick."

"What about suck it?"

"I don't need you for anything other than a lie. Do you understand me?"

She nodded. Money was money, and it didn't matter what she had to do for it. Carrying her up my torso, I wrapped her legs around my waist and walked us to one of the bedrooms. Kicking open the door, I shut it behind me.

Everyone at the party saw what had just gone down.

Especially Christian.

After all this time...

The ups and downs.

The heartache.

The betrayal.

It felt like I'd finally done something right.

Thirty-Four

Autumn

NOW

ONE DAY.

Twenty-four hours.

Our month was almost up, where we'd lived and breathed our family. We were playing house, doing everything together, and our time was coming to an end soon. I didn't know what to do, and I barely knew how to feel. Still, I kept Julian at arm's length.

We flirted.

Teased each other.

Kissed a few more times.

However, that was it. When things started to get too heated, he'd stop, and despite being frustrated and wanting him to keep going, I was relieved. If we made love, it'd only fuck things up further than they already had been. We never touched each other in front of Capri, but kids had a way of picking up on anything. She could feel our love in the same way my family could.

Christian had stopped by a few more times to see us. We were still close, especially now that I had Capri. In a way, he'd stepped up and helped be a male role model in her life, and he wasn't going to stop just because Julian was back. The last two times he was here, Julian and he exchanged more words than they had before.

"Where's Kinley?" I questioned while finishing up dinner.

Julian was grabbing a beer from the fridge, handing one to Christian who was sitting at the kitchen island.

He nodded, silently thanking him.

See … progress.

"She's out with her girlfriends for the day."

Julian nonchalantly asked, "How are you and Kinley?"

"We're good."

"You guys have been together what? Twenty years now?"

"Coming up on it, but as you probably remember the first couple of years we were on and off."

Julian chuckled. "I was a bad influence."

"You sure as shit were. Who would have thought you were fucking my little sister the entire time?"

"Christian!" I exclaimed. "We didn't even kiss until I was sixteen, and we didn't have sex until I was eighteen, so no … we were not hooking up the entire time. Your best friend was still screwing any girl in a skirt."

"Hey!" Julian scoffed out. "She didn't have to be wearing a skirt."

I chuckled, but it was the truth.

Putting his hands up in the air, my brother mischievously smiled. "Relax, I was kidding." His eyes shifted to Julian. "You actually waited until she was eighteen?"

"First girl I ever waited for anything." He winked at me. "She was worth it, though."

"Alright, alright," Christian chimed in. "Let's lock that shit up."

Julian smiled. "Any kids in your future? Capri needs a cousin, don't you think?"

The expression on Christian's face quickly turned somber, and before either of us could call him out on it, Capri walked into the kitchen. The rest of the night, we all hung out as if it were old times.

Now don't get me wrong, they weren't friends by any means, but at least they were talking and on friendlier terms with one another.

Christian said he was doing it for Capri and me, but I knew better. He was full of shit. He missed his best friend, and the more he was around him, the further his guard came down. It helped that Julian was determined to have Christian back in his life the way he used to be.

Julian didn't lose.

Ever.

I shook off the constant thoughts, making my way into the garage to tell Julian and Capri dinner was almost ready.

I stopped dead in my tracks when I heard Capri ask, "Daddy, what's going on with you and Momma?"

My heart dropped to the floor as did my jaw. I'd been waiting for her to start questioning things between us. I just never imagined she'd ask him over me. My heart began pounding against my chest, and I placed my hand on top of it, willing it to slow down for a second. I hid behind a wall, able to hear but not see them. They couldn't see me either which only aided my current situation.

"Sweetheart, that's a difficult question to answer."

"Why? Don't you still love her?"

"I'll always love her, baby."

"Then why don't you tell her?"

"I have. Many times."

"Then I don't understand? I know Momma loves you too. She looks at you like Ariel looks at Eric from *The Little Mermaid*. Besides, she's never had a boyfriend or even been on a date, so I think that means something because Momma is super romantic. But since we've been here, she's smiled and laughed more than I've ever seen. You make her happy, like really, really happy, so I don't understand. Can you explain it to me?"

He sighed. "You're too smart for your own good."

She giggled. "I'm a genius like you."

Julian didn't say anything for what felt like forever, and when he finally did, he admitted, "Capri, I've messed up so many times when it comes to your momma."

"What do you mean? Like from before you left her?"

"Yes."

"Why?"

He inhaled another deep breath. "I let everyone influence what I wanted. I didn't want to ruin my friendship with Christian or my relationship with your grandparents."

"Oh … so you broke Momma's heart instead?"

"I did, baby. I'm not proud of it, but I broke your momma's heart so many times I've lost count."

"Then just say you're sorry. When I'm a bad girl, I tell momma I'm sorry, and she always forgives me."

He teased, "When are you ever a bad girl, Capri?"

Not backing down, she added, "Daddy, just tell how sorry you are. I know she will forgive you if you do. Momma is a super forgiving person."

He laughed. "Sweetheart, sometimes people can forgive, but they don't ever forget. I've hurt your mother deeply, and I don't know how long it's going to take for her to forget about the damage I've caused."

"But I don't want to leave. I want to live here forever with you. Can I stay, Daddy?"

Hearing Capri say those words to him was like taking a fucking bullet to my heart.

Did she want to stay with him over me? Would I lose our daughter to him if we left?

I shuddered, causing an eerie feeling to course down my spine.

"Capri, you'll have both of us. I promise. You don't need to worry about any of that."

"Then we're living here forever?"

"Baby girl, I pray that you are."

"Daddy, this is so confusing."

"I know, and I'm sorry. If I could go back and change things I would, but all I can do is keep trying to make things right with your mom. I don't want to lose her again."

"I don't want to lose you."

I rubbed my face, feeling the weight of her statement.

How can I do this to our daughter? How can I rip us apart when we only just found each other again?

The truth was I wanted to stay for Capri.

My parents.

Christian.

Me.

The sound of his footsteps crept close to where I was hiding, and I swear I stopped breathing until I realized he'd moved closer to Capri, probably crouching to her eye level.

The tone of his voice was laced with sincerity. "You won't lose me, sweetheart. No matter what happens with your momma and me, I'll always be your daddy, you'll always be my baby girl, and nothing can ever come between that. It's me and you forever, baby."

She sniffled, "You promise, Daddy?"

He didn't hesitate in replying, "Cross my heart."

"Okay. Do you want me to talk to her? Maybe I can tell her you're super sad and how much you want us to stay. I can help, I know I can. Momma listens to me."

Wiping away a tear that escaped my eye, I waited on bated breath for his response.

Disappointed when he said, "You need to let the grown-ups handle their business, Capri."

"But I want to help you. I don't want to leave. I want to live here forever with you."

"I'd love that more than anything."

"Then make her stay, Daddy. Please…"

Several tears slid down the sides of my face, and I never wanted the ground to swallow me whole more than I did in that second. I wasn't only hurting Julian, I was also hurting our daughter, and that pained me deeply.

I couldn't listen anymore. Hurrying back inside, I busied myself with finishing up dinner and tried to keep my emotions in check in case either of them walked in. I didn't want Capri to see me upset, or for them to know I was eavesdropping on their private conversation.

Through my haze of what-ifs, I opened the wrong drawer and came face to face with *The New York Times* article. Like a fucking beacon shining bright, it was staring right at me. From then on, I moved in autopilot. Opening the magazine, I found his interview and read it from his first words to his last. He opened up about everything. There wasn't one thing he didn't tell the public, especially his feelings and love for me.

Our history.

His remorse.

It was all there in black ink on white paper.

"Autumn was born to be mine."

"She was made for me."

"I fought to not love her, realizing early on how much she completed me."

"She's the only woman I've ever loved."

"She's my soulmate."

My head was spinning.

"I don't know how I've lived over a decade without her."

"She's my beginning and end."

"The first time we made love I knew I was done for."

"I'll spend the rest of my life proving to her how much she consumes me."

"I want to marry her. Make her my wife and the mother of my children."

Faster and faster it spun with no end in sight.

"She's my everything—she's always been my everything."

"I didn't know what love was until I left myself truly have her."

"There's nothing I wouldn't do to keep her by my side."

I slammed the magazine shut. The emotions were one right after the other as I stood there frozen, unable to move, to think, to do anything other than feel like the floor was caving in on me.

I wanted to run to him.

To tell him I loved him.

To forgive him.

But I couldn't get my feet to move or my guard to come down. Something was holding me back, and I couldn't ignore that. Instead, after we eaten dinner and Capri went to bed, I found him in his office. Lost in his own thoughts, staring blankly out the window.

"I read the article," I shared with him.

He turned around and locked eyes with me.

Without reservation, I coaxed, "I forgive you, Julian."

His bright blue eyes flashed with a blaze of happiness as he stepped toward me, but I lifted my hand, halting his descent. Peering around the room for a few seconds, I battled a visible internal struggle in my mind.

It didn't take long for him to address the obvious. "You're here to say goodbye, aren't you?"

Thirty-Five

Autumn

"**J**ULIAN." I PAUSED, WAVERING FOR A MOMENT. "I CAN'T DO THIS with you again. It almost killed me the last time. I'm here to say my piece because we leave tomorrow."

He narrowed his eyes at me. "Do you honestly think I'm going to just let you leave?"

Taking a deep, solid breath, I willed myself to tell him the truth.

The one I'd been holding in for so damn long.

Opening my mouth, I confessed, "I wanted to get pregnant with your baby, Julian. It wasn't an accident. I purposely stopped taking my birth control."

His face paled, and it felt so fucking good to finally admit that out loud.

"You lied to me?"

"Yes."

"Why?"

"Because I knew you. I knew how you were, and it was only a matter of time before you pushed me away again. It was the only way I could ensure you wouldn't anymore. You always wanted a family, so I gave you one."

He immediately closed his eyes, the hurt evident all around him. It burned deep into my core. I hated knowing I was hurting him, but I needed to tell him the truth. He had to know.

As much as it killed me inside.

"How the fuck could you do this to me, Autumn?"

"I didn't do it to you, I did it for you."

"You did it for me? Are you fucking kidding me? What exactly did you do *for me*, kid? Get knocked up on purpose and then not tell me about it? What the hell kind of plan was that?"

"I didn't know you were going to tell me you were leaving. I had no clue you were going to take it that far."

"That's your fucking excuse? How could you do this to me?"

"I thought we were going to be a family."

"We still could have been! All you had to do was open your mouth and tell me you were pregnant!"

"I know. I'm sorry."

"You're sorry? For fuck's sake! I can't even look at you right now!"

"I swear the last thing I want is for us to leave and for you to hate me." Fresh tears streamed down my face, the ones I had been trying to keep at bay. "We've both hurt one another so much, Julian! How could we possibly come back from this? I don't trust you with my heart, and you resent me for not telling you the truth! That's our reality, not this made up happily ever after you've created in your head!"

In three strides he was in my face, backing me into the wall. "You fucking betrayed me, and still—I want you!"

I couldn't fucking breathe.

I hated myself for destroying him.

"We have to let each other go. It's what's best for our family."

"You leaving is not what's best for our family, and you know it!"

"Stop screaming at me! I'm hurting too! You broke me! Can't you see that?"

"So this last month was what, Autumn? Fucking payback?"

"Of course not."

"Bullshit!"

"You left me! After you fucked me over!"

Julian

My resolve broke like a chain that had been stretched to the max. I heard it snap, loud and clear. With wide eyes, I ran my hands through my hair, wanting to tear it out. Trying to remain calm but becoming defeated with each passing second.

I couldn't keep up with the torment—it clasped onto me like a vice as I stormed around my office, my feet stomping everywhere I stepped, leaving a path of destruction in its wake. Throwing anything and everything I could find, I unleashed my fury on my office instead of her.

"Julian, stop!"

Hearing the desperation in Autumn's voice halted the chaos coursing through my veins. Neither one of us said a word for I don't know how long, facing each other, panting profusely. We didn't need to, though. Our eyes spoke for themselves.

Our connection was present, and she wanted me to see it, giving me the hope I needed to go on. I growled out my frustration, releasing the craze, the wrath I no longer had any control over. It pounded into me as furiously as what she'd just admitted.

"I'm hanging on by a thread here. So unless you want to see a side of me you haven't seen in years, I suggest you weigh your words before you come at me with more bullshit. We're far from fucking over. Nothing will ever be done between us!"

"Just let me go!"

"I can't! You belong to me! You always have, and you always will!"

My mind was spiraling with more thoughts and questions, trying to find some clarity. Some truth within the haze. I shut my eyes and bowed my head in between my hands. Needing a minute to process what the hell she'd just said.

She could see it.

Feel it.

She could feel me.

I never wanted to shake her and hold her as much as I did in that moment. Showing my weaknesses wasn't something I ever did, but it had always been different with Autumn, and she knew it too. I couldn't think about the future without contemplating the past, and for the first time it had me questioning how we would make it through this.

I stared up at her through the slits of my eyes, longing to feel some sort of connection through what I was about to say to her. "I fucked up! How many more times do I have to say it to you?"

"But that's always been the problem between us, Julian. You fuck up, and I forgive you. It's an endless cycle I want to put an end to. I don't know what you expect from me because the woman you see standing in front of you—you made her this way."

I jerked back. With each blow she delivered, I felt a little more of myself die inside. I didn't know which one was worse—her lies or her truths.

"You're so full of shit," I confidently countered. The thread I was hanging on to snapped. "You've loved me your entire life. I'm embedded in your skin. I'm flowing in your blood. I'm beating in your heart." Before she knew it, I was standing directly in front of her, pulling her hair away from her face and grazing my knuckles against her rosy cheek. "I'm a part of you, sweetheart, and you're not going anywhere." I moved away, even though it was the last thing I wanted to do. I wanted her to miss my touch before my resolve exploded.

With the way I was feeling right now, I was damn ready to throw her over my shoulder, kicking, screaming, putting up one hell of a fight, and lock her the fuck away until I proved my point and made her mine again.

"I can't talk to you when you're like this."

She turned around to leave, but I gripped onto her arm. "Don't you walk away from me." Stepping right into her personal space, I backed her against the nearest wall. My six-foot-two muscular build loomed over her petite frame as I tugged her hard against my chest.

She didn't cower—if anything she stood taller. I cocked my head to the side, sweeping her hair away from her eyes to stare deep into them as I locked her in place in front of me. Her chest rose and fell with each brush of my hand.

I held her tighter.

To look at me.

See me.

Feel me...

I switched my grip to the back of her neck in a possessive act, running my thumb up and down her windpipe. Her breathing hitched, and her lips parted when my other hand lightly grazed her inner thigh.

"Julian, stop," she weakly let out as my fingers inched higher and higher up her leg.

"Stop what? I would've been there for you, taken care of both of you, like I still fucking ache to do. Please," I begged. "Just give me a chance to make it right. I can't live without you."

Before I even realized what was happening, she was crying against my chest, and I wept with her.

"I'm sorry, baby. I'm so fucking sorry for everything I put you through. I put us through. I ruined us when all you did was try to save us. Losing you will be the biggest regret of my life. I love you so much, and I need you to please never forget that," I pleaded in a tone I'd never heard out of my own mouth.

"I love you too, Julian."

She stayed there in my arms, both of us knowing this was our end.

This was goodbye.

I kissed her, she kissed me back, and for a moment we lost ourselves in each other. She pulled away first, and I wiped away all my tears, kissing along her face for the last time. She sucked in air that wasn't available for the taking as my arms fell to my sides.

Empty.

Alone.

Broken.

She took one last look at me and left.

For the first time in our love story, I watched her walk away from me instead.

Thirty-Six

Autumn

WE'D BEEN HOME FOR TWO WEEKS.
Home.
It didn't feel like that anymore.

Capri and I were miserable.

Why was I doing this to us again?

She was mad at me, devastated I'd actually made us leave. My mind kept thinking about that morning, and it killed me every single time.

"Momma!" she pleaded with tears streaming down her precious face. Please don't make us a leave! Please, Momma! I want us to stay with Daddy!"

"Capri, please don't do this to me right now."

"I love you, Daddy!" She ran into his arms. "Please don't forget about me!"

He picked her up off the ground, and she clung to him like she'd never wanted to let him go for anything.

"You have to be my big, brave girl, okay?"

"But I don't wanna go!"

"I know, baby." He kissed the top of her head, looking at me with so much hurt it crippled my stance.

He held her in his arms until she cried herself to sleep before he gently laid her down in the SUV. Kissing her head one last time, he quietly shut the door.

Shaking his head, he bit, "I hope you're happy with yourself. You didn't just break my heart. You broke our daughter's too."

Her words played in my mind as if they were a broken record on endless repeat. My head was pounding, overly thinking about what I'd done to us when my phone suddenly rang.

"Christian," I answered it. "I can't talk right now."

"Good, because I'm the one who needs to do all the talking now."

"What are you—"

"Are you happy?" he questioned out of nowhere.

It was all it took for me to breakdown. "No…"

"Don't cry in front of Capri, Autumn."

"I'm not. She's out with Emily. What did I do, Christian? What did I do to my family?"

"Autumn, stop crying."

"I can't. I feel like I've been crying since I left him. When all I want to do is go back, but I can't."

"Why can't you?"

"I don't know. I just can't."

He deeply sighed, breathing out, "It's because of me, isn't it?"

"What?"

"You heard me."

"I don't understand."

"Yes, you do."

"This has nothing to do with you."

"Bullshit, Autumn. This has always been about me. Mom and Dad would have accepted you guys—fuck, they probably would have been thrilled about it. The only thing holding him back was me, and we both know it."

"Christian—"

"No, it's my turn to talk, and you need to listen. I fucked up. My job was to protective you, and I protected you from the man you needed most. He's always loved you. I saw it clear as day. The way he'd look at you when you were speaking, when he'd never give any girl his sole focus. The way he'd smile when you were around, when he was usually a broody bastard. How he'd think of you even when we were at the fucking grocery store, buying you your favorite candy or magazine. He was completely devoted to you."

"What are you saying?"

"I'm saying that I was wrong. I never should have kept you two apart, and for that I'm truly sorry, Autumn. It's your life. He makes you happy, and for years I saw you suffer with Capri alone. Knowing deep down in my heart that he was more than likely the father."

I gasped. "You knew?"

"I wasn't a hundred percent positive, but he started changing. He wasn't bringing girls home anymore. He was always busy, and when I saw you in his room that night, I knew he was busy with you. He didn't hit on girls when we'd go out. My best friend became a man I didn't recognize because of you. I saw through the bullshit charade he did during my bachelor party. Julian would have fucked her on that chair, not giving a shit anyone was in the room. He wouldn't have taken her to another room. He was trying to prove something to me, and I saw it for what it was."

"Oh my God."

"When you told us you were pregnant, I tried to reach him. I called around to all our friends, everyone who knew him, the places we used to hang out, trying to see if I could find him, but I never could. For months I tried, only to come up empty."

"I didn't know that."

"I wanted to fucking kill him, but I couldn't prove he was the father. All I had was my intuition. Than Capri started growing up, and I could see so much of him in her. Her mannerisms, her confidence, the way she holds her fucking fork, it's all Julian."

"Why didn't you ever say anything to me?"

"What could I say? I couldn't offer you anything, give you any information on his whereabouts. The only thing I could do was be there for you and her. I felt so fucking guilty she didn't have a father because of me. It was the least I could do. Again, I'm so sorry, Autumn. I never meant to hurt you. I fucking love you."

It all made sense, and I had no idea how I couldn't see it until now.

"It was never him, Christian. It was always me." I paused to let my words sink in. "I pursued him. For years it was all me. He never wanted to disrespect you, our parents, or me. For the longest time I didn't understand his reasoning. A little part of me resented him for it. I felt bad I didn't feel that way and he did. Even up until his article, I was terrified of you finding out. Not Mom and Dad. I didn't want to lose you like I'd lost him."

"You're not going to lose me. I promise. All I've ever wanted is for you to be happy. You're always going to be my little sister. Do you love him?"

"More than anything in this world."

"If he hurts you again, I'll fucking kill him. You've been warned. I'll always be here. I'm your big brother, and you're stuck with me for life."

"I know. You've been the best big brother a girl could ever have."

"He's a mess, Autumn. You need to come home."

"Wait? You've seen him?"

"Yeah, the owner of the bar we used to hang out at called me at three in the morning a couple nights ago to come pick his ass up. He was fucking hammered. I could barely get him in the car. He passed out in our guest bedroom, and we talked the next morning."

"Wow. Julian losing control. That's never a good thing."

"No shit. We're fine. I'll get over it. I want you happy. I want my niece to have a family. The same one we have with two loving parents who want what's best for her."

"Do you mean that?"

"Of course I do."

"Where is he now?"

He chuckled, and the doorbell rang before he added, "At your front door."

Julian

There she was, finally standing in front of me. Before she could say a word to me, I bent forward and threw her over my shoulder.

"Julian! What the hell?"

I walked into her house, looking around for Capri. Ready to throw her over my other shoulder and leave with what belonged to me.

"Where's our daughter?"

"She's out with Emily. Put me down!"

"Not a fucking chance. You're coming home with me. Now!"

"Julian—"

"Where are they? I'll go get her."

"They'll be home any minute. Will you please calm down?"

"This is me calm."

"Really? You're literally carrying me on your shoulder like a freaking cave man. What's next? Going to hit me over the head with a club and drag me out of my home?"

"This isn't your home. Your home is at the ranch with me."

"You're right. It is."

Now that got my attention, and I set her down on the entry table, caging her in with my arms.

"Are you fucking with me?"

She smiled, shaking her head. "I never should have left, and I'm so sorry I did. I'm also sorry about the birth control and Capri. I was young, but I don't regret it. I couldn't imagine my life without her in it."

"How could I be upset with you? You gave us our baby girl."

"I love you, Julian. I've always loved you, and I always will."

I laid my forehead on hers, rasping, "You mean I don't have to spank you into submission?"

"No, I'm not really into that."

"Unlucky for you, I am."

Grabbing my face, she looked deep into my eyes. "Take me home. Please. I want to go home."

I didn't have to be told twice, claiming her lips like she did my heart.

"I love you, Autumn. I want to forget about the past and just focus on the future. Can you give me that?"

She nodded. "Yes, I can now."

"You're not going to run away from me anymore?"

"No. My life belongs to you. It always has. I love you, Mr. Locke."

"Say it again."

"I love you, I love you, I love you!"

Kissing her passionately, I almost made love to her right then and there, but Capri walked in with Emily beside her. Through my craze, I didn't close the door.

"Daddy!" The expression on my baby girl's face almost brought me to my knees.

I let go of Autumn, and Capri jumped into my arms.

"You're here!" Capri celebrated. "You came for us! I knew you would! I just knew it!"

Holding her close, I pulled Autumn into the side of my chest. Embracing both my girls after what felt like forever of missing them.

My world.

My heart.

My soul.

Was finally with me, and I was never going to let them go again.

Thirty-Seven

"MOMMA!" CAPRI EXCLAIMED, RUNNING INTO THE KITCHEN with a little ball of fur in her arms. "Look what Daddy brought me home!"

"Oh my God, no he did not."

Julian walked in after her. "Capri! I told you to let me talk to your momma first. Now I'm in trouble."

"Oh, yes you are, Mr. Locke."

"We just flew back this morning, and I'm already Mr. Locke?"

"You bought her a puppy? Without even discussing it with me first?"

"I was planning to, but Capri beat me to it."

"You're supposed to discuss it with me before you buy the puppy, Julian."

He grinned. "Is that the way it works? I got it confused, but thanks for clearing that up for next time."

"Next time?"

"But, Momma, look how cute he is!"

I rolled my eyes, shaking my head.

"Kid, it's just a puppy."

"A puppy I'm going to have to take care of."

"Not true, he's my puppy. I will be responsible for him. I promise."

I shook my head again. "I'm not going to win this one, am I?"

"I think you already lost, Momma. The puppy is here."

"You're not winning me any points with your mother, Capri."

She giggled. "Sorry, Daddy."

For the rest of the afternoon, we played with Capri's new Miniature Cockapoo. He was adorable, weighing only five pounds.

Later that night while Julian was putting Capri to bed, I listened at the door without them knowing.

"Daddy, I knew you'd come and get us. I just knew it."

"And now I'm going to make sure you stay forever."

What did he mean by that?

"That's a good idea, just in case Momma gets mad at you again."

"Baby, Momma is definitely going to get mad at me again."

"Facts."

I scoffed out a chuckle. She truly was too smart for her own good.

"Would you like me to make sure you guys are here forever, baby?"

"I would love that, Daddy. I think it's a very good idea."

"Good. You can cuddle your puppy for a little while longer, but he needs to sleep in his crate, okay?"

"Okay, I promise. I'll be a good girl and put him in there before I fall asleep."

Yeah, that wasn't going to happen.

I made a mental note to circle back before I went to bed, knowing she was going to sleep with that puppy if I didn't. To say I wasn't nervous to be sharing a bed with Julian would be a complete lie. I was so freaking anxious I couldn't control the emotions.

Making my way back to our bedroom, I jumped in the shower to wash away the unease I was experiencing. After I was done, I slipped on my cream silk robe, and when I walked back into the room Julian was sitting on the edge of the bed, waiting for me.

"You're nervous," he stated, fully aware he was the reason.

"Maybe."

He grabbed my hand, tugging me forward to stand in between his legs. "Why the anxiety, kid?"

I shrugged.

"Don't give me that."

"Well, we haven't had sex in over a decade, so I think that's reason enough."

He smiled. "Oh, we're having sex tonight?"

"Julian … don't tease me."

"But you used to love it when I teased you, especially when you were sitting on my face."

Arousal crept through every inch of my body, and my skin heated immediately.

However, it quickly decreased the second he informed, "Your house in San Diego went on the market the moment your feet touched my plane, Autumn."

My mouth dropped open. "Julian! I didn't say I was selling my home."

"It isn't your home anymore. This is our home."

"What if I wanted to use it for investment purposes, like renting it out?"

"I'm worth 3.2 billion. You don't need the money."

"Exactly, you're worth that. Not me."

"How many times do I have to tell you that what's mine is yours?"

"We're not married—"

I almost fell to my ass when he simply stated, "Marry me."

Julian

There was no hesitation on my part. I reached into my pocket and pulled out a Cartier ring box.

Her eyes went wide as I opened the box, showing her a five-karat princess cut diamond ring.

"That ring probably costs as much as my house, Julian."

I nodded. "Give or take."

I pulled it out of the box and slid it down her ring finger. "Perfect fit."

With a mischievous smile, she exclaimed, "I didn't say yes, Mr. Locke."

"I didn't ask, *Mrs. Locke.*"

"Mrs. Locke does have a nice ring to it."

"I've had that ring since I bought this ranch."

Her face paled. "You're lying."

"I always intended on coming back for you."

"I don't know what to say."

"How about we start with how much I want to make love to you for the first time in over a decade with you only wearing that ring?" I opened her robe, gliding it off her shoulders, and it pooled at her feet.

My breath actually hitched as my eyes devoured her bare flesh. She was fucking sexy as sin, looking better than I'd remembered.

"Do you have any idea how many times I've fucked my fist to the image of you like this? And it wasn't even close to how you look right now. Christ, Autumn. You're stunning." Cupping onto her tits, I grinned. "These are bigger."

Shyly, she smirked. "Motherhood, I guess."

My hands skimmed her skin down to her stomach. "I can't wait to see you pregnant."

"Pregnant? Jesus, Julian. You're not wasting any time."

"I've wasted over ten years." Shifting my fingers to her pussy, I rubbed her clit back and forth with the palm of my hand, and she melted into my touch. "Your body has always been so fucking responsive to me. It's one of the many things I love about making you come."

"Okay, cocky sir…" Her knees buckled as I thrust two fingers into her warm, welcoming heat.

There wasn't a place on Autumn's body I hadn't explored, and tonight I'd planned to revisit each one several times.

Finally, I had everything I ever wanted.

Hoped for.

Loved.

I didn't care how long it took us to get to this place, all that mattered was we were there, and we weren't ever going back. She was lucky I didn't have a wedding officiant at the house, wanting to marry us this instant, but I knew she'd want a wedding with her family and friends, and it was my job to make all her dreams come true.

"Mmm…" she moaned, her eyes closing as she leaned her hands on my shoulders, trying to hold herself up.

It didn't take long to have her coming down my arm. Gripping onto her waist, I laid her on the bed and kissed her pussy with my mouth. She still tasted the same, and I couldn't hold back, going to town on her cunt.

"Ahhhh…"

"You think you can do something for me?"

"You're asking me now? When your face is buried in between my legs?"

"Less chance of you saying no."

I sucked her clit into my mouth, moving my head side to side and up and down.

"I'm going to come…"

I stopped, and she jolted forward glaring at me. "Julian! Why did you stop?"

I licked her nub before speaking with conviction, "Give me a baby."

She smiled, big and wide. "I'm not the one who determines that—it's your seed."

"Do you know when we made Capri?"

She nodded.

"Care to share?"

All she replied was, "The Audi R8 drive."

"I always did love that sports car."

"And now you own three."

"Five actually." I began fingering her, and her head fell back. "How long were you off the pill?"

"Oh… I see where you're … going with this."

I finger fucked her g-spot, and she was having a hard time answering my questions. "I'm waiting."

"Your balls are on point … Oh God … at least they were … back then."

"That doesn't answer my question."

"I got pregnant…" Her eyes rolled to the back of her head. "The first month."

It was all I needed to hear. "Good to know. I plan on knocking up right now."

"You're such … a cave man…"

I growled, hitting her sweet spot while I fucked her with my mouth. "That feel good?"

She panted.

Legs trembling.

Body shaking.

She exploded in my mouth, soaking the seam of my shirt in the process. Her legs tightened so hard around my head as she came all the way down my face. I savored the taste of her against my tongue, swallowing all her come before I kissed her clit one last time and crawled my way off her body.

"I'm not even going to get undressed. I'm going to fuck you just like this, and then I'll make love to you when I'm done."

I could never get enough of her sweet, sweet pussy.

Not then.

Not now.

Not ever.

Mine.

In one swift motion I pulled out my cock and thrust inside of her so damn hard that her body flew back toward the headboard. Never letting up, I angled my leg and took her like a madman.

"You going to give me a baby?"

"Yes…"

"I want at least five more."

We locked eyes.

"Five?" she countered as I pounded into her, wanting my seed to go as deep as possible.

"At least."

"Julian! I'm not a cow."

I slammed into her, relentless to get her pregnant while shoving my tongue in her mouth. "Fuck, I missed you. You've always had such a tight pussy." I angled my leg higher, making her leg incline. Our mouths parted as I roughly took what had always been mine.

Feeling myself start to come apart, I fucked her like a man who was starved.

"I love you," she moaned.

"Say it again."

"I love you, I love you, I love you…"

Her cunt squeezed the shit out of my cock and after I made her come a few more times I finally let myself go. Spreading my seed so far inside her core, there was no way I didn't get one in there. I kissed her one last time, peering deep into her eyes.

My world was staring back at me, and it was hard to breathe.

I was home.

Where I belonged.

Without any uncertainty, I told her the truth of how much she always owned my heart and soul…

"I love you, Autumn. Now, then, always.

Epilogue

Julian

"**D**addy, how do I look?"

"Like the most beautiful flower girl in all the world."

Capri beamed, grabbing onto her uncle's hand. "I'm ready now."

"Are you?" Christian questioned, nodding at me.

"Never been so ready for anything in all my life."

"Good to hear." My best man patted me on the back.

The last three months sped by, and I'd wasted no time in demanding Autumn to begin planning our wedding. We were exchanging our vows on the ranch, and she was adamant on it being in our home. Saying it was part of her dream from when she was a little girl.

It was small and intimate. I was still very much a private man, and I didn't want to share our day with anyone other than family and close friends. The press was having a fucking field day with our wedding, and I had to hire security and built tents because reporters were flying over our estate, trying to get the first picture of us as man and wife.

Although, I didn't let any of that get to me. There wasn't anything I wanted more in this world than to have Autumn take my last name. Capri's last name was also changed to Locke.

By law, my family was mine now.

As soon as I witnessed my girl coming down the aisle to become Mrs. Locke, all I could think about was how lucky I truly was. My gaze never left

Her hair flowed loosely down her face, wearing very minimal makeup, fully aware I wanted to see those freckles. She wore a fitted white gown that accentuated all the curves of her body, but I was the only one who knew what was really beneath her wedding gown, triggering my cock twitch at the mere thought.

I smiled a reassuring smile as her old man placed her hand in mine. "I couldn't be happier for you."

"Thank you, Dad."

He nodded, loving the fact that I'd called him that. Even when I was younger, they always insisted I address them as Mom and Dad, but I couldn't bring myself to do it. I no longer had that issue. Winking at her mom, who was sitting in the front row, I turned my attention back to the woman who was moments away from becoming my wife.

The minister proceeded, until he finally arrived to the part I craved the most…

Our vows.

"Autumn, if it weren't for you, I'd be living a lonely life. I found my soulmate through my best friend, and I will forever be grateful for the gift that is you, kid. You make me a better man, father, and human being. I'd be lost without you, and I was for over ten years. Everything I've made for myself is because of the love and faith you had in me. Words can't express how much I love you, how much I need you, how much you mean to me. Capri and you are my entire world, and your parents and brother make it better."

Tears slid down her face, and I wiped them away.

"You were made for me. I knew that then, and I know that now. I can't wait to spend the rest of my life with you. I love you."

Although she was still crying, she'd never looked more beautiful in my eyes.

Autumn

"Julian," she breathed out. "You're everything I ever wanted. From the first piggy back ride I was yours."

He scoffed out a chuckle.

"I fought for you and lost, but a part of me thinks we had to go through that to appreciate and value what we really do share. Our love has always been all consuming, and I wouldn't have it any other way. You're the best thing that's ever happened to me, and I can't ever thank you for giving me Capri. The way you love her..." I sucked in a breath. "It's just … everything I knew it would be. You're everything I knew you would be. I love you so much. I never stopped, and I never will. You're the best part of me. I love you, Julian Locke."

The minister proceeded. "By the power vested in me by the state of Texas, I now pronounce you husband and wife. Julian, you may kiss your bride."

He gripped onto the sides of my face and brought me over to him. I went effortlessly, and we claimed one another's lips for the first time as husband and wife. We spent most of the evening dancing in each other's arms, enjoying all the wedding traditions. Wanting to savor every second of our day. Until he grabbed my hand, leading me to the barn where we could be alone for a couple of minutes.

"I can't believe no one suspects."

"Julian… stop it."

He kissed my lips. "Kid, you're six weeks pregnant."

"I know! I didn't want the press to find out and say you're only marrying me because I'm pregnant."

He laughed, kissing me again. "I don't give a fuck what the press thinks and says."

"I know. It's one of the things I love the most about you. It's why you have me as your publicist. I put out the fires you love to start. Well, that and your huge cock."

He laughed so hard his head fell back. "God, I fucking love you, Mrs. Locke."

"I love you, Mr. Locke."

Crouching, he kissed my belly. "I can't wait to meet you."

I rubbed his head, and when it disappeared under my dress, I exclaimed, "Julian!" before I could stop him—who was I kidding. Before I could come in his mouth, we were interrupted by Kinley's voice.

"Christian! I can't be here! I need to leave!"

"For fuck's sake, Kinley! You can't leave my little sister's wedding!"

"I don't care! It's your fault that no one knows the truth, and the longer I'm there, the harder it is to not tell everyone."

Julian popped back up, staring straight at me. The concern evident all over his handsome face. We were both rendered speechless when Christian announced…

"We're not ruining their wedding because you want to tell everyone right now that we're getting a divorce!"

The end.

For Julian and Autumn.

It's only the beginning or is it *the end* for…
Christian and Kinley.

I met my soulmate when I was thirteen years old, never imaging our love wouldn't be enough to save us from circumstances beyond our control.
Dr. Alpha (Standalone/Second Chance Romance)

Meet
M. ROBINSON

Wall Street Journal & *USA Today* Bestselling Author M. Robinson loves her readers more than anything! They have given her the title of the 'Queen of Angst.' With several bestselling novels under her belt, she loves to write and couldn't imagine doing anything else with her life.

Her readers are everything to her and she loves to connect with her following through all her social media platforms, also through email! Please keep in touch in her reader group VIP on Facebook, if she's not in there than she is on Instagram or her author Facebook page.

She lives in Brandon FL with the love of her life, her lobster, and husband Bossman. They have one Wheaten Terrier, a Miniature Cockapoo, and a user Tabby cat. She is extremely close to her family, and when she isn't living the cave life writing her epic love stories, she is spending money shopping or living boat life. Anywhere and everywhere. She loves reading and spending time with her family and friends whenever she can.

She truly appreciates her readers being on this writing journey with her. She thanks God every day that this is her life of telling stories to make people feel and disappear to another world.

Being an author is her first passion in life. It was what she was meant to do on this earth. Be a portal for characters who want their stories told.

Acknowledgments

Executive assistants & all around the reason I can write: Silla Webb & Heather Moss

Editor: Silla Webb

Cover Designer: Lori Jackson

Paperback, Ebook Formatter: Silla Webb

Publicist: Danielle Sanchez

Agent: Stephanie DeLamater Phillips

Bloggers/Bookstagrammers: Without you I'd be nothing. Thank you for all your support always.

My VIPS/Readers

Photographer: Andrew M Gleason

Cover Model: James Joseph

Street Team Leaders: Leeann Van Rensburg & Jamie Guellar

Teasers & Promo: Heather Moss & Silla Webb

My VIP Reader Group Admins:
Lily Garcia, Leeann Van Rensburg, Jennifer Pon, Jessica Laws, Louisa Brandenburger

Street Team & Hype Girls: You're the best.

My alphas & betas:
Thank you for helping me bring this book to life.